PENGUIN BOOKS

WHICH OF US TWO?

Colin Spencer had his _____ *zine* at the age of twenty-o_____ ub- lished and five plays _____ mi- autobiographical sque_____ *Love*, with the overall title *Generation*. In the last decade he has been writing a regular food column in the *Guardian* and has published twelve cookery books.

WHICH OF US TWO?
THE STORY OF A LOVE AFFAIR

———————

COLIN SPENCER

PENGUIN BOOKS

920

PENGUIN BOOKS

Published by the Penguin Group
Penguin Books Ltd, 27 Wrights Lane, London w8 5tz, England
Viking Penguin, a division of Penguin Books USA Inc.
375 Hudson Street, New York, New York 10014, USA
Penguin Books Australia Ltd, Ringwood, Victoria, Australia
Penguin Books Canada Ltd, 2801 John Street, Markham, Ontario, Canada l3r 1b4
Penguin Books (NZ) Ltd, 182–190 Wairau Road, Auckland 10, New Zealand

Penguin Books Ltd, Registered Offices: Harmondsworth, Middlesex, England

First published by Viking 1990
Published in Penguin Books 1991
1 3 5 7 9 10 8 6 4 2

Printed in England by Clays Ltd, St Ives plc

Contents

.

Preface

·

I met John Tasker in 1957. My first words to him were, 'Dull, isn't it?' Not a prophetic utterance, as the letters in these pages reveal. But as the phrase was an observation on life immediately prior to our meeting, maybe it had a certain significance.

John died of cancer in June 1988; before he died he asked that all my letters be returned to me. I re-read a few at random, finding that I was nauseated by the callow youth I was forced to recognize after thirty-one years. I then thrust them aside thinking the dust of the grave must continue to settle upon them. But something within me had stirred in its sleep: shapes and colours, nicknames and laughter, the Vienna of the late fifties, ghosts that were not always reassuring or pleasant. In fact there was something monstrous lurking within the memory. In time, I thought, all this would settle back into the sediment of amnesia and dreams.

But a few weeks later, having long forgotten where I had stored them, I stumbled on my cache of letters from John. Immediately, I began to wonder how many of our letters would dovetail, whether putting the two together might explain anything about my past or our love. Foolishly, I was unprepared for my reaction: the letters still had a terrifyingly turbulent effect upon me. I found so much within the relationship impossible to fathom, but most of all I could not understand why I ended it and why we had not continued to live together. The apparent reason revealed in the letters seemed to me then to be a defence against John, the only way I had of warding him off for ever; but why should I want to do it, given the intensity of feeling that is shown here? Would I, I wondered, if I put both sets of correspondence together, and attempted a long cool look at the relationship, now be able to uncover the truth?

In one of my letters, confused and furious, I wrote, 'What do you want, a book?' Perhaps then, this is it. But the relationship we had, so fierce, so short, has already been used in my novels. It was almost as if I ended it in order to bury everything, so that I contained his rage as well as my own, which I could then fuel my fiction with. Perhaps books are the only place for such emotions as these, highly wrought, deeply complex; maybe such feelings do not belong in life, because they have nowhere to go except in violence and frustration. Yet this I know is nonsense. We each have a responsibility to understand ourselves better, and books are but one way of helping the process. They reflect much that is inchoate in a way we can absorb, yet never delineate in any rational manner.

I think now we felt too much too soon. There is something very gauche and adolescent about these two twenty-four-year-olds. We were not equipped in any way to deal with the savagery and the torrential rawness of it all. I fled. But of course, I know now that I fled from myself as much as from John. I have had to return. I have had to attempt, however cautiously at first, to understand the danger and threat that loving seemed to hold.

The material that we gave to each other I used in some degree in the four semi-autobiographical books that make up the still unfinished sequence, *Generation*. John in a small way was Reg. Our first night together and the farce of a thrice coitus interruptus I used in the first chapter of *Anarchists in Love*. Our relationship together in Vienna is seen very clearly in *Asylum* in the relationship between the brothers Carl and Angelo.

Bad autobiography deals in superficial disguises, a cover up, or it can even blatantly lie. But I have long felt that good or truthful autobiography often tends to wander unconsciously into fiction. The reader might think that as this book uses the actual letters it could escape the emphasis of unconscious fiction, but I must declare that within me I still feel guilt, and where there is guilt, there is also disguise and dissembling, understatement and exaggeration.

I have used the letters in two ways. Where in some sequences they speak for themselves and carry the narrative, as in the last few chapters, there is no need for a commentary, only a few explanatory notes. But generally I have used the letters as spurs to comment on the action and to examine my younger self. In no way do I think the letters are particularly interesting in themselves. They are not well written: mine often parody experimental literature or descend into camp and bathos, while John's tend to be emotional screams. I hope, nevertheless, that they have some interest as social documents: they are gay love letters, and should therefore tell us something about gay love. Yet ultimately they seem to me to be simply love letters.

This is the story of the first great passion of two young men and my inquiry on why I murdered its future. Is that statement in fact true? I can give a dozen reasons why it could not stand up in a court of law, arguing that in the first case it neglects to mention other earlier passions and why in the second case there were strong self-destructive tendencies. Yet it has the power of an awesome truth for me.

I

First Meeting

.

We picked each other up in the upstairs bar of the Greyhound Pub in East Street, Brighton. In an anniversary letter two years later I even state the time as 9.30 in the evening on 8 June, almost bequeathing it a royal natal award. An immediate empathy came from one of us completing a quotation of T. S. Eliot's, no doubt from 'Prufrock'. The second common ground we discovered was a love of the theatre – Brecht in particular. Though the Berliner Ensemble had been in London the year before, Brecht was still a fairly esoteric passion to have. These were the first obvious bonds, but something much more powerful occurred as we strolled the sea-front through the night. I believe we knew each other's vulnerability instinctively and so the beginnings of mutual trust formed. But upon the surface we were so excited at all the books, plays and poems shared, that little time was given to thoughts of physical attraction. We were discovering much in common, the basis for most relationships. Some time during that weekend I suppose I must have noticed the omission that John was most vulnerable about. Or did he tell me the story before he undressed and climbed into bed? Or did we make love, as we did later in the summer, on the sitting-room carpet? I cannot recall, but cancer must have begun our first meeting as it closed it. For cancer stalked him all his life.

John was then teaching in a school in London. We met at the beginning of his taking a week's holiday at half-term; by the last half of that week he had moved in with me. This time together was crucial; the events moved swiftly but we became of some importance to each other, though neither of us was free. John shared his London flat with G., a lover from South Africa. I had a girl-friend, Lucy, who was a research botanist, and I was also having an affair with a rather grand Anglo-Catholic priest whom I genuinely adored, even though I was an atheist and he was thirty years older. This kind of complexity seems to be characteristic of a major part of my life, as much as calling myself an atheist is a gross over-simplification. The facts I would have told John, as he would have painted in the details of his own life.

I knew that at the age of sixteen he had seduced his drama teacher, Kester Berwick. This was in Newcastle, New South Wales, and such an act in 1949 would have been more monstrously taboo than it is now. John was not discreet by nature either, so it would have been difficult to hide in a small circle, however big the community. But I think he also told me then that inherent in the seduction was his longing for Europe, and Kester was seen as the means to it. I can remember him saying that he wanted Kester's potential as a theatre director and teacher to be recognized in Europe rather than the cultural backwater they were living in. I am sure John made this a most urgent plea, building up a persuasive and convincing case. Certainly the picture I received was of John persistently nagging Kester. His parents' permission must have been sought, though I suspect if John said he was going to London to study drama it would have been a *fait accompli*, once it was clear no financial burden was placed upon them. I see now in his nagging, in the urgency of wanting the best for the beloved, in hiding the greater egocentric impulse, a reflection of what was to happen to us. But then all I saw was John's enthusiastic creativity, his addiction to European culture and his longing to be part of it.

So in 1950 they set sail, reaching Europe and journeying from Athens to Vienna and thence to the Austrian Tyrol where Kester had friends. They would have roughed it, for Kester had very little money. Later, when I knew him in Greece, I would notice almost a celebratory delight in the husbandry of farthings; so the budget would have been carefully worked out. This parsimony would bug my days with John later, for such caution can seem miserly. Eventually they reached Holland, hearing throughout their European journey terrible tales of British food rationing. In Holland John, with his few savings, bought one whole Edam cheese, only to discover when he reached Britain that it was the only foreign cheese available. Kester found work teaching in London and John studied at the Central School of Speech and Drama, a contemporary of Jeremy Brett among others.

From the first I was much struck by John. I had never before met a young and attractive homosexual who was sensitive, intelligent and widely read. If we had both been at university, there would no doubt have been several possible mates, but out on a limb, as I was, John seemed unique. Youth and culture entwined is also a potent force if you stem from a philistine context as both John and I did.

After John left it took me two days before I wrote the first letter. The use of the possessive pronoun at the beginning of a letter denotes, I suspect, a certain stage in a relationship – when one is keen but still very much unsure, when one wants to show warmth but still be formal.

18:vi:57

My Dear John,

I suppose it is as difficult for you as it is for me to write this letter, what to say and how much to say, the adroit inference that is self-consciously planned. It is all vastly complicated and I can't pretend to understand a quarter of it. One has, of course, a few clues. (1) I miss you. That is only natural, I suppose, but worse, I feel miserable without you and regret the times I was unkind and certain. That again is only human. (2) I keep on seeing you everywhere I go in Brighton, your head or hands or body appear suddenly, flash forward and then I hear your voice. I am full of ghosts. And then there is (3) it is not enough to remember, but my mind insists upon recreating moments we should have experienced and wondering if life is going to allow us to. Like midnight bathing ...

I bathed naked in a warm and darkened sea in the early hours of this morning and this afternoon bathed in the same sea, naked again. I'm brown all over.

After you left I had dinner with Allan and Sugar Dad who was staying at the same hotel as poor Esmé P. (To think we had discussed him when he was dead.)

3

I am too dazed and quite unable to make plans. I hope we shall be able to see each other again soon.

C.

John's week in Brighton had concluded with us going to a performance of *The Country Wife* with Laurence Harvey and Joan Plowright. *The Country Wife* had also in the cast playing Sir Jaspar Fidget the singular actor, Esmé Percy, and his dog, a rather overweight spaniel looking like a sack of second-hand clothes. Percy was staying at the Royal Crescent Hotel where, after the Saturday night performance, he died. He had a very idiosyncratic voice and delivery – I can still hear him as one of the Chinese Gods in *The Good Woman of Szechuan* and the way he said, as he rose on a cardboard cloud, 'It will be all, all right in time.'

Where did I bathe naked in Brighton? At night, at low tide, it was dark enough to enter the water anywhere along the front. But in the daytime? I can only think it was the beach at Fishergate, just before the gas works, a fifteen minute walk from Tennis Road. Few people ever went there, and because of this it had a vaguely gay reputation.

My regret on being certain linked to a regret on being unkind, was, I seem to recollect, my refusal to commit myself emotionally in any way. The pace of the affair seemed a little too frenetic for my taste so I stressed that I was *not* in love with John, though my letter seems to contradict that. I posted it on the 19th, and that evening John wrote the following.

London SE 14

My Dear Colin,

It seems very strange to see your name beginning this letter. All last week I took pleasure whenever there was an immediate contact between us. That meant judging your mood of that moment, watching your first reaction. That, I take most delight in, the moment when an idea bridges two people, an electric moment when a word, an idea, without necessarily being deep, joins one to another, when the word doesn't have to be formed and spoken, then it is even more exhilarating. That happened between us many more times than once I think.

4

In comparison a letter is a poor substitute. What I thought might happen is happening. I already distrust and disbelieve all that I felt we achieved when we were together. Why? I'm not quite sure. Perhaps there wasn't a strong link forged? Perhaps it's an unconscious effort at protection in case *you* no longer believe in it.

Perhaps there's something else. A third wish. This is all a cousin of 'further being farther than farther'. You might call it exploration. Perhaps that's what hurt most leaving you, a sense of so much more to explore, intellectually, emotionally, physically.

I was shocked to read of Esmé Percy's death. It created quite a stir in Brighton, I suppose. In one way he was a link with a much younger me. I'll explain one day.

I've only just now read 'Nightworkers', I don't quite know why I didn't want to read it before. Perhaps it was to do with sharing an experience.

How strangely alike it is to your other story. The 'hero' retiring into a closed personal world. That's the sensation I found from your self-portrait. In a much slighter way I felt it sometimes when I was with you, that I was intruding. Is that unsympathetic?

Strangely, yesterday I found a character straight from something you could write, selling 'Fragrance' soap along my street. It seems a strange linking. I couldn't help but buy some.

Now the sun is low and golden. It makes me gleam much bronzer than I am – yes, it's no longer pink.

Send me a sane letter. Or even flippant. Not earnest like this one.

Warmly, love, John.

PS And thank you for being a better landlady than dear Mrs Gibbs.

PPS On rereading this, everything important seems unsaid. Fill in the gaps please.

'Nightworkers' was my first short story published in the *London Magazine* in 1955. I had based my main character on Allan Sills, a friend I had met while doing my National Service in the RAMC. Later the same character reappeared in the novel series as Steven. Allan had a room in Brighton on the front next to the Grand

Hotel and had lately acquired this Sugar Daddy who was patience and generosity itself. So Allan/Steven now lived in some style and we, in the next few months, often benefited from it.

The salesman selling soap strikes me as coming straight out of Tennessee Williams. I don't much care for the connection, nor did I then, I suspect. I realize now that John was never very much on the wavelength of those stories and somehow resented their existence. This was because the Colin who was the professional writer was a creature in himself that John could never possess. And possession played a key role in the struggle of our relationship. I touch upon John's equivocal feelings over my work throughout this book, for they had always puzzled and disappointed me.

Brighton, the place itself, was important to my work and became over the years the setting, and almost another character, in my novels. If I was alone in the town, I would visit each bar, pub or club to see what talent there was. The public holidays brought into Brighton a great horde of strangers, and then the known gay venues, though crushed and uncomfortable, never failed to have some attractive and idle youth on the same search as one's own. I did not much care for these flesh-pots where human dignity was reduced to how the genitalia performed, but, like many others, I could not resist doing them over, having a look to see who the newcomers were. However, what I loved most were a couple of bars which they never used, Piggots and the Beach Bar. The first was a pub off the lower end of St. James Street, where the saloon bar with a piano was kept almost exclusively for lesbians. The odd gay was endured, but not encouraged. The lesbians were all locals, middle-aged or older, some of them had faces out of Hogarth, and in their astonishing ugliness I found a fascinating poetry. A short stay, half a bitter's worth, was long enough, just to remind me of some aspect of a life within myself I needed to revitalize. But I was capable of spending a whole evening at the Beach Bar, which was a microcosm of gutter life. As its name implied, the bar was on the beach, at the end of West Street. I've no idea what it is like now, but thirty years ago it was crammed with what politicians refer to as the dregs of humanity. Spivs and tarts, yes, but spiv failures, alcoholic crooks who even fudged a simple theft, tarts with hearts of gold so pure

they did it for free, because they were too far gone to care much what they were doing. There was a midget and a dwarf, old women of vast corpulence dressed in torn satin and grubby lace, men with make-up smeared over their faces and toupees put on crooked, women in wigs and feathered hats, gay boys of devastating ugliness, deformities and amputated fingers. They had names like Banana Lil, Hot Rod and Baby Bee; there was asexuality, bisexuality and anything else one could dream up. I loved it: it fired my imagination, though I was always a little petrified and ill at ease. I never picked anyone up from these bars, but I used both in various novels and set my first play, *The Ballad of the False Barman*, in the Beach Bar, trying to catch something of the depravity that a mere onlooker might see, yet showing that underneath the squalor there were many misfits and failures, people living out dreams on a pittance. Happiness was as transitory as a free drink from a stranger.

I must have shown John all this Brighton life, but I cannot remember us doing the rounds. As a couple we were self-sufficient, yet I think we liked to be seen. We wanted, I suspect, to go to bars to be admired as two young, desirable men. We did not hide our love, nor, I believe, did we flaunt it, though there might have been aspects of that, for our homosexuality was very much a radical weapon against society. We used it to unnerve the conservative Establishment, to poke fun at it, to undermine it. It is, of course, child's play in its literal meaning: rude words and gestures are pathetic weapons to fight with, but we did not see that. We saw homosexuality as a huge area of truth which had been swept underground, and we saw the Establishment, filled as it was with so many 'closets', as hypocritical and immoral. On that, of course, we were right.

We are inclined to forget now the appalling effect on young homosexuals of the fact that we were outlaws. The act was illegal between privately consenting adults. We grew up to fear the police. I do not exaggerate. When there can be a knock on the door at night, the house invaded by uniformed men who then examine the way you live and the condition of your bed linen, you exist in a social tyranny ruled by bigots. This, at an early age, teaches you what the concept of freedom and democracy is. In Britain, we have never approached anywhere near those fundamental rights which all citizens should have. This knowledge of the moral and sexual tyranny we are born in is liable to give one a compassionate understanding of all oppressed minorities, an emotional solidarity with them. As my father said, and it sums up one view of life nicely, 'If you are up to your neck in shit and some bastard throws a brick at you, do you duck or not?'

We were illegal and we resented the rest of society for making us so. But we had to survive, be ever watchful for the approaching harassment from police. Yet sometimes you forgot. Happiness always made you forget. One night, beneath the stars with the sea rolling in at our feet, John and I, our arms entwined in romantic lover fashion, were walking the Brighton esplanade back to Hove. We were also singing Brecht. Not loudly, but softly, as lovers do, singing 'The Alabama Song' and laughing as we sang. Suddenly without a sound two torches were switched on a yard in front of us and they played over our faces and bodies. 'Who are you? What are you doing?'

The shock of the surprise was more terrifying than any other aspect, but as the grilling went on one felt a new terror. We were criminals in the eyes of the law. They let us go after five minutes, and we went on walking, hurrying through the darkness now, miserable and shaken that we should be made to feel bad when we knew we were not. In bed, in each other's arms that night, we slept fitfully, afraid of the sound of the knock on the door.

The first paragraph of Charter 88 begins thus:

We have been brought up in Britain to believe that we are free; that our Parliament is the mother of democracy; that our liberty is the envy of the world; that our system of justice is always fair; that our guardians of our safety, the police and security services, are subject to democratic, legal control; that our civil service is impartial; that our cities and communities maintain a proud identity; that our press is brave and honest.

None of this is true to the oppressed minorities. It is blatant nonsense to a black lad, an Asian girl or a gay boy. Throughout my growing up I was aware that these were concepts believed by many but I knew there was no substance behind them for me.

I received John's letter on the 21st, a Friday, and wrote back immediately.

My Dear John,

What a strange and curious letter.

Why should you be afraid of such a normal reaction to last week? We may well go down in a cataclysm of thunder, guts and tears and have nothing at the end of it all to remember. I don't think life bothers or even worries about what we secretly want. It gives us something quite different from what we asked for. And then of course one can always play that delightful game of adaptability. When one is about ninety, bald, paunchy and addled (and maybe wise) one can't cry like the young or long like the frustrated because one has 'adapted' oneself. And that is probably a living death. Which is all to say that if you want something enough, scream for it until you get it, don't, don't be reasonable. Love is rare enough after all, for one to tear one's own guts out in order to get it. And we all play that game in some degree or other. You know I believe, think, feel, that something real did happen last week. I don't think I've doubted it once. But I think it can die through undernourishment quickly.

So if you can, and if you can bear to see me washing, ironing, packing, why don't you come down next weekend? I leave on the Monday.

C.

I must say I find this letter off-putting. I seem to ignore the power of the unconscious, to reject 'secret desires' as inexplicable. How could I have been so dim? Perhaps it was a method of distancing myself from the mysterious and the inexplicable. The use of 'one' is, of course, another distancing trick. My idea of what it is like to be old is also way off the mark; it had not occurred to me that the old might feel more frustration and weep over lost hopes far more than the young. Obviously I saw the old as conservative, rigid, puritan, the ones who had not lived. On the positive side, the letter does express a wish for risk, for adventure, for exploring the uncharted seas. There was also plenty of cataclysm of a memorable kind.

I was about to leave for the Côte d'Azur and Venice with my vicar. John wrote back on the Sunday.

London SE 14

Dear Colin,

Thank you for both your letters. Our first must have crossed in the post. I spent quite some time trying to answer your earlier letter. I was more than displeased with what I wrote. If you thought my earlier letter obscure and rambling then you should have seen those efforts which ended in the waste basket.

I was in a daze all last week. I couldn't get you from my mind, I was more than miserable. And I felt frustrated, that we were so far apart and that, at that moment, if we had been together we could have been very happy. I found myself looking for you in the streets, in cafés, at the theatre, hoping by some strange quirk of chance you had been able to come up to town. Needless to say I was constantly frustrated. And just then so many people at once began making demands on my interests or time or affections. All of it seemed to be taking us apart. It was all rather distressing.

Colin, liebchen, I never doubted what happened last week. I simply couldn't stop wondering if it had affected you as it had me. I was afraid to say – I want to be with you – see, here I'm shying, because I really want to say, I love you. And that is true. I *want* us to find time to explore that because we would be very happy very often.

Last week, for the first time for *many* months I gained confidence in myself. That was your work. You did it in many ways. Summer started last week.

I'm coming down at the weekend if it's still all right. I'll give you a hand in packing and preparing. Please, though, not too much of that. Leave some time for lying in the sun, bathing and being happy.

Friday – I went to Sadlers Wells to see the Kurfurstendamms' production of *The Dream Play*. How very modern Strindberg is! How much plays such as *Camino Real* owe to him. What good theatre-use of the theatre. And yet how difficult to accept his moralizing and heavy-handed use of symbols. It seems very much lacking in subtlety now, though when I was at school, this was one play I particularly wanted to produce.

Tuesday evening I took charge of a drama class at an LCC evening institute. The first time I've worked with adults. It was exciting and exhilarating. Their work was very good and they seemed very pleased. A pity it was only for one evening. Thursday and Saturday I attended classes and demonstration dance studies at Sigurd Leeder's studio. Do you know him or of him? He was the co-founder of the Jooss Ballet famous before the war for *The Green Table*. The work I saw was most interesting and one lad's attempt to mime riding a horse was better by far than the famous 'horse' of Jean-Louis Barrault. At the time I was angry that you weren't there to see it.

John

The Kurt Jooss Ballet Company was another bond between us. I had seen them perform *The Green Table* in the middle of the war at the Theatre Royal, Brighton, and I fell in love with modern dance movement there and then. Astaire and Rogers paled into insignificance compared with this modern and passionate anti-war tract. I returned home and, aged about ten, declared to my mother that I wanted to study dance. She looked horrified and declared: 'Oh no, you'll become one of them.' The tone of voice was so shocked, the words reverberated with such deep revulsion, that I never dared to mention it again. It was not until my late teens that I realized what she had meant.

John rang next on the Wednesday. I was out for a moment, and he spoke to the girl-friend who was staying with me.

26:vi:57

My Dear John,

I'm very sorry to have left the house for the ten minutes last night when you chose to telephone. Lucy seemed somewhat mystified by the message.

I'm sorry it can't be Friday, but I want us to have a wild and ecstatic thirty-six hours, with nothing in the way. I think of you at all the times I shouldn't, but I find now that you're growing vague and distant, that I no longer see you about or hear your voice, nor can I close my eyes and bring back by force, the visual memory of you.

There have been masses of things I wanted to say. But your last letter made me feel happy. Oh John . . .

C.

My relationship with Lucy was not primarily a sexual one, though occasionally we shared a bed. This, I think, is the reason why the girl is so casually dismissed. I believe strongly that in the first half of our lives, until we achieve greater self-awareness, our psycho-sexual nature is commenting fiercely upon our parents' programming. The reader may be bewildered by the fact that, at this moment, there were girls, lads, men and clergymen mixed up intimately in my life, but I believe this owes more to my parents' real nature than to mine. I was frantically trying to struggle out from beneath their unresolved, labyrinthine problems. Because my relationships with women are an inevitable part of this memoir, this programming is explored later. The bisexual is one of the last taboos in our society. (A more odious figure now, of course, because of AIDS.)

My next letter drops the possessive pronoun but ends in love. It is written from Cap Ferrat, from the villa next to Somerset Maugham's.

Bontoc
2:vii:57

Dear John,

I couldn't understand exactly what it reminded me of (the villa, I mean) with its facile modernity, until this morning. Do you know it is incredibly Scott Fitzgerald, the hardness, the sharp brittle unfriendly lines, built in the 30s – if you haven't read *Tender is the Night* do so, and you will get a picture of what this is. Though I must say, the garden, the pool, the sea, the cicada, singing, the balm and the luxury, the frogs at night, and above all, a thin orange moon, like a flame, subsiding behind a hill is all more beautiful than one had ever imagined. This is my first quick note in the beginning of the morning.

3:vii:57

I swam and sunbathed all day, naked by the pool. In the evening we drove to Villefranche to see the new Jean Cocteau Chapel of St. Pierre, only opened on Sunday for the first Mass. It used to be a place for the fishermen's nets, though it was built as a chapel in the thirteenth century. He has painted it completely in a series of the most fascinating line drawings, incredibly beautiful, very thin and spiritual.

There is a German affair here also. A very pretty boy of 19, Wolfgang, and a possessive, rather jealous man of about 30. It's all very quiet and tends to be boring, for one can only soak up the sun and read and write, etc. But anyway perhaps I shall enjoy the gay life of Venice all the more. Must say I'm rather longing for a gay bar and masses of pretty things to stare at.

Write a letter that will welcome me to Venice on Sunday when we arrive.

Love,
C.

PS The journey was superb. Not a tremor or a bump at 23,000 feet.

It interests me that I use 'gay' in the modern sense, but I rather regret there is no detailed picture of this villa. Somerset Maugham came to tea one day, but the house guests were told firmly by our host to remain out of sight by the pool. I was so furious at this snub that in later years when I might have engineered a meeting through mutual friends, I refused to sink so low. I was also then not an admirer of Maugham's work, thinking in my arrogance that it dealt merely with the surface of life.

The Villa Bontoc was so named by the American owner Bill Sherfesee after a tribe who had a particular mating ritual that beguiled him. The story as told to me was that in the long house there are a series of parallel hammocks with naked youths and maidens in opposing lines. The youths swing in the hammocks until they penetrate the virgin girls. This seems to me now a most bizarre and difficult feat, though for some reason it was a story that my vicar lover adored.

The villa was full of staff, maids and menservants. For the first time I had a taste of the rich life. We dined from a long polished table with lighted candelabra, and a manservant in white gloves served us. But I found the whole ambiance claustrophobic. I could not view this context in any other way but as a rather involved joke, a piece of surrealism, with me observing people who basically deceived themselves. Our host was married but gay, a paradox I considered then in my inexperience to be a form of self-hypocrisy. I felt sensitive to the wives and their possible humiliation in this uneasy alliance. To make this worse our host was also a Christian, like Billy, my vicar, and I found this the most embarrassing idea of all. On the Sunday morning, the maids had disturbed me still sleeping beneath swathes of mosquito netting, as the staff had been certain I would have gone to Mass with everyone else.

I must admit I was also then part of what sometimes seems like a homosexual conspiracy – once gay, always so. I now believe this not to be true. Yet I detect in myself then, and in gay people now, a refusal to admit that women could exert the same power over a man that perhaps a young lad could. Gossip abounds with stories of staid married men running away with a golden boy. These are, I am certain, part of the myths of sexuality, always with us in some form or other. At Bontoc I think we all believed that Bill had married as a conventional cover to hide his gay entanglements. However, I have now no way of knowing whether that was true or not. All I do know is that the truth is far more complicated, astonishing and subtle than gossip ever wishes to reveal.

After a week we moved to Venice. Here, the tone of my letters radically changes. It was as if I knew I was not part of Billy's smart rich world, that I couldn't tag along as the young 'kept' lover, that I found the whole situation humiliating and slightly disgusting.

Lido di Venezia
8:vii:57

Darling –

I love you, I love you, I love you and I miss you and I want you and I don't like it at all. All the things I have I find I want to share with you and then you're not there.

The heat is intolerable, the sea like a hot bath, at night sleep is almost unbearable and at the moment I still haven't seen Venice, but I will in an hour. So I'll write tomorrow and tell you the first impressions. Oh, darling, why are you such a long way away? Last week I wasn't sure of anything. This week I'm sure of too much. But I simply want to be with you. I think I enjoyed those last two days as I have never enjoyed anything before.

Write to me quickly for I'm starved of hearing from you, parched and desolate.

Love,
C.

This, I remember, brought a cool response from John. (The letter is missing.) I write again, my letter posted on 11 July.

Dear John,

Your letter is both bewildering and confusing. When I had thought things were vaguely clear. My dear John, it's understandable I suppose that you should be feeling confused, but I would have thought that that last weekend cemented something which made me feel sure of two things. 1. That I loved you. 2. That I wanted us to live together. Where we live together depends mostly, I think, on the Army business. Now if this is what you feel uncertain about, for God's sake tell me in plain words, so that I can get the knife out and sever you thoroughly from my system. I know it is difficult in that I had to be away just now. But I want you constantly here, and perhaps one day we might come to Venice. It is the most incredible and romantic city filled to overflowing with tarts.

We fly back on Thursday 18th in the evening. I could be somewhere in the West End about 9.00 p.m. Can I meet you and can I stay the night somewhere? Keep Friday clear as well, we might go back to Brighton together. Mama doesn't come till Saturday evening. I don't know what you are doing in August but I want you near, if possible.

Darling, don't let us slip through our fingers, for the first time in my life I feel that there is a tremendous amount for us to give each other and masses of things to explore. I want us very much to be happy. I believe we can be. I want us to be as happy as the night we bathed, naked and dark in an even darker sea. I hate being away from you and we must try and not let it happen again. Does all this, I wonder, make things any clearer? It doesn't for me.

All my love,
C.

PS What do you want me to bring you back from Venice apart from myself? A gondolier perhaps?

I hear the sound of John's voice in this letter of mine, as if I have taken over the role of the passionate seducer. John was to learn painfully that when I wrote in a letter 'I knew I had to be away just now', it was generally because I was with someone else. Here, too, is the first mention in the 'Army business' of the National Service that John would have to do if he stayed on in England. Though he had an Australian passport, he had lived in England for eight years and he was likely to be enlisted. He had decided to avoid it by leaving the country.

This second letter brought an answer likely to calm any anxieties I had.

London

My Dear Colin,

Thank you for both your letters. The second arrived on Friday and then one was waiting for me at home yesterday evening when I came back from my exam.

Sweet, I'm sorry if my letter upset you or worried you. It was a very unfortunate fortnight for many reasons. I missed you very much, so much I hardly admitted it to myself. Then school was *so* busy with some exam reports and got a bit on top of me. I tried to achieve too much for this exam, making a model of the stage, costumes, plots, etc. and perhaps I got a bit frantic. Then with G. life has been very confused. One moment he would be very elated and wonderful, then next very depressed and considering suicide. And being capable of it. That was very distressing. One moment he would be as I have always wanted him to be and felt he was capable of, kind, thoughtful, very sweet, very loving. After many months of unhappiness this unexpected 'flowering' tore at me. And then he would become so depressed, that I felt that I was walking a razor edge in what I said to him, to keep him from doing something crazy. It's all been very exhausting. Sorry love, even to write this now but it's something easier for me to write than say.

I'm so pleased you're coming back on Thursday. Can you meet me in town at 9-ish? Easily? What would Billy (?) say or think? Would he mind? I'll be in Faulkner's Coffee Bar, Leicester Square, from 9.30 to 10.30 p.m. Do you know it?

I'll try to arrange a place for us to stay. If you can come then come.

I hate your being away. Because I want so often to see you, touch you, say something to you. And you're not there. And to make do I must imagine it with an imagined you. And when I do see you, that imagined you goes and there is a blank pause while it sinks in that *you* are there.

Sweet, I want us to be so very happy. And I want us to be resilient to mistakes and upsets and difficulties. We know each other as yet under ideal conditions – lots of free time, sun, money to spend. I want us to strengthen the bonds between us so that they could take the strain when conditions are far from perfect. And I want to see that area of common ground on which we meet extend and grow. It would kill me to watch it shrink away.

And I want to learn to accept you as you are without in any way wanting to change you into what I might want you to be. For me that will be hard!

I love you sweetheart. Darling. Very much. Come back very soon.

My love, my thoughts and even more.

John

PS Yes, a gondolier, please.

What Billy thought, he kept mostly to himself, but he knew in that three week holiday where my thoughts were. He must have known too that it was the end of our relationship.

Whether John and I stayed in London that night or not, I cannot remember, but what had been arranged soon after I returned was that once the school had broken up for the summer holidays John would leave G. and his flat in London and come to live with me. We did not decide anything else for the future except for that month of August.

Before Billy departs from these pages, though he was to remain a considerate and loving friend throughout his life, I ought perhaps to say a word on vicars and my early predilection for them. I was, in my youth, somewhat addicted to a handsome vicar, rather in the way many devout churchwomen are. However, I did more with my vicars than they would ever have dreamt of, or perhaps they did and still do dream of such carnal pleasures.

My addiction then as now was a good joke, but I did not at that time look any closer at it, to try to understand why I needed to seduce every vicar in my path. Was this my unchristian duty? For that is what it felt like. What was the nature of the motivation which compelled me? They were, after all, easy prey. There was certainly no challenge in this activity, and any group of people conquered so easily, you would think I might find boring. In fact, it amused me profoundly; but why? The nature of most addictions is only understood after they have either vanished or been conquered. Mine faded away with the knowledge that the whole activity was a kind of unconscious revenge upon my mother. She, married to a Rabelaisian womanizer, had a series of obsessive infatuations with various vicars, from Richard Rees of the church in Hangleton where my sister was married at eighteen, to Gordon Strutt of a church in Addiscombe. They were all low churchmen of great and earnest worthiness who advised my mother to honour and stay within her marriage vows, thus imprisoning her for life to an egocentric and inconsiderate husband. As a child, I was aware of how I resented their advice and their power over my mother. At fourteen, when I begged her to divorce my father, leave and start an independent life of her own, she rejected my advice and continued to take the counsel of her vicar. Need I say more?

My revenge, I suppose, was even sweeter when my mother fell violently in love with Billy himself, though a more sophisticated woman would have seen easily not only his own nature but the strength of his obsession with myself. This last infatuation was, in fact, to prove embarrassing. In Billy's presence she became quite coy, and rationalized his failure to pursue her by the fact that she was still married. One might think that alone would be the spur for leaving my father, but her infatuation was kept within the limits of fantasy.

I cannot end this chapter without returning to its beginning. On the first night we spent together John told me of the cancer he had suffered. Testicular tumours are associated with undescended testes, though it is not clear how or indeed whether one causes the other. Certainly in John's puberty, only one testicle had dropped into the scrotum and no one did anything about it, for ignorance in these matters reigned supreme in those days, especially in his family. The tragic irony is that a young man with only one ball is so vulnerable to developing a tumour. In the year before we met the tumour and the testicle had been removed, and the treatment had included radiation and chemotherapy. They gave him a false testicle so that the scrotum would look normal, but in a few weeks John had suffered a reaction to this alien object and was in great pain. When I met him the wound had healed but there were no testicles, the scrotum lying flat against the underside of the groin beneath the penis. No companion of John's could be fooled by this. Oddly enough, the hospital had also provided tablets which produced fake spermatozoa; they told John that a woman would be fooled. Odd view of women they had. John took the tablets daily. His physical state did not, of course, make the slightest difference to an orgasm or the mechanics of love-making. I stress this because so many people seem to think that having no testicles in a mature man means he is a eunuch without the ability to experience orgasm. What it did mean was that he was sterile, but certainly not impotent. This cruel fact is basic not only to his character, but to the whole nature of our fraught yet idyllic relationship. Looking back now, I curse my own insensitivity which never took the matter into account as one of the factors which made our life together so stormy.

2

Living Together

.

Astonishingly for me, throughout the whole of August we were relaxed and happy. This first experience of sharing my life neither alarmed nor confused me. Post-war Britain was then beginning to come out of the gloom of austerity, though the pressure during the war years to economize, garner the scraps, and never waste anything, had left residues of daily trivial guilt. My youth was lived in an atmosphere where everything was pared down to the meagre, but John's Australian, expansive enthusiasm, the kind of largeness of vision he had, tended to shatter all the small-minded, nit-picking worries. Everything was touched with exuberance. The simplest tasks, from the moment the curtains were pulled in the morning, were invested with a possible meaning and an almost certain celebration. The summer was hot, and Brighton felt like the Mediterranean, crammed with people swimming and sun-bathing. We made a sun lotion out of olive oil, a touch of vinegar and a drop of iodine for added colour. John baked croissants, leaving the dough out in the garden all night for a cool rise. They were the first croissants I had eaten. He knocked two apples together and asked me to listen. Listen to the interior, to the heart of things, feel it, he was saying. Like Rebecca West's father asking the children in winter to rest their palms upon the bark of trees and feel the sap rising.

He bought me from Heal's a small breakfast tea set; it wasn't by Bernard Leach but it was very like and it introduced me to the warmth and pleasure of good shapes in pots and cups. I used the teacup for morning coffee for the next twenty years. He also brought with him various pieces of china, including an art deco teapot, which I still have, a small plump shape in the Chinese manner with one spray of leaves forming part of the spout and lid. A tiny example of perfect, unpretentious design

I worked on my novel in the mornings or made line drawings of John in sybaritic poses. My description of his body was of Picasso Blue period (his torso being thin and undeveloped) with baroque or Michelangelo legs. However, this combination was perfectly suited to a thin pen line and over the years from those months I sold a good fifty drawings. He had a shrewd eye for art and would point out architecture that he thought was suitable for this pen treatment of mine. The Royal Pavilion was ideal. I began it that summer. I was to learn again and again in the next two years that John's particular talent was to fire others, to direct them into the paths they could best flourish in

In those days National Service loomed large; for me it was something grotesque and formidable. At eighteen, though a pacifist, I had chosen the RAMC and opted to treat venereal diseases. As part of that I was sent to Hamburg, where a queue of Allied servicemen waited to be diagnosed and treated. Later the experiences were used in stories and novels, but I barely survived and was discharged after fifteen months when I attempted suicide. John was now liable to do his two years service and was determined to avoid this by leaving the country. Thus we knew that whatever happened in the relationship, the physical living together could not continue unless I went wherever John travelled. I was aware of this and I think at first did not much care. In youth one is not good at making decisions, tending to put them off or use them as an excuse to hide deeper motivations. We did not discuss the future, and if I said, 'Why not stay and do your National Service?' he would answer gloomily, 'Look what it did to you.'

That month I met Harry Fainlight, the poet, down from Cambridge, and an admirer of my published short stories. He was also determined to avoid his National Service, but this did not prove to be a bond between him and John. Harry's presence made everyone – except myself – uncomfortable. His face was amazingly fragile as if made from bird bones; he would stare at the company with his huge, slightly protuberant eyes which seemed to absorb so much that was going on beneath the surface, then suddenly laugh, a sound totally without humour. This sound would

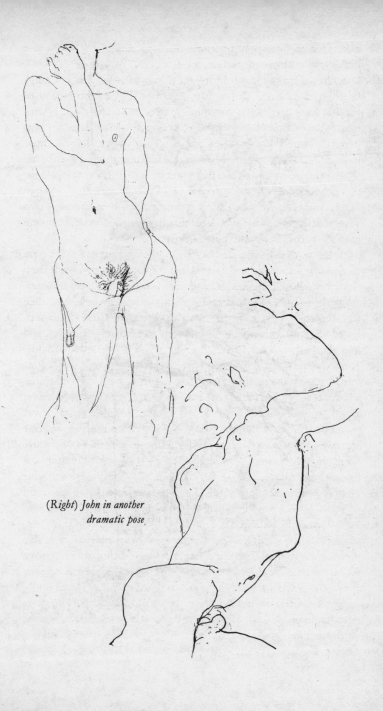

*(Right) John in another
dramatic pose*

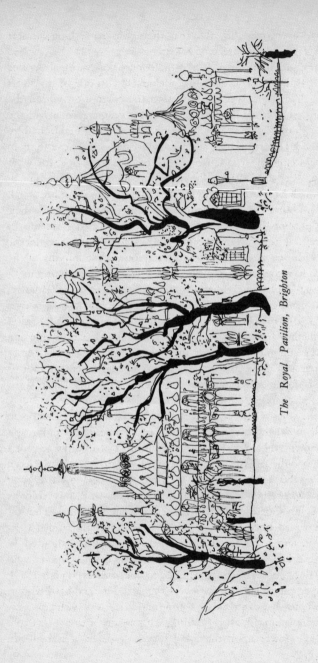

The Royal Pavilion, Brighton

unnerve everyone; they felt that there was something sinister about Harry which threatened them.

Harry and John, then, feared the concept of National Service while I had experienced its brutal character. In one of my short stories, 'An Alien World', I stressed the corruption within the military which they both dreaded. A few years ago many of the memories of National Service by people of my generation were published. I was intrigued and somewhat puzzled to read in them a tone of enjoyment, a sense of it all being a jolly jape, for what I remember, and loathe still, was the total erasure of the human individual. I regard the individual as an art form: the more we all celebrate our individuality and our distinction from each other, while pooling our talents and resources, the closer we are to civilization. Yet warfare requires the exact opposite: it wants the herd with one voice, it wants two million people moving at the same split second in the same gesture. Film of pre-war Nuremberg rallies gave me as a child an instinctive horror of the mass voice, of the mass emotion, to such a degree that on rare occasions when I have marched in London with CND or the Trade Union movement, I have been unable to chorus any slogan or sing any song of commitment. I fear the human animal when it comes together as a mob – for whatever cause. And when the mob is trained, under orders and given weapons, then the human spirit has no place to go, but hides and trembles in shame.

In the year of my National Service, I watched lads of eighteen beaten into submission by the use of psychological ploys and punishment. There was little revolt in most of us anyway, but I had joined the RAMC as a pacifist and I was given orders to learn to shoot the enemy. This was the time of the war in Korea, and North Korea did not recognize the Red Cross so RAMC soldiers were being shot and killed when tending the wounded. The rest of the squad obediently lay in the sand dunes and aimed their rifles on target. I refused to touch the thing. I was shouted at, kicked, called a faggot and eventually sent to the Captain who listened to me wearily but said I had to obey orders. It ended with me being punished with two weeks' guard duty and hard labour, which consisted of attacking a stone and brick wall with a pickaxe and demolishing it, then building it up again. This work had a numbing power upon the mind. Psychologically it is brilliant:

make them see that their labour is useless, then they will understand how inadequate and insignificant they are themselves. I kept my individuality burning deep inside but it was a frantic and bitter struggle. I would not have wished the experience on anyone. I knew I had had a small taste of hell.

We had few friends in that short summer. We did the bars at weekends, walked and swam. John introduced me to contemporary American poetry, to Stevie Smith and William Plomer, while I introduced him to Djuna Barnes's *Nightwood*, the novels of Faulkner, Joyce, Woolf and Gide. We read plays together aloud and never dared discuss the future.

But there was Brighton and its astonishing quality. The showbiz aspect was always beguiling. I had had my confrontation with various personalities. Some months before I met John, Allan and I were having supper in a modest coffee bar in Duke Street, owned by Skeffington-Lodge, a Labour MP in the Attlee Government. Across the room Gilbert Harding was also eating with what seemed a couple of lackeys. Gilbert was very loud and offensive, complaining of everything. When there was a pause in this aggressive monologue I said to Allan in my loudest and clearest tones, 'Who is that very rude man over there so intent on ruining everyone's pleasure?' Silence from Gilbert, who was possibly the most famous man in England. He called over a waiter and whispered to him. A moment later a bottle of claret was brought to our table; we raised our glasses and spent the rest of the evening with him, when he behaved with great charm. I intrigued him and I was to be taken up in a big way. I endured the process for two days.

The next day Gilbert rang and invited me to pop over for lunch. He was charming, the best raconteur, except for Angus Wilson, I have ever met. I was then whisked up to London to see *What's My Line?* As Gilbert bent over to get into the back seat of the chauffeur driven car, he farted loudly four or five times. As he did so, he turned and glared at his fat Pekinese Shampoo, shouting the dog's name and complaining of his behaviour. A little nearer London we passed two lads on bicycles. Gilbert leant out of the window and sniffed the air. 'Fish, fish,' he called out. 'Can't you smell it? Wanking, that's all they do, all the time.' He relished the thought.

After the performance we went out to dine. Good food then was based on the grandeur of the ingredients, not the style of cooking. Lobster would be smothered in an alcoholic cream sauce, Dover sole covered in Hollandaise. It was *haute cuisine*, very filling and very bad for you. Gilbert was treated in the restaurants as a discerning gourmand, waiters fawned. We returned to his flat. On the piano there was a signed photograph of Marlene Dietrich. 'Marvellous creature,' Gilbert said. 'She wanted to marry me.' I looked astonished, and I still am. I was relieved to see that I had the guest bedroom all to myself and I slept alone, but I was awoken in the morning by Gilbert's heavy hand descending upon my crotch, accompanied by his individual roar. 'What! No erection. Every boy has an erection in the early morning.' Then plunging his face near to mine with every hair of his moustache outraged, he shouted, 'Why haven't you got an erection?'

After being called in to do up his braces and help him on with his jacket I said I was not his valet and walked out. We hardly ever met again. Poor vulnerable, tortured Harding, he longed for affection but had no way of managing to cope with it or even of knowing how to find it. He outraged all my sensibilities and pride, but if I had been older and wiser I would have been sharp with him, as in the first meeting. He bloomed with such treatment. The trouble was that most people feared him and indulged him. He did tell the most amazing stories, all true he claimed. There was one about a sailor who exposed himself with a crucifix hanging from his penis. All because he had a Roman Catholic mother who became a whore, I seem to recall. Gilbert's main troubles were his Catholicism and his mother – maybe that's why he told the story so brilliantly.

John and I lived in the upstairs flat of a small terraced house in Hove – 15 Tennis Road, opposite the lagoon and a few minutes from the sea. This was the house that my Spencer grandparents had once lived in, moving there in retirement from East Croydon. They had been looked after by my spinster aunt, christened Edith and nicknamed Dede by the first granddaughter – my sister Thelma, who was named after a Marie Corelli novel. The house in Tennis Road belonged to Dede, but as it was too big for her use only, my father had turned the top floor into a flat and used it for weekends. But he had grown tired of this arrangement and

I had now taken it over, bought a few pieces of second-hand furniture, taken the worn purple carpet and curtains from the vicar's bedroom and had quickly made the place not only comfortable, but stylish. From my late teens I searched junk shops and collected furniture, china and glass.

It is difficult to write this without sounding élitist or superior, yet a gift for interior design is as much a natural characteristic as the ability to play the piano or do sums. It is almost wholly visual. A Suffolk woman recently commenting on my painting said, 'Your brain must be in your eye.' There is something in that, for the visual sense has an extra dimension. The painter's eye? Something which assesses shapes, dimensions, colours, the play of chiaroscuro, the sheen of wood and fabric, the fusion of patterns. The Vermeer interiors have it to perfection: it is an essential part of the profound satisfaction they give. Money can be a barrier to taste, whereas I have known friends with no money at all go into a bare room and make it live within a few hours, with the sparse possessions they have. It is a natural facility but where it comes from is a mystery.

My childhood environment was plebeian with touches of gross vulgarity. I knew as a small child it was ugly, knew it made me uncomfortable and unhappy, knew from then that there was something out there called 'antiques' that I liked. My sister recalls me saying at the age of seven that 'one day I would have a house filled with antiques'. I have to conclude that as a very small child I must have flicked through magazines, seen illustrations of Edwardian and Victorian romances, and that scraps of interiors which I found pleasing lodged in my memory. Once in my late teens, I, of course, visited other houses which sometimes, as in the vicar's, simulated taste through wealth and inheritance. Though I was appreciative I knew that this was a kind of house uniform worn by the affluent; these furnishings did not derive from a distinct personal choice, they were inherited and maintained as part of social status. For this reason, they too included unhappy juxtapositions of unappealing shapes and colours, as ugly in their way as the furniture of my childhood. Perhaps it is partly genetic, for my maternal grandfather had been a cabinet maker. It was his furniture, a bookcase and a desk, I took to my own bedroom when I was small.

One incident occurred that August which was unforgettable and the above explanation about my part of the house in Hove sets the scene. My aunt, if she came to the flat, knocked on the door and called out. The door, of course, could be locked but I never bothered. My aunt, in fact, hardly ever did come up the stairs. If she wanted to see me she would wait and run into the hall as I was going out of the front door. I remember her once calling out and banging on the ceiling, but that was understandable enough as our bath water was running through into her scullery. We had taken a bath together and the inevitable had happened: in the midst of love-making most of the water went on to the floor and through the ceiling.

But what was traumatic was the visit of my mother early one morning, travelling down from East Croydon and bringing with her my five-year-old niece, Sandra. My mother decided she would surprise me. She, in fact, surprised herself. Dede was glad enough to see them and went to put the kettle on, while mother came straight upstairs and, without knocking, walked into the flat through the sitting-room and opened the bedroom door.

It was about ten in the morning, very late in her view but not in ours – we were often up talking and reading till two in the morning. We slept naked and often on waking would make love. But that was not the scene that met mother's eyes. We were both naked, yes, but were now deep in horseplay, fighting and rolling over on the bed. I had pinned John's wrists behind him and was seated on top of him, when, hearing the door open, I looked up to see mother staring at us. She said, 'Crummy lorum,' and left. I crawled beneath the bedclothes, dwarfed to the size of a toy that the Gods were kicking around the world. John then came into his own: with great decision he told me to dress and go downstairs immediately. But could I face her? I felt ashamed and humiliated. John was insistent. Go on, he commanded. And I did. Unwillingly, with a kind of nightmare screaming within me, I went down the stairs. Did I know what I was going to say? There was no apology from me needed, we both knew that. I suppose my plan was just to see her and say nothing, pretend the whole scene had not occurred. However, in times of emotional conflict my mother nearly always behaved magnanimously – this time was no exception. I kissed her on the cheek and said, 'Good morning.' She said, 'It was my fault. I should not have walked in. I should have knocked.' The incident was closed.

Yet it remains open still to me. Why should I be ashamed, humiliated, suffer nightmares of torment over this incident? Why should I recall it so clearly thirty years later?

The act of homosexuality essentially questions the masculine identity. It looks at masculine role-playing and understands its instability and vulnerability. All this and much more I was quite unconsciously saying to my father. I also see clearly now that in being gay I was taking my revenge on him. He loathed poofs, queers and pansies and celebrated all the derogatory notions; his conversation was riddled with demeaning jokes about them. That his only son and heir – a phrase he was fond of – might be one, humiliated him, but he carefully, until the day he died, never let on. Besides he was confused: girls came to my bed in the family home at East Croydon and he would give us an early morning warning, 'before your mum gets up'. So the girls would climb out of the ground floor window, and as dawn hardened around Park Lane I would see them to the station. My gayness then was a kind of performance for my father, and something my mother should not have seen.

But this won't wash at all. The vicars, after all, she was supposed to see. I was showing her how the Church had clay feet, but of course she never did see it. Vicars were fond of her son, she thought cosily, because her son had such an air of sensitive spirituality about him, or some such nonsense. (I think secretly she had longed for me to take Holy Orders – until in my adolescence she had to face the fact that I was a natural rebel.) My shame was obviously to do with my early programming, but in what way?

John and I in those first few months had told each other about our backgrounds. In these stories we found another bond, since our fathers had fought in the First World War, and what was more, were both at the Dardanelles. John's father, Tasker, was a few years older than Spencer, for my father, aged sixteen in 1914, had, like many others, lied about his age when he volunteered. I can never quite digest the terrible enormity of those youths being pitched into that traumatic horror; indeed, my father was marked for life, and because he was, I am too.* Early film newsreel, novels, songs and poems about that war reduce me to emotional chaos, and in a sense I weep now still for my father, that sixteen-year-old, and all the millions like him who were savaged and corrupted by the experience. Of the Dardanelles he said, 'We came after the Aussies; when we tried to land under Turkish fire, we were helped by the thousands of dead Aussies entangled in the barbed wire in the shallow water. We trod over them and got to the beach that way.'

Tasker had been at the Dardanelles and survived; he went on to France and was gassed. Back in Australia his health was ruined; he was past forty when he married and started a family: first a daughter, and then in 1933 John was born. But his father always seemed to John grim, humourless and taciturn, always sick and at home, something to escape from as soon as possible.

It wasn't until 1917 that my father was wounded and 'sent back to Blighty'. This was his account which I wrote down ten years ago as he told it. I place it here, because terrifying experiences like this were endured daily by millions, including John's father and mine, and inevitably they were part of our heritage in our emotional life.

'We were going through the Hindenburg line, attack started at dawn, the first lot had gone through, we were the second lot, I was all on my own, trotting along, ahead of the others...'

'Ahead?' I queried, never seeing my father as a hero.

'Well, I wanted to get there, holding my rifle with my right arm. I'd dropped the ammunition for the Lewis gunner, too bloody heavy, was going to look after myself. He had shell shock, Bennett was his name, started going round in circles with the Lewis gun, pointing it back at our lines he was. Too bloody dangerous. Best to be out ahead and on your own. So there I was, trotting, and suddenly me arm wasn't there, back like this behind me, it was, as I was running. I thought Christ, who's taken me bloody arm away? I look back and there it is hanging

*Dirk Bogarde – born 1921 – recently referred to himself as the last survivor of the First World War, reflecting the observation above. He had forgotten that those war survivors went on producing children well into the thirties and the experience was always far worse for the private soldier.

31

there, no feeling in it at all. Cor, I thought, what a bit of luck, been hit and now back to dear old Blighty. So just then I saw this shell crater, quite shallow it was, and there was a Lewis gunner lying in it. "Been hit, mate?" I said.

'"No," he said, "but it's safer here." Like Colonel Cudden, who hid in an old tank all day miles from the fighting.*

'"I have," I said, and sat down in the crater with him. He helped me off with me old Sam Brown and the jacket, looked at me arm. Just a little hole in the biceps, that's all. What a bit of luck, I kept on thinking.

'"If I were you," he said, "I'd hop it back."

'Just then a bloody shell exploded and a ton of mud came on us.

'"Suppose the Germans' counter-attack starts?" he said.

'Then we see a chap hopping on one leg, flashing past us like a bleedin' Olympic runner. Well, if he can do it, I thought. So off I trot back, holding my arm up. Then some officer waves at me, gestures for me to go around in a circle. So I do that. Machine-gun post that was. Sergeant there gets a bandage and makes me a sling.

'"How the hell do I know which way to go?" I ask.

'"Follow the red telephone cable, lad," he says.

'It's half buried in the mud and he points which way I'm to follow. All alone, off I go trotting across the mud, when suddenly I see the main road from Arras to Paris and it's packed with the Scots Infantry. I was longing to have company, someone to chat to, so I join 'em.

'"Jock," I say, "it's a hot day." And this chap just gurgles. Been shot through the throat, he has. Then we come to the first aid tent, just a shell hole with a bit of canvas over it. And the chap there bandages my arm and says to three of us, "look, you lot can walk five miles to Arras. If you see any vehicles leave them for the other wounded who can't walk."

'No sooner were we on the road when a horse-drawn ambulance stopped.

'"Want a lift?" he said.

'Sod the others, we said. Get to Arras and I wanted a tom tit badly,

---

*Colonel Cudden was father's CO in his Hampshire Regiment. Our childhood was full of stories about him. He wore make-up, was never in the front line, and was a petty tyrant over matters of dress. Father swore to us children that if he met him in civvies he would kill him. How? I asked. With the car, hit and run, he answered.

but I couldn't get my trousers down, stuck to me arse they were, with blood. Couldn't see what me arm was like behind, see. The orderly gave us a tetanus injection, couldn't put it in me arm, so he jabbed it into me chest and wham, I passed out, flat on the floor I was. Then we're told to get on a little train, across the town, forgotten the name, just a bench either side, remember seeing this soldier opposite me and the pool of blood at his feet. And I thought, he's going to pass out any moment, then I looked down and there was a pool of blood at my feet too.

'Got to the hospital and a sergeant said: "Right, form up in ranks, ready, march." And I got cheeky.

'"No mate," I said, "we've had enough of that. Just tell us where we've got to go and we'll get there."

'Quiet as a lamb, he was, just pointed across the square. And that's when the doctor said to me, have to have the arm off. Two o'clock in the afternoon, that was.

'"Amputate that arm. Have to lose it, lad," he said.

'"Look," I said, "this tattoo cost me a quid in Winchester. I'm not losing my tattoo."

'"Nothing for it, lad," he said.

'Next morning we were waiting and he comes back and says: "You three will have to wait. Got a lot of leg cases come in, in the night. Those are urgent." And he sends us off somewhere near the coast. When I think of all those poor blighters with only one leg and that saved me arm. Do you call it luck or is it providence?

'Hospital was good, proper bed, lovely nurses, they had to operate then, nerve gone, put some gold thread in and great bloody iron splints clamped to your shoulder. Wore it for ten months, when they took it off, me arm was bent, me fingers up, couldn't budge it and Major de Wynter said – this was a hospital in Surrey – he said,

'"You man. Why aren't you moving your arm?"

'"Can't sir."

'"Can't!" he said. And he took me arm and tried to break it across his knee like it was some bloody log. He couldn't. Got red in the face, he did.

'"Look, sir," I said, "if you go on like that I'll have another fracture."

'Then they gave me electrical treatment, but it took another two months before I could move it.

'So I'm back home, wanting two weeks holiday with me bike, but my

33

mum wouldn't have it. "Mr Law," she said, "needs a clerk and he is one of your father's tenants."

'Him being Chief Clerk in the Income Tax Office, Park Street. Well to please mum, off I go. And I'm given lists of figures to add up, but I see someone had done it before me in pencil in the margin. So I get those right quick and they hire me. What am I being paid? Thirty shillings a week. Then I start and I'm addressing envelopes. I didn't pass that exam to do that, I think. So perky, I complain. And they give me forms to vet. I come to one about a captain who was a prisoner of war and hadn't paid his tax for three years and I thought, blimey, fight for your country and that's the thanks you get. Tore that up. Got bored. Started tearing a few others up. Then they wanted me to get piles of big books from the strong room and carry them up three flights of stairs. Enough of that. I put my splint back on.

'Then Armistice Day came. November. I heard the band in North Street, wanted to join them. Opened the window to listen and some bloody spinster says, "Harry Spencer, there's a draught. Please, shut the window."

'So I said, "Bugger the window, bugger you and bugger the income tax office." Out I went, never went back, not even to get my last thirty bob.'

The term 'lovable rogue' is not big enough to describe my father. I used to say that he belonged more to fiction than to real life. There was something of the frustrated artist about him. He had a pleasant tenor voice and had ideas about singing professionally, but he failed to win a competition and gave it up. This was not like him, for he was a fighter. I learnt, of course, to love him, but he was hardly a role model for a young boy. From him all I learnt was that heterosexuality caused great grief. He had a series of mistresses before I was born and the one that he was involved with immediately prior to my birth had a husband who died in the throes of tertiary syphilis. As a direct cause of that I spent most of my teens convinced I suffered from congenital syphilis and was a doomed creature. No wonder Mann's *Doctor Faustus* was a seminal book of great significance to me. This was, of course, the main reason I chose to treat venereal disease in my year in the RAMC. Because of that I learnt about the various diseases and knew that I quite obviously was not a sufferer, for one of my parents would have shown symptoms long before that. Did my father realize how near to danger he was? He told me, 'I visited Elsie's husband in hospital, he was in a horrible mess. Gave me the willies, that did.'

As a child it was yet another caution, and a terrible one, to forgo women. But I had more devils to deal with in my sexual awareness of girls than this. Father's main mistress was his secretary at the building works, a married woman called Maisie.

We lived in Hove throughout the war, but father stayed in Croydon in the week, through the Blitz and the buzz bombs which devastated much of the town. At weekends he drove down with the car boot crammed with black market food obtained from Percy, the butcher, a member of the Communist Party. Sometimes, Percy and his wife would stay, sometimes just Maisie. At these weekends Maisie took over the duties, calling father Mr S. and insisting to my mother that she knew how he liked his tea, 'the top of the milk only'. Outraged, my mother would storm out of the house. She was, alas, entirely innocent. She never suspected that Maisie and father had a sexual relationship. The whole family, however, sensed that Maisie was an intruder, taking something away from us, though we couldn't understand what.

As a small boy, I suffered from acute embarrassment if father and Maisie insisted on taking me out with them, for I did not want anyone to believe that Maisie was my mother. Physically I thought she looked absurd. She was very tall, with long gangly limbs and a huge round head. But now when I look at photographs of her, I see a very sweet face, a kind and generous expression. I am sure this is the truth. She and my father gave each other a huge amount of happiness and I know that sexually they were in a state of bliss, having an imaginative turn of mind when it came to performing variations on the missionary position. I fear, though, that all this was part of my trouble. I knew from my father so much about what they did together, that the whole subject filled me with revulsion and horror for many years.

The first time I made love to a girl and we spent the night together, I had to drive off visions of Harry and Maisie coupling in all their diverse ways, for the visual obscenity of these pictures had the force of Bosch demons. So it was much easier for me to give up the struggle, to shut the door on all the nightmares and

Eddy . Mabel

*. . . as I called them in fiction, but this was my late adolescent perception
of father and Maisie*

on women too. To accept love and sexual pleasure from men and
leave it at that. Except that the human animal is so made that
there is no escape when he closes doors upon the unconscious.
Sublimation or suppression leads to all sorts of ills and somewhere
within me in my gay persona I knew I was lying, knew I was
being false; then I would panic and drown my sorrows in drink.

All this, however, still does not explain the particular knot of
contradiction that made up my nature when I first knew John. I
hope to pursue the unravelling as the story of our relationship
continues, but it must be said now that much of the above doubts
were almost laid to rest in that short summer of 1957 in the midst

of the first flowering of our love. For John taught me much, lessons I have since often forgotten and had to relearn many times. He taught me about tenderness, he taught me that loving was the most intense concern for the other's welfare, he taught me that the softest touch was the most erotic, that kindness is a better seducer than lust. He taught me that loving each other was a celebration and that the whole world should join in, for our love was rare enough for us to wear it proudly. I had been loved

John

before, I had felt sexual passion, felt affection and yearning for someone, but what I was feeling for John and what he was giving me was something entirely different. On one level we had become totally immersed in each other's lives, our tastes were fused down to the way we demanded that our coffee was selected, roasted, ground and made. Such things may seem trivial to some, but the style of life, the way we all live, the mode of food, clothes, interiors, have psychological significance more than we often wish to credit. I may have been called fussy; I would prefer to say selective.

John was in agreement with all this as true lovers have to be. Our sense of humour and our literary tastes were also close, and our enthusiasms were passed on easily to each other. Sexually we never stopped. I can remember making love three or four times a day, in probably more positions than Harry and Maisie had yet to discover. We were, as they say, horny for each other. I have to say here, for it is too significant to be left unsaid, that it was John who taught me, by first allowing me, the ecstasies of penetration. I had not buggered a lad before, and few since for that matter.

The art of penetration in sex needs a book to itself. The shape, size and character of orifice matched to organ are all vital if a loving relationship is to give lasting and varied pleasures. I never cared to have it done to me, always finding it full of pain and without an iota of pleasure attached, so the fact that John enjoyed the activity was vital to the success of our love. I am not suggesting that a relationship cannot be fulfilling without penetration, but for me it is basic and necessary. I have found that the psychological rapture of sexual fulfilment, the multi-layered sexual experience, the series of worlds that unfold seemingly towards an epicentre, all this and more only comes with being inside the other's body. That final coupling, so miraculously and beautifully animal, fuses two into one. All this I first discovered with John. Though I had made love to women some years before, the experience was never as metaphysically exciting as it seemed to be with John.

My father once asked me the difference. I put the exchange in a novel and a reviewer, Julian Symons in the *Sunday Times*, rapped me over the knuckles by saying no father ever talks to his son in this way. My father had said, 'You've had both, son. What d'you think is the difference?' I replied, 'On the whole, arses are tighter.' He looked meditative and murmured, 'Yes, I seem to remember.'

The Army was now at John's heels. The autumn term was about to begin and he should be getting a job abroad, if he was to have an income. 'You must make a decision,' I can hear him say to me almost every other day. But a decision was almost impossible. I loathed committing myself to anyone. I was terrified of losing my independence, of throwing in my lot with John and of leaving friends to live in a foreign country where I knew no

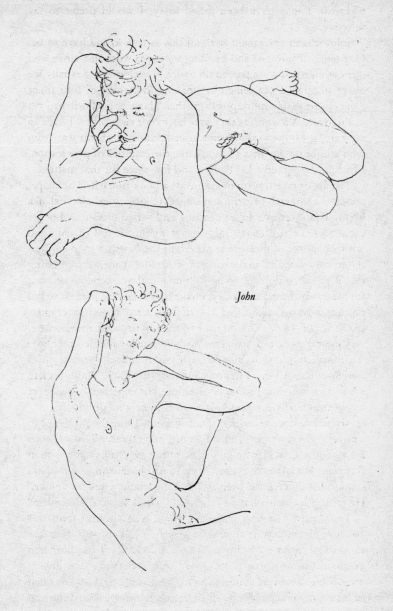

John

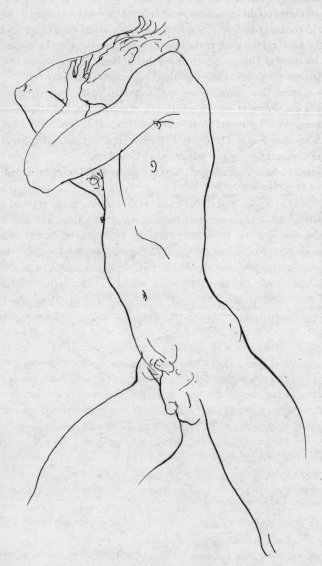

John, in dramatic pose (I added balls, not very successfully)

one and could not speak the language. Perhaps it was not these elements in themselves, but the fact that it all meant a domination by John of myself and my world, which I feared. In Brighton our personalities could just about hold an equal balance. Abroad John would control our lives completely. Yet we loved each other and surely such matters are commonplace and are there to be sorted out by lovers. Thus, we continued throughout September to live in Brighton, but knowing that time was rapidly running out.

Sometime that summer we met Edouard, who was to figure largely in the next six months, but who in the end changed nothing. For I suspect if it was not Edouard, it would have been another Sugar Daddy as John referred to them with great bitterness and fury – and who could blame him?

Edouard was middle-aged, highly cultured and intelligent and in the Diplomatic Corps. Thus he was on intimate terms with the artistic, the famous and the cultured rich. He saw me in the same bar in which I had met John a few months before. He had a remarkable basilisk stare, the look of an enigmatic beast who would first turn his quarry to stone before gorging himself. He came over to us and introduced himself. We conversed for a while, and then he asked for my telephone number and we parted. John and I thought nothing of the meeting, nor did we think much about Edouard; we were too engrossed in each other for much of the outside world to impinge. But the next evening he telephoned and fixed a date for us to come to dinner in London. Edouard had asked Paul Dehn* and Jimmy Bernard and the five of us had dinner, waited on by a manservant, Burns, who figured later in the pages of my novel, *Asylum*. There must have been two or three other occasions in September when Edouard saw us, and somewhere in that time he managed to declare for me an intensity of love which astonished me. It was the depth and the fierceness of emotion, kept very strictly under control, which mesmerized me and certainly slightly terrified me. In all the time I knew him, no physical act of affection ever took place. I actually felt physically revolted by him and shrank from the idea of being touched. Yet I was becoming more and more fascinated by the elegance and

* Poet, journalist, film critic on the *News Chronicle* and author of screen plays.

the style of his world, by the familiarity with which he spoke of screen and stage idols, of ballet and opera stars. His world, of course, was the one I wanted to belong to, yet I also knew that I was becoming swallowed up into John's life. Young, inexperienced and naïve, I suppose I thought I could have everything I wanted, everything I felt I needed: John's love and Edouard's world. Yet I also knew that was impossible. I did not love or care for Edouard – it was his basilisk stare, the enigma of his obsessive concern with me, his apartment, manservant and friends I was fascinated with.

I chose John, of course. He was going to live in Vienna, he spoke German, he could teach; I would survive by selling drawings and writing short stories. Together we would make it.

I can remember that after saying I would go, a black gulf formed within me, that sick feeling of the unknown, that crater of insecurity. But together we would survive. John returned to London to pack. I dealt with other matters and wrote this note. My lack of punctuation is, as I mention later, partly a kind of literary exercise, which would have exasperated my mentor, John Lehmann.

Brighton
10:X:57

Just to tell you that I love you and that I have talked to Dede which makes everything all right about the flat but I fear though I've hinted I haven't said outright to Edouard but I will as it is only 7.00 now God bless the Queen and keep the Golden Gates wide open for someone who full of love and trust and need and desperation – will enter and please darling come down if you can Saturday morning I feel happy again and infinitely loving, tell Paul and Jimmy that I think they're nice and even more than that and have a nice dinner because you're a nice boy and don't be naughty and flirt too much always remembering me and that I am not too far away.

Yours etc.
C.

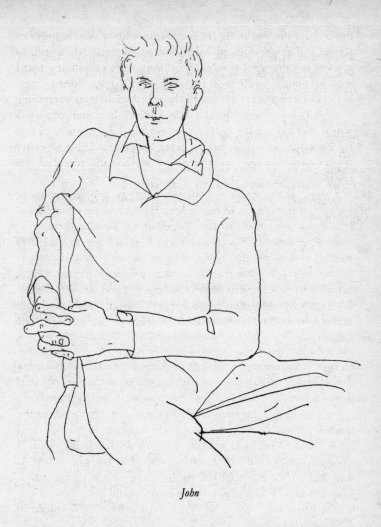

John

The following day I wrote to John again. I never told him the details of my discussion with Edouard who had played Satan in the Wilderness, offering me the world. It was a seed I rejected then, but it grew inside me and gave me, in the next two months, little peace.

Thank you darling for your letter. I had forgotten that you will probably be very busy in London Saturday, so I shan't expect you until later – though it would be a nice surprise if you did come earlier.

The money position isn't too bright – but don't worry, I'll make it. I was up till 2.00 this morning talking to Edouard – a terribly harrowing business. Now I'm longing to get away – the sooner the better, but I suppose I ought to have Monday free in order to see papa and get something from him.

Come back to me very quickly – we've got all that olive oil to use before we go.

Love,
C.

Edouard had made a bid for me to stay. He had recounted everything he could do for me – the contracts, the galleries which would exhibit my paintings, the magazines which would publish my stories, the directors who would see my stage designs, all this and so much more. His enthusiasm for my work, for my talent, for myself was charged with such potent force it seemed sometimes almost malevolent. I was hypnotized, yet knew that my physical revulsion was so great that the whole scenario was impossible.

I was to meet John soon after dawn at Liverpool Street for the Harwich train. I spent that last night again at Edouard's, and again the same pressure was put upon me to change my mind. It went on until two in the morning when I at last got to bed. It was then I remembered I had forgotten to pack my passport. A Freudian slip, I dare say, but the error would have put off our leaving for a day, that is all. Yet it would have been crucial to John, seeing in this absentmindedness a significance that was only too clear. However, Edouard when he heard of it said he would drive me through the night to Brighton and back again, and that is what happened. I can recall sitting in his car being driven very fast down the A23 and thinking, I cannot possibly understand this man. His action struck me as so generous I was almost seduced, and perhaps that was the point of it.

A few hours later I was sitting in the underground with my

passport, aware that another, deeper anxiety had never been voiced to John, or to anyone else for that matter. I had accepted from him that Austria was an entirely different country from Germany, but I knew I was uncertain of it. Born in the year Hitler came to power, my first twelve years had been dominated by his shadow. As a small child I had seen photographs of Belsen and I feared Germany and the Germans. The thought of living in a German-speaking nation worried me intensely. But it seemed a psychotic, irrational response, therefore one that should be coped with, tamed and suppressed in that stiff British upper lip manner. I should have known better. I should have listened to those inner voices, but I was overwhelmingly in love for the first time in my life and in that state – a fool's paradise – we always think everything will sort itself out and must come right in the end.

3

Poverty and Parting

·

We crossed that bleak plateau of heavily industrialized central Europe which seemed endless to me, changing trains at Munich before arriving at Innsbruck. We were to stay close to some friends of John's in the Tyrolean village of Schwarz – Kester had taken John there in 1950, to visit them. We arrived in October in the midst of autumnal shades iced with a dusting of snow. The orchards around Schwarz were clustered with unpicked fruit, the trees gnarled like a Dürer etching. John's enthusiasm in this setting got a little on my nerves, for the Tyrol was not to my taste. We would climb the mountain past cattle grazing beneath the trees, their tiny bells tinkling, oddly at variance with the cows' lumbering gait. This inappropriate mixture irritated me – kittens had bells, not cows, I remember thinking. John had told me that the peasants in the Tyrol greeted each other with the words 'Grüss Gott', Greet God. I had misheard him thinking they said 'Greek God', and for some days I meditated on how the Hellenic influence had come to be of such importance in the Austrian Alps. I ought to explain perhaps that my hearing is not particularly good in the sense of distinguishing the nuance of sounds. Worse than that, it takes more than one attempt for me to tell the major key from the minor. This explains my appalling track record in trying to learn languages. A foreign accent gives me great trouble, and even, alas, where I now live in rural Suffolk the brogue can give me difficulties. No wonder my next few months trying to learn German was a struggle.

Schwarz was terraced, and, with its white and yellow houses apparently clinging to the mountains by the tenacity of their small black iron balconies, to my eyes was trying far too hard for the

46

picturesque. The windows, balconies and tiled roofs were covered with tubs and boxes of geraniums. In the centre of the village there was a baroque church with an almost oriental gold dome and cupolas. Above the town lay the small schloss, with one round tower left, its roof painted red. The castle had been used by the Germans as an observation post throughout the war, and allied bombing had destroyed the other three towers. Here three sisters lived, Kester's friends. These we visited; they were timid, spoke almost in whispers and politely offered us tea. They each wore hunting jackets and carried walking sticks with heavy ivory heads as they showed us the gardens. It was all alien to me, even this brand of spinsterish grandeur.

We stayed in a large and rather empty room at the top of a chalet. The loo was a huge pipe running straight down three floors deep into a cesspit. Sitting astride its wooden seat was rather dizzy making, the turds for a moment left one in eerie silence then made an almighty splash. I recall soon being tired of beef goulash and Wiener schnitzel with very watery potato salad, though liking the cabbage soups and dumplings. John had begun, Kester-like, to husband the farthings, and my fondness for wine was watched rather too closely for comfort.

We visited Solbad Hall and the church and a chapel filled with crumbling bones. Here there are hundreds of skulls, swathed in silk and gauze, lodged like valuable manuscripts upon velvet shelves, tier after tier of 'bones of reverend contemplation', I wrote at the time, 'with beady eyes of sequin and semiprecious stone. And what of a hundred headless skeletons, martyrs, scholars and saints . . . were they embedded in these walls? Their limbs like a gigantic creeper fastened deep into stone and brick like the nerves of the church.'

One night to celebrate a legend we joined the locals in a pilgrimage. A dove, the legend claimed, flew into Schwarz in the thirteenth century at the time of the plague. It flew into the town holding an olive branch and was wounded; and the people, leaving their sick and their dead, followed the dove across the river as it shed its blood and up across the other mountain. Then, at the place where it died, an olive tree grew and the people built a monastery and a church there and the monks that came looked after the sick and cured them. The pilgrimage followed the dove's path. We held candles and fell to our knees on the spot where the legend said the dove's blood was shed.

The medieval church fell into the river and a baroque church was built in its place. We attended Mass in an interior with bleeding hearts dripping with sequins and a Madonna whose cheeks were rouged, her pink cupid bow lips parted to show gleaming teeth pearly white. After Mass, we were given coffee and hot rum before walking down the mountain and into the dawn.

Ironically enough, John could not have chosen anywhere which would leave me aesthetically so cold. To my taste, Alpine culture of whatever nationality is too picturesque, and the symbol of the edelweiss somehow too coy to be anything but irritating. But I did not allow these prejudices to mar the experience, for I was with John and he was idyllicly happy; he had won me, as it were, taken me from the pernicious influence of the older besotted admirers into his world, rather homespun, 'arts and crafts', and very unsophisticated. A reflection of Kester, in fact, as I was to learn.

John was both thrilled and eager, watching my reactions closely, longing for his enthusiasm to be matched by mine. (I made the pilgrimage into a short story, but never got it quite right.) Yet his passion never fired me; the Alps of course had their magnificence but I was not inspired by them. Innsbruck and its churches had a Mozartian elegance that I did respond to, but we paid only one visit before we caught the train to Vienna.

We found a room in the Heinestrasse which ran along the side of the gardens of the Belvedere-Schlosser. The city struck me as ornate and heavy, the baroque gave me no pleasure, as it does now; then I found it oppressive, comic and very alien. It was also bitterly cold and getting colder every day. What little money we had was getting low, the academic year had begun, there were no teaching posts available and John could find no work. I drew the Viennese monuments with hands that grew purple with cold, but there was nobody to sell the drawings to. We found a workers' restaurant which provided soup for something like two pence. I can see it now: it had a layer of fat about an eighth of an inch deep upon the surface, with bits of gristle and vegetables below swimming in a tasteless stock. With a slice of bread this was our lunch, and according to John, who seemed to be in charge of the money, this was all we could afford.

One incident stands out in those six weeks. John managed to get us invited to a party given by the drama society attached to the American Embassy. By this time we went around Vienna in a state of perpetual hunger; we walked everywhere, huddled in several layers, with me feeling more and more homesick. The party came as a godsend, with all that booze and food. We ate our fill and then later I searched for the kitchens, where I filled my pockets with frankfurters and bread. Then we slipped away and visited a gay bar. Here we drew the attention of two Scandinavian guys, tall, blond and very impressionable. The most attractive one said something to his friend who left the bar, then came over to us. We were just leaving. He was from Sweden and spoke to us in heavily accented English. We paused outside the bar, exchanging small talk for a moment, when suddenly a car drew up. The passenger door flew open, the Swede thrust me inside and fell in after me. As the car, driven by his friend, zoomed off he snapped the locks, leaving John outside banging at the windows.

I was bemused. I had been kidnapped, I thought. 'Why have I been kidnapped?' I asked. I cannot remember what the Swede said; all I can recall is how mightily amused I was. I think I treasured the moment most because it was adventure; the weeks before had been meagre, dun coloured, without spice and I was so bored, apart from being always hungry. The thought of being whisked away and murdered made not the slightest difference. At least something was happening.

The car took us to the Swede's flat, where his friend disappeared and we were then, as the story-books go, supposed to enjoy a night of lustful love-making. Alas, this story becomes more bizarre. The handsome Swede with a hard muscular body had one basic imperfection: his penis when erect was shaped like an umbrella handle or a periscope – it went up, curved over and then it went down again. It was quite impossible to think what to do with it. No wonder the poor man had to kidnap his partners. I left at dawn and walked home, my coat still trailing frankfurter sausages. I let myself into the flat, rather fearing the wrath to come, but outside the door to our room, laid neatly over the

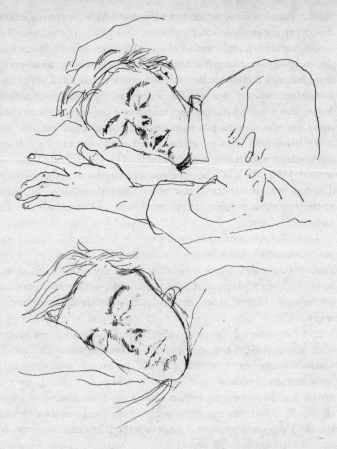

John asleep

mat were more frankfurters. They spelt the word, welcome.

An adventure like this certainly coloured the unremitting gloom of our lives. There was plenty to draw, but the cold made such a task unendurable. I sat at the window and drew my view. The corner of the street had a late nineteenth-century ornateness, a kind of bourgeois Imperialism which appealed to me. It appeared two years later on the front page of *The Times Literary Supplement*. But our room did not have enough windows or enough views for my pen. I tried to write, but ideas for stories would not come. I was getting restless and depressed. Our passionate relationship could not satisfy my creativity; there must be an end to drawing John. I had painted a gouache portrait of him back in the summer, but portraits did not sell. I needed to earn money. I felt I had imprisoned myself in a squalid backwater. Basically the problem was – and I was to meet it several times more – that Vienna was John's world. Austria had been the first European country he had travelled to and lived in when he left Australia and its cultural significance within him was powerful. The stronger its influence within John, the less it seemed to have anything to do with me. I could not see where I was going, and there were, to make these frustrations worse, letters from Edouard which stressed my cultural isolation.

I told John I wanted to return to England. But secretly I had told Edouard I would meet him in Paris. I am shocked at this deviousness now, but I was ashamed to admit to John that I longed for the flesh-pots of Paris. I wanted quail eggs, caviare and champagne, French food subtly sauced and, above all, warmth. I had no will to devise the priorities of life, no way of understanding that these enticing flesh-pots might wait a little for me. I just found Vienna painfully spartan and left the following day.

All my life I have underestimated the power of my feelings, thought that I could cope perfectly competently with actions based on a rational appraisal of a situation, and then been swept under by an emotional torrent which quite unexpectedly has descended upon me. I had decided that life in Vienna was sparse, tedious and alien, and I would be much happier back in England. My life with John was over. Yet once I had left him I was thrown into one of the worst depressions I have known, totally unable to do anything. It was like suffering the sudden death of a soulmate, a twin, an only child. I never knew that this was what loving meant. I was desolate, and it was little help for me to say to myself – I should have known. It was youthful ignorance and I suffered the consequences of it. John's first letter only deepened my despair.

Two original drawings by Colin Spencer, made in Vienna

28:xi:57

Colin,

It's very hard writing to you. Very hard, and I guess I only do it to ask questions. Why did you leave? Darling, do you know? Please tell me now. If ever you loved me, tell me so that I can understand. I can't grasp it at all.

Sweet, yesterday and today I've been quite numb. I went home on Tuesday expecting to find you in, not realizing you were gone and today and yesterday and Tuesday I've kept thinking you were at home waiting for me and then I'd make myself understand that there's no reason any more to hurry home and so I come back here as late as possible and as infrequently as possible. I can't stand the flat and thinking how happy we often were and where we made love and when and how often and why we laughed or were happy or silly and somehow began to understand, no that's the wrong word, to be at one with each other.

Never once did you suggest my going to London with you. And so I feel that I would have been in the way there and stopped you getting anywhere. Sweetheart, a very huge doubt grows in my mind that for you what was between us was not so rare and necessary. If that's true, then for the love of anything tell me. Now. Without any decision. At this distance tell me. You could do me nothing more. Do you realize now what you did when you went away? In just packing up and leaving? If you haven't felt numb inside and if your whole body hasn't felt lost and reasonless then this letter is merely embarrassing and any reply from you pointless.

There were many reasons for coming here but the two most important were to get into an atmosphere where we could really live with each other and to be able somehow to work together. I feel I have no reasons to stay here any longer.

But if you feel as I feel, now, hold on to all that tenderness and longing and tell me how we can soon repair this terrible rift. How somehow. For Christ's sake do something. Once you wrote me a long letter about the horrors of continually adapting oneself to all the second-hand easier things of the world. Darling, I love you such a lot. I don't want us to do anything cheap but something which can stand on its own two feet, something hard, and really loving someone I guess is the hardest thing to do. More than leaving them. What was between us was the rarest and most important thing I have *ever* known. I can't give it up easily. If I had known what pain your going would cause I would have railed against it with my whole being. Don't let us go quietly into this dark night.

If you write me whatever you want to say, don't let it be a pretty letter meaning nothing, one which just eases the realization that nothing is any more. All the time we were together we looked for truth. Don't lie to me or give me soft answers any more.

I love you such a lot. Darling, what have we done?

John

Among the papers sent to me after John's death, there was a rough for this letter. The aerogramme he eventually sent me was much the same, it only omitted another Dylan Thomas echo, after writing 'Don't let us go quietly into this dark night'. He had added 'Rail against it'. This wild fighting spirit of his I always found seductive. But I detect that he was as astonished as myself at the depths of despair he was suffering and how intensely we missed each other. He also sent a postcard of the crown of the Holy Roman Empire, with this message:

This too for you. Though it gives no real impression of its barbarous ferocious nature. Except for the Brueghels it's the best reason for visiting Vienna. If you could get a little of its nature into your work I'd be so excited. If you'd only seen more here. If only.

This is John, the teacher. I fear this was lost on me; I have never seen the barbarous ferocious nature of this crown. Though I detect what John meant to see in it, I would have thought Orson Welles' film of *Macbeth* or Eisenstein's *Ivan the Terrible* caught it with more monumental vigour.

I wrote back at once. My letters – as the reader must see – were very under punctuated, the reason being that my spirit was breathless and I was in a continual panic. But I was also under the influence of the experimental literature that I was addicted to at this time, from Apollinaire to Firbank and Faulkner.

1:xii:57

No, I don't know why I left – I've been trying to understand. And the answers, the obvious ones, don't seem to me everything and I try and find the others, the real ones, so please be patient with this letter. I'll try to find the truth.

It is something to do with living together. That loving for you is living together and for me it is suffocating but the other way about, not over me, but beneath so most of the time I'm not even aware of it, but that suddenly it just produces an action like packing a bag and leaving while a part of me is horrified and just doesn't believe I'll do it and in the train at Vienna at the station I prayed and prayed you'd come and then I'd have to go back with you and the other part called me a romantic fool and that if I'd really wanted to get out of the train I would but that I either went then or just not at all. And then I told myself I'd get out at the next station and find my way back but the part I didn't know about just went on sitting there.

And it is something also about us being all too late – that the part of me that wants and loves you is the part that was all of me three years ago when I would have given all and everything for just that – to live with you anywhere and put up with anything. I've always been frightened of your *VIRTUE* and because of that never dared to state in plain words the more callous parts of me. Your letter made me love you so that I thought I'd break – and I want you in my arms so much. I don't know what we've done, I just don't know. How could I ask you to come to London with me when we've got no money and when you can't get a job here and I suppose I refuse too. You say, loving someone is the hardest thing to do – perhaps that is just what I've failed at. That if I really loved you I'd work here or stay in Vienna. I'm just not big enough any more.

I don't *want* to love anyone else. I don't want to sleep or live with anyone else but you. I've known all this for a good four months. I should like to spend a good part of the rest of my life with you. I know that I felt as *desolate* and as suicidal on that train journey as I did when Jan left me.

You say too, that if I feel as you feel now, hold on to all that tenderness and longing and tell you how we can soon repair this terrible rift. But suppose our loving has to be the slave of my ambition? What then? For that's where it's got to be. And leaving you was telling you that.

What chances are there of us living in England? What chances of you not going home to Australia? Do you remember you said to me once: If ever you see me with someone else, *come and get me*.

C.

Again, I am shocked at my deviousness, at my barefaced omission of a few facts. No mention of those four days in Paris or of Edouard. I have the vaguest recollections of Paris at that time: of Edouard meeting me at the station and of him gallantly carrying a suitcase and then complaining of the weight; of my being whisked to a party given by a French count where there were rivers of champagne; and of my going out on to a balcony which overlooked Paris at night, and feeling so miserable because I longed for John that I was shocked at the depth of the self-inflicted wound. I thought then it would go away

In this first letter I am also somewhat puzzled at my thinking John was virtuous. I seem to remember thinking this about almost everybody I got entangled with and it seems to me that they always made me feel so dangerously amoral, made me feel I was almost a threat to society. Therefore they thrust themselves, in comparison, into a virtuous light. John was, of course, no more virtuous than the next man, or woman, nor any more moral than myself, as in the coming two years I would discover. But in those early days, I think John used the concepts of loyalty and truth as weapons to possess me with. I should have had the wit to see it was all bunk.

Jan was my first male love, whom I described in the *Guardian* in its series, First Love.* I was nineteen, he was twenty-seven. After six months of bliss, Jan, a Roman Catholic, confessed all to his priest who then damned the relationship and Jan refused to see me any more.

The following day I wrote a second letter.

2:xii:57

John, I don't think I've thought about much else except how *somehow* we can be together – in the evening everything seems so simple and I feel so sure of you and of me and what I shall do: in the morning (which is now) everything becomes frightening.

Your letter was like a war that engulfed me. The flat is so hollow and Dede has sold the house. I shall go home for Xmas and stay there until I can find a room in London. I have sold a drawing to the *Paris Review*, but not a story. Lehmann has taken the Xmas card, Martyn has sold some drawings, Allan is at the Art School, and there are so many other odd pieces of news. But I have neither the enthusiasm or the belief that you'll be interested

*See Appendix.

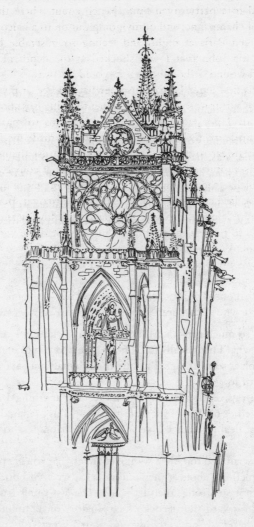

Paris, St Chapelle

in order to tell you. Have we got any chance? Please tell me, and please don't feel bitter or too angry.

All my love,
Colin

I had done a drawing for John Lehmann of a doorway in Vienna where the porch was held up by caryatids; in this drawing they were reading the *London Magazine*. Martyn Goff had bought some line drawings of John and sold some for me to friends. My Aunt Dede, alas, had sold the Hove house, precipitated by my leaving, and bought a bungalow outside Worthing to be near her sister. It was a mistake: the sister died and Dede felt stranded; away from her beloved esplanade where she walked to Palace Pier and back every Sunday, she became a recluse and quickly declined into old age.

Wien
4:xii:57

My very dear,

I wish so much now that I did send you the letter of yesterday.

It was what I truly really felt. I hope it helped you to understand how I look at some things. I'm sure though that you have answers for a lot of it.

Please, my very sweet darling, more than anything I want us to be together happy. More than just want, I'm prepared to give up a great deal of what I have of any other happiness to be with you.

If you want that too, then want it so much that you are prepared to do something about it then tell me what we are to do.

If it's not so strong, then let it die. The last thing I want is a back and forward shuttlecock of explanatory or incriminating or tenuous letters. And certainly no pretty literary love letters. Darling, what I feel for you is so vital I couldn't bear to see it pine away without food. Letters and words are no diet.

I love you, long for you so much.

J.

Darling,

The things I have with me that make me most unhappy are the only two letters of yours I brought with me. The two just before we left when you wrote so happily and ecstatically* and made me so wondrously happy. I want to burn them and can't. Oh sweetheart, what is happening? Do we have to adapt again? To living apart?

This letter puzzles me: it is not clear whether John sent me 'the letter of yesterday' or not. It is not among the others, unless it is the undated highly morose one reproduced on page 65. But I did find the following letter of Paul Dehn's. It is worth including, not only to show what a kind and gentle creature Paul was, but also how I must have struck others – a dyed-in-the-wool sybarite. Yet the letter is perceptive, and it sums up pretty well the conflict I was battling with.

London SW3
8:xii:57

My poor, dear John,

Please forgive my not having answered your letter for so long, but a particularly hectic film-going season has coincided with Jimmy catching the flu. My eyes ache from seeing three films a day, and my wrists from squeezing lemons! He is better this morning, but still rather washed out after four days' high-ish temperature, and not yet fit enough to write letters.

We both feel so sad for you, and can feel about a billionth of what you must be feeling by putting ourselves in both your places. If it's of any consolation to you, I get the impression that Colin is by no means happy himself. I've seen him twice since he got back, and he is quite unable to keep you out of any conversation for more than a minute on end. Every time the Paris train stopped at a station on the way home, he contemplated getting out and going back to Vienna. Of course, in the end, he didn't. He has persuaded himself that, in his particular case, any kind of creative work is impossible under conditions of physical discomfort. He needs his daily bath, his weekly haircut, his warmth and his wine –

*Letters on pages 42 and 43.

and I truly think that his decision to return here was based on a resolution *not* to be kept gratis in all these comforts by a retinue of rich admirers but to get a job that will make him enough money to earn them himself. Indeed one can't deny that he is more likely to do so as an Englishman among Englishmen than as a non-German-speaking foreigner in Vienna; and I've found it no good to try and talk him out of his refusal to rough it, because the refusal is ineradicably there.

Meanwhile I know that his perpetual longing to be with you is setting up one of those inner conflicts with which he will simply have to live and struggle until your return. This conflict is the price he knows he's got to pay for the choice he's made; and because he must realize in his heart of hearts that the choice isn't entirely courageous, I'm certain it will increase his admiration and love for you rather than diminish it. Do hang on to that thought, until it's time for you to come home.

No one knows about your letter to me except Jimmy – and I know you'll forgive me for showing it to him because we can't have any secrets from each other and anyway he's so fond of you! Somebody rang up yesterday (no name) to say he's forwarding another from you. I shan't blame you if it's full of wrath and vituperation for my not having answered your first one earlier. Write whenever you want, and we shall reply whenever we can.

Meanwhile, please accept vast hunks of love from us both – which we hope will fortify you a little in the horrid, lonely time you must be having.

Paul

PS Jimmy will write soon.

This following letter of mine also sums up the conflict and appears one of my more balanced efforts. At least I see clearly that the price of every opportunity I coveted was giving up John.

9:xii:57

John – most of the last 24 hours have been spent (and I mean most of the night too) in thinking how to get back to you. In rereading your letter – God knows how many times – in loving you and wanting you. In finding out airport times and railway times. In thinking how mad I am and the ridiculous business of rushing across Europe and now, only now when it's nearly Tuesday have I come full circle and tried to be sensible and practical. I can *use* your £10 in getting back. (I certainly can't borrow any more money from any SDs.) But what the hell have I got in Vienna – how long did £30 last? In a few weeks' time I might be able to get a job here – that much-needed independence that I've never had. Of course I want you and need you and want you here but how can I say we will be happy any more than I can say I won't be unhappy in Vienna? You can't change me, of course, you can't – and a part of me will want and need the sops to my ambition which Vienna cannot give and London does. I'm now on the brink of every discovery that I have most coveted. But at what price: I'm not even sure of the price, except I know it's you. I thought there was only *one* way to answer your letter and that was to go to Vienna. I still think that. You must think that this is full of excuses because I haven't. But it isn't – my darling, it isn't – it's just that I can't see a way for us longer than those few months in Vienna. I can't think or contemplate Australia. I just refuse to.

Things got to such a state this afternoon that I tried to ring you and find out your number from a street directory of Vienna but I couldn't if I didn't know your landlady's name – the cakes and tea one. Then I was going to send a telegram – Oh my God, my arse was moving, I wasn't even feeling tragic, just that I wanted you more than anything else. But now I've got to be sane. And the only sane thing I can think of – is for me to get a job in television or BBC and to attempt to get some place.

Tuesday

I couldn't go on with this last night as I felt too tired with the flu and no sleep the night before. I didn't get your letter until Sunday as I was at home being nursed by mama but I rang Dede up to see if a letter had come and came down here. Now this morning I got the other one and I think I feel the same, sweetheart. I wouldn't be happy in Vienna, but if you want me more than anything else and if you're sure that we can't be happy in England, then I'll come. Oh my God, I wish to hell someone could help us. Are we bad for each other I wonder? But I will try too to be happy in Vienna. I shouldn't have come back so early except that doing that perhaps illuminated this particular problem – that love just isn't enough. Even though we want it to be enough. Of course there's always Ireland. No National Service there – but I should think no jobs either. We might go there in the spring and try to live there – it's closer and I wouldn't feel so cut off and there would be no language barrier for me. Is all this so small? I don't know. You see I just can't think everything out clearly and put it all down. I think your letter was right. I can't even discuss or argue it – for it seemed like sense. And I must do something about it. But it's like being in a self-erected cage and having lost the key to get out. Coming to you would only make me battle against the other side of the cage. We must find some way of living together and giving me the means (it may be the illusion) that I'm getting somewhere with my work. I want a job so badly.

That's all I can find to say – because it's not words I want but the only answer to be just with you. Believe me I'm going to try and do something very very soon, for us in London. Sweetheart, I hate asking you to give up things – because I want to. But though I could make the grand gesture, of rushing back to Vienna as I *want* to do – I know I wouldn't have the strength to keep on doing that through the months, to keep on in my mind giving up the things I want. Are you so sure we could be happy in Vienna together? If I didn't love you I would never have come out in the first place or ever have felt as I have done these last weeks – never, never as torn or as incomplete. I wish to hell we could just be together, just love each other quite simply without all this terrible complexity of problems – I thought too that I'd get to come out to you because you needed me to do that, because I hate you to doubt what is so real in me, besides I want to hold you in my arms more than anything else. But it's just not enough is it? I can't bear the thought of that big doubt.

All my love,
C.

I am relieved to see a certain honesty here. I am adamant about Australia, and I see that if I did return to Vienna it would only be for a few months. I also hold out no hopes of John being able to fight off the authorities over National Service if he returned and we lived in London. We should, I believe, have explored Ireland. I think, if we could have survived, we would have loved it. I wrote again three days later.

Edouard had arranged various meetings to which I had taken my folder of stage designs and drawings. He was, in fact, being marvellously helpful with all his contacts, and the various opportunities that appeared upon the horizon were not all wishful thinking. Ettiene was a French pianist who had connections with the Third Programme.

12:xii:57

My Darling, I've been thinking more and more and I hope reaching some kind of sanity. I did ask Paul a good week ago to tell me if he heard from you as I thought he might. And I saw him last night and he said he had. I didn't ask any questions and he only said one thing. Which was that the strange thing was you seemed to assume that everything was all over. I always thought I was impatient and I suppose I am, but please darling be *patient* about this. It's easy not to be. To get into an emotional whirl and fly off to each other, but sweetheart it is terribly impractical, from your point of view and from mine. I could never earn enough money in Vienna to keep myself and if you helped to keep me it would begin the little humiliations that eat away a relationship. I don't want to keep on saying what I've already written and what we know anyway. You *must* believe me that I don't want to live my life or spend the next ten years with anyone but you. But it would be *unfair* to us and unbearable to me, if we couldn't live it where I feel my work has a chance of growing, selling and being appreciated. It is just bloody bad luck that at the moment I feel it is London and I must strike and use all the contacts I can grab in the next few weeks. Both Gielgud and David Webster have seen some of the designs and like them and the television woman seems to be enthusiastic too. Ettiene seems to think that I can land a £1,500 a year job if I work these people properly. It's important for my happiness to do this – important for me to feel that people think my work is good and can use it. I've had too many years of the other and I'm sick and tired of them.

I'm writing from home as mama has gone down with the flu and mine is still about – she doesn't ask any questions and is being very sweet. But the rest of the time I'm looking for a flat in town – a studio if possible. Sweetheart, let me get a job, and a place here for us to live in – I might get them both before Xmas but if not it will be soon after. And save all your money now or try to, and darling, don't think that I don't want to catch a train and come to you. I want it so badly, but I'm convinced it would be madness, that I can't be happy for long, even though I try very hard. I want to give something up for you, and am unable.

And please if you think our life here would be plagued with Sugar Dads – I will secrete the amber that will immobilize them like flies. I'm beginning to feel quite strong again. Is this a literary love letter? I hope not.

But think hard about all this – darling, if we love enough and if everything you said in your letters is true – then we can endure a month or two being separated. I've never stopped wanting you since I left. I never stopped and won't, feeling torn in two. But somehow, strangely enough I've become more sure that we mean enough to each other for this problem not to be solved somehow – even the Australia one, which is part of this, sweet sweet darling. I'm sure we can do it somehow –

So think about what I've said and if you feel you can't then we must think again and I'll try to give up and try to do something with myself but perhaps now you feel you can be more happy alone in Vienna. I can't be happy here without you. But also we must think what you are going to do in England. I'm sure it is possible to circumvent the Army problem and to get some money.

A wonderful, wonderful great book. Jean Genet's *Our Lady of the Flowers*, all about a boy called Divine and a man called Darling. I wanted to rush to you, so that I could read you parts of it. But I will soon.

Please, we will be together soon.

All my love,
C.

Jean Genet was to oust Faulkner as a literary influence very quickly. John wrote to me on the same day, and about this time

I received two other letters from him; they are both undated, but the second one is, I am sure, the letter he refers to a week before. They were all powerful ammunition. The poem he wrote out for me is 'Which of Us Two?' by Peter Viereck, from our favourite anthology, *The Penguin Book of Modern American Verse*, introduced and edited by Geoffrey Moore. It is, of course, from this poem that I have borrowed the title of this book.

I don't know when you'll get this not knowing your Croydon address.

My dear Colin,

This I wrote last Saturday after two letters of yours. I've kept it till now, not posting it. Now I have to, not because I'm so upset at the moment but so that you know how painful for me your letters are. It's an unfair letter I know but it's hard sometimes to be 'sane and sensible'. Don't write any more. It upsets me very much now. When you want us to *do* something then write. Maybe I'll still be around. I love you very much. I can't be happy here without you. I lead a day to day life. If we are not to be together then I must try as hard as I can to forget you. Then we can write pretty witty camp intelligent letters to each other. You can hardly enjoy getting my long moaning letters.

The poem says more, than I can find words for, of what I feel. I understand it now. Really.

Oh, sweetheart, if I could but once kiss you. I want to discover you all over again.

J.

Saturday

I went off to the ballet this evening by myself, posted a letter to you and then after watching the tarts by the Opera House, came home by myself.

I don't cry very often. I'm a good stiff upper lip Englishman now if never before. But in the half hour walk I just bawled, I couldn't help it.

Somehow I've reached a salvation point. When you first left I just couldn't believe it. It took me two weeks to realize it. And tonight I knew that I couldn't trust you at all. Not a fraction.

That though you talk about our coming together, somehow you are binding yourself hurriedly and most willingly to London. That if you left so easily, quickly, then the reason to come was not that you loved me. Perhaps it was the idea of the wine, high life, I don't know what. And when that wasn't straightaway coming it just wasn't worth the effort to stay.

If you give it up so easily why should you be willing to sacrifice anything – any little thing – for it? I don't want any more letters. It's late tonight but tomorrow I'll burn all there are. I just *hate* the idea of any letters from you at all. For I know what they'll be full of. Words and words and vague promises and ideas and things like 'It's bad LUCK! that I need to be in London'.

It is the most terrifying thing to suddenly discover that you don't trust someone you love very much.

Oh, I can't say how *much* I need you to *do* something for us and I know you won't, won't care and you'll substitute pretty words again. It's terrifying to realize that what you feel for someone, big and rare and important though it be for you, yet for *you* it is simply one part of a large fabrication. And a replaceable part at that.

I've never been so low. Please no more words. I hate them so much.

J.

What can I do when my *whole body* doubts?

Which of Us Two?

When both are strong with tenderness, too wild
With oneness to be severance – reconciled;
When even the touch of finger tips can shock
Both to such see-saw mutuality
Of hot-pressed opposites as smelts a tree
Tighter to its dryad than to its own tight bark,
When neither jokes or mopes or hates alone
Or wakes untangled from the other; when
More-warm-than-soul, more-deep-than-flesh are one
In marriage of the very skeleton; –

When, then, soil peels mere flesh off half this love
And locks it from the unstripped half above,
Who's ever sure which side of soil he's on?
Have I lain seconds here, or years like this?
I'm sure of nothing else but loneliness
And darkness. Here's such black as stuffs a tomb,
Or merely midnight in an unshared room.
Holding my breath for fear my breath is gone,
Unmoving and afraid to try to move,
Knowing only you have somehow left my side,

I lie here, wondering which of us has died.

12:xii:57

Oh darling,

What am I to say to you and your letter. This is my third beginning and I'm in the dark.

There's nothing I can write any more. I can't say come to Vienna. I can't say I'm coming back. If you want, want, want us to be together, then *you* must say one or the other. I had to persuade you to come, persuade you like mad. I tried like hell to persuade you to stay. I can't do any more. The responsibility of what happens is very squarely on your shoulders. If I made up your mind for you, you'd resent me too much. Remember once on the Brighton train you said that you would like to come away with me? Remember how hurt you were when I said it was a pretty conceit, meaning very little? That one had to *want* it more than anything, not just *like*? But you see it's true.

This is one good but unpleasant side of loving. It makes you take responsibility for your actions. Squarely take it. Now this is for you to take. If you come back here, then try to make it work. Try like mad. Meet people you don't know, learn a language, get work and not allow yourself to give up. With plenty of loving it's not really such a terror.

Or ask me to come back. And take responsibility that we are somewhere where we can breathe, where there's a bit of light, where we can be quite independent of SDs. Where our being together can be creative and close. I don't want a bed-mate,

67

theatre-companion, assistant. They're two-a-penny. That's all most lovers are in London.

I want what is between us to be vigorous and lusty and strong and inquisitive and courageous and very happy. And with us it was so. I want to say *is* so but I dare not. I don't think either of us really appreciated what grew between us, binding us. But it grew in easy days in Brighton. We had to make it harden. That was one good reason for coming to Vienna. And I can't bring myself to think it was so weak after all. Never have I been so able to be so much myself, without having to pose or hide. Never have I been able to explore so much with someone. Never have I felt such countries and worlds of thought and emotion waiting to be explored.

Darling, when I write like this a great pain hurts deep inside me and I feel myself beginning to cry – I haven't for more than a week. Suddenly the full impotence of these words comes upon me. One part of me hammers at me that I'll be writing such a letter next week, that I'll still be trying to explain why we are, were, should be, must be, in love and still I'll be only able to reach tenuously across many, many miles and know that words can't say one smallest fraction of all that I feel, that can't ever be said.

Darling, do I have to tell you that I love you more than anything else in the world? Do I have to tell it, suffer the humiliation of having to remind you of what was between us, to have to tell it again? I can't. I did that again and again when you were thinking, planning to go until I hated myself. What new words can be used if so much that was torn right out of my heart can't tell you?

But now you must be willing if it is important to you – you see this big doubt I can't rid myself of – to come here or to ask me back. Whichever way to take responsibility.

Of course I want you back here. Do you think I am at all happy to think that what was to have been our effort by both of us was a failure because it made demands?

Darling, I'm lost now. People have been clamouring to know whether I was staying or not. They want to know in order to plan spring and summer terms. And, waiting for your letter, I've put them off. I wanted this letter to say come back or I'm coming. I opened it and the first thing I read was in the middle saying 'I will try to be happy in Vienna'. I put the letter down and dared not read it for an hour. And now after reading it I know that, no I don't know anything, except the letter is so afraid to say anything that it flounders in words. Darling, accept complexity in loving. Do you still think love is a cage? Then you must learn to love more and more, until you are bound about with love, because then you are free. Darling, our love was no cage. If it was, I would have railed and ranted against your going. I would have gone to the station and grabbed your bags. I would have refused to give you the money for the fare. In its freedom, you had the freedom to go, without hindrance. But it gives us both freedom. For me to say we belong together. For me to say to you, 'If you see me with anyone, come and get me.'

Do you remember our very first afternoon in Austria? In the forest. With the sun and much ease and selflessness. Never be so mistaken to think that just a nice memory. That happens few times in a lifetime. Darling, was that being caught? In a cage? Or was that being made free?

I've come and gone from this letter many times. My pen wants to write I'm coming back but it can't. But deep in me is such a need to end this pain.

I am horrified that it will be at least a week before you reply to this. Nearly Xmas. Don't let us hesitate more than then.

Why aren't I to doubt? Though you don't mention him, I'm sure you're using Edouard again. That he is putting chains on you to stay in London. They're velvet covered all right but they're chains none the less. Then how can you say I'll come to Vienna 'if you really want'? Oh, darling, I just can't take it any more. I can't fight for you any more. All I can say is you need never doubt what I felt/feel for you. Doesn't that give surety of any action? And isn't that freedom? And are you free in London? Your letter has made me feel so unhappy, it is as in the first days when you left. For you talk in your letter about being sane and sensible. Three times you write this glorious phrase. It seems you too have been subjected to all the moderate common-sense, dull second rate, half dead banalities I've had. 'That you get over it'. 'That spring comes again'. Do you put so much worth on them? In your letter you seem further from me than I've ever known. If I could hold you very tight in my arms it would be all right. My body is absolutely bewildered. It doesn't want anyone else. It's not even a matter of wanting to be faithful to you. It's simply that my body rebels. It doesn't want the second rate, the sly, the half-hearted, the hesitant. It just wants to be bloody randy with you. It wants to spend long hours with you naked and passionate and at ease with you.

If you can find loving as good in London, take it. With both hands. I can't find a single word for everything that hurts inside me, because it will out.

Darling, save what is between us, NOW. Or *kill* it. Don't let us play with it like this, don't let it just disappear in a cloud of words.

I love you. So much I am afraid. Oh darling, why are you so far away?

PS Darling, I'm sending this letter not because it says what I really want to say – I don't know what that is – but I must feel in touch with you again. And so even these very fumbled confused words are better than none.

More than anything, I want you to be happy with me. We achieve much together.

If going away has made you deeply realize that *we* are important then come back. If it would make you want to try harder to make a success of it – and it will be easier now – if we wanted it we could earn about £13 a week together working at everything that has come up – then come back. I guess I need that more than I can say. Even *we* need it more than I can say.

Darling, a whole world lies in front of us. Waiting for us to take it. I don't ask anything of love, certainly not that it is a be all and end all. But it gives us eyes and ears and tolerance and sympathy. You as a writer need all of them, I as a human being who loves life need them too.

Love can never be a slave to an ambition. It can work side by side. These all sound like platitudes. I guess they are. But they're true too. As all I feel for you, love.

This long, passionate and painful letter did, of course, over-whelm me. It didn't clear my mind or solve any of the conflict, but it persuaded me that I had to return. John in Vienna was a huge and powerful magnet, and everything else in my life seemed to shrink in comparison. Yet now I see more clearly the defiant moral tone: I must knuckle under, learn a language, work in this city he had chosen. The idea that we came to Vienna to harden our love I find a specious argument. John doing his National Service would have hardened our love and him as well. But I did not approve of thinking such thoughts, nor could I take seriously his claim that he would return to England, for I knew his fear of National Service would drive him away again, though perhaps I should have done. Another failing I see in myself is not to allow my lovers the choice to be generous, magnanimous or selfless, but to judge them as being unlikely or unable to be so.

But two days later his next letter was written, which showed an entirely different John, shell-shocked, bitter and often vile, yet still magnificent.

Vienna
14.xii.57

Thank you for your letter. It's very happy and obviously extremely excited. I'm glad that you're so happy and that things are going as you've wanted them there. To have a studio and £1,500 a year and a satisfied ambition should set you up as the happiest young dog in London. I hope it does. I guess that's all I can say. Except, well really nothing. This is where I should end. With best wishes for Xmas and 1958.

Don't go into all this with your eyes purposely closed or saying to yourself that things are motivated in ways other than they really are. No one is going to *give* you a £1,500 job. The competition's too stiff. Such jobs you have to pay for, by being pleasant, toadying a little and usually bedding willingly with the right people. If Gielgud or the other cunt takes your designs and says he wants to use them, ask yourself honestly if it's because they're good designs or because you were good in bed. As I don't think the designs are much good that won't take long to work out.

Secondly, £1,500 a year is a price usually including body and soul. Don't think it'll be only two afternoons a week. Don't think it'll give you time to paint and write all you need. Don't be mistaken in thinking it won't influence your work, real work, for the worse. Don't think, for God's, sake, it'll give you any time to love someone very much.

Then, if the job doesn't come through what do you do? Content yourself with a mere £500? A job not so glamorous? Does the studio or the job come first? If you get the studio and then no job who pays for the studio? Rent, etc.? Who pays from the beginning? All right, you needn't answer that either.

And lastly, what on earth makes you feel you are worth £1,500? Are you really so good, so brilliant? Or is it charm? And being accommodating? Darling, when you land something or you've worked your connections and you're whipping your pants down and climbing into the necessary bed of the moment and you're thinking of another high priestess scalp – perhaps of the drama, this time – then don't get it mixed up with *ars artis*. And don't fool yourself that you're the only one doing the using.

Sweet, I'd like you to not have anything published or accepted for the next five years at least. I'd like you to rough it, to work hard, no matter how menially, to stand on your own two feet and I'd like you to love someone – not, not even necessarily me – so much you'd go anywhere with them and stay, *want* to stay, even when the going was far from easy, even when he pulled you quite away from *all* security, all fixed ideas, all one mindedness. Much more than I ever wanted to. Or did. And then you might have something worthwhile and really important to say.

It would be hard to come to London. Harder than it was for you to come here. My ambition isn't furthered here. We came to try and live together. In air you could breathe. Neither gained an advantage from coming. If either did you could have by working and writing somewhere new. I can't sell the fact I've given private lessons. And it just *wasn't worth* the effort on your part to stay. To try a bit, a month. Two months. I just can't even begin to fathom out how you could have left so quickly, giving it all up. Do you wonder that I doubt, highly, so much you say? Unwillingly doubt so very much? If I came back – forgive the histrionics but – it would seem like our love being slave to your ambition – I refuse that. It makes it seem that we can only be happy when the gold flows and life is easy and comfortable. Such loving isn't worth the effort of wiping your cock clean. Is it really so weak and emasculated?

Are you really astonished that I give Paul the impression it's all over? Isn't it? Really? Is there really a place for me in London? Will you ever bestir yourself, take the responsibility to come back to Vienna? Won't we continue to substitute for *doing* something for us to be together, the easy device of letters? If our being together was really *so* important, as you say too it is, how could you have left so soon? Why am I so insensitive as to think you still want us together? How could it have gained worth for you?

Three weeks is hell to be away from you, loving and wanting you as I do. Two months – God – is too long. But it might be bearable if our being together were certain, were going to be solid and worthwhile and fruitful. What do you want me to do? Wait till you've made a niche for yourself? Hang on, wait until one month, two months or how long till you say I'm coming or come back? And what of all the permanent plans here? For the new year. And don't tell me there is no work for you here.

Two hours ago I wanted to write that I was fed up with just words, that I didn't want any more letters, that yours I was burning, I wanted to send this last literary – excreting amber – back to you for your collected works. It's not just a matter of patience, of waiting. What you do is outside me. It's seeing what's between us take second place to something doubtfully good and possibly dangerous. Seeing you revive all the deadly situations. I guess I'm just one huge thick-headed fool who doesn't really know when to call it quits. If I was sane and sensible as you are continuously referring to yourself in your letters, I would have called it quits long ago.

And how much longer do we thrash around in the dark? How much longer must words for things say so much of what I wordless want to do? And can't you tell me of something 'important for us' as a change from 'important for me'? And can't our loving come first? Just sometimes. Even in making the grand gesture.

Or perhaps in the next few days I should become sane and sensible too.

J.

John seems to me far more in control of words than I am, far better at the *mot juste* or barbed comment. Yet in many ways this letter was grossly unfair. I was not getting into anybody's bed; I was managing to keep Edouard at bay with several excuses, the main one being that I had to have time to get over my grief for John. Nor was there any question of paying for any favours bestowed. Ettiene was a happily married man, and my meeting with John Gielgud and David Webster was businesslike and formal. I recall that Webster genuinely liked my stage designs; it may have led to him suggesting me for some small touring company knowing that I had to have experience, but that is all conjecture. I suppose I repeated 'sane and sensible' so often, hoping it might work like a magic charm. Sane and sensible called up in my mind a kind of serenity that I wanted to achieve. I would hazard a guess that serenity is something I often enjoy now, but the reality of sense and sanity is not mine to have, nor ever will be, for they seem like tokens of good behaviour created by a society that is naïve enough to believe that it can achieve order out of chaos. But then they appeared to be everything I was not and all the things that others felt I ought to be. No wonder, after these letters of John's, that I wrote back starting the letter as I did; though I hadn't as yet received his letter of the 14th, printed above.

Croydon
16:xii:57

My Darling,

I have never known this ever before – I cannot think of anything else all day and most of the night, but you. Do you believe me? I wouldn't write it if it wasn't true – I'm sunk in a perpetual gloom writing letters to you in my mind longing for the sound of your voice and the touch of your body. I think it is driving me a little mad. And when I say every minute, I mean literally that. I can't write a thing, if I force myself I feel I am breaking inside – the only time I forget *you* is sometimes at the theatre or the cinema but three-quarters of that time is spent in things which jar you back into my memory. I need you, need you desperately. I feel my heart is very slowly breaking and with such pain.

John, are you coming back here soon after Xmas? I'm only a little nearer to getting a job, but I think I'm having an interview at the BBC tomorrow – I only hope I land something worthwhile. And where are you going to spend Xmas? I can't send you a present now, it's too late. I hope you'll be in Schwarz but I don't know the address, and I'm frightened this letter will take a long time in the Xmas rush and you won't get it for some time – I'm terrified too that my going away has lost you for ever.

Please sweetheart, I want very much to make you happy and if you come back I'll do everything I can for you even to drowning all the sugar dads that ever was in a large sack like a litter of kittens.

I'm abysmally unhappy without you. I'm quite sexless too, I haven't come for a week and I don't think I've had a hard on either. My body belongs to you and wants you as much as I hope your body needs mine.

One more thing: if you find it and think it really impossible for you to leave Vienna. Then somehow we must think again and I'll get out there. I know, I've just got to be with you. I know it more every day.

I don't want *us* to be destroyed. Because of my fault we have come perilously near it.

I love you with all my body, with all my heart and I think now it must be, with all my soul.

Colin

I had an interview at the BBC with the Controller of the then Third Programme, but after this received John's letter of the 14th.

Hove
19th

So it's come to this: a silly bickering letter refusing, in a welter of excuses attacking me, to do what you've said and wrote enough times you would do. Come back, because I've asked you to come back. It wasn't very impressive. But if you can't come back that's it, isn't it? Please darling, I'm not angry or hurt but just puzzled. Why the mention of success should make you blaze with such righteous anger, I don't know. But I'm sick and tired of reading letters from you and writing them myself and just going on splitting hairs – the next phrase is plain bitchy, which your last letter bordered on. So if you'll still have me I'm coming back to you. Why? Because I love you.

Give me a week at home over Xmas and I'll catch the train on the Monday – the 30th which gets into Vienna midday Tuesday – then we can celebrate New Year's Eve. If you have time this next week, try and get some work for me. And kick the Austrian student out of your bed on the Tuesday night – I'd like you to myself.

Now please darling, don't get into a flap and start regretting that I'm coming back. (A telegram will always stop me.) And don't think that I'm coming back for all the wrong reasons. I've told you, I love you. It's as simple as that. And don't think that I'll change my mind in the next week. I won't. I've been through quite enough these last weeks to know what I'm doing now. You made it quite clear in your letter that you thought I couldn't make you happy in England. Mind you I don't believe for one moment that a life with you would make me into a writer and painter of worth – and that anything else will destroy me in time. That's balls, and what is more bloody pretension on your part. I'm down here to pack, just for one night, go back to Croydon tomorrow.

I shall have to fight this next week and I don't care about anyone, except mama. I hate to see her hurt.

All my love,
C.

PS   Strangely enough I still FEEL sane and sensible.
PPS Both Gielgud and Webster (the other cunt) saw the designs before they met me. They were impressed by them. I'm sorry you were never.

I like the *coup de grâce* of my PPS but I detect a kind of exhaustion in this decision. I could not ignore his despair, any more than my own.

Edouard had found a studio off the Fulham Road. It was for sale for £2,000, and he wanted me to ask my father for the money, or half of the money and take a mortgage on the rest. I could not bury my pride and ask father for anything, so it was out of the question. Such a loan from him would have been a token of his love and esteem, neither of which he had ever given me. All I had from him, as I grew up, was criticism which showed envy, jealousy, an urgent competitiveness, and a wish to denigrate. He had the money, there was no question of that, but he was mean, keeping my mother on a housekeeping pittance while he lived it up on Mediterranean cruises with Maisie. In the early fifties he backed a boxer and bet £300 on a fight, which he lost. We, the family, knew there was affluence but we never saw it.

In the following letter John admits to being jealous of my life in London, and again he says he will return; again I never took such a claim seriously. Nor do I now. There was something incredibly resolute about him. Life had to revolve around his decisions while he condemned others for not seeing and following the light of reason, which inevitably emanated from himself. This, of course, is perfect theatre director psychology. I wish I had deduced that then. All I saw was a kind of divine madness in him, the fanaticism of a Savonarola which you had faith in or not. Our trouble was that my faith flickered like a faulty light switch and I kept on finding the comical within the drama.

Vienna
23:xii:57

Darling,

I love you, I love you, very, very much.

When I got your telegram on Sunday I thought the good news was a job. Your letter only came two hours ago. Please do not be as angry as your letter is. Nor so resentful.

I have a feeling that without wanting to we've pushed what we feel for each other over a terrible precipice. If we can save it without either being resentful, then we *must*.

Darling, you can't come here. At least not feeling so bitterly resentful as your letter. If you have no job or no chance in London in the immediate future then come here. There is work.

Or I shall come back. I've already given up one job because it would have bound me too firmly here. Another two I must give a decision on by 7 January. I don't need any big gesture from you any more. Please believe that. And I hate myself for the last letters I've written. They stem from being aimless and just plain wanting you – I've known no one, not in the smallest degree since you left. Try to understand why I couldn't help writing like that. Darling, I've never thought I was in any way a 'Saviour' – least of all of you. But about that and everything else, especially the designs – the more I try to explain now, the more you'll misunderstand.

If you *need* to stay in London, I'll come back. Very soon. As soon as I can square off everything here. But, feel sure, that we can be happier there than here. And I shan't be resentful about coming back. At all. Though what to do I don't know. Certainly not to be a schoolteacher!!

I sent your mama a card. Because I like her so very much and I so much want her to like me. Don't, if you can help it, hurt her.

> All my love.
> And then even more,
> J.

PS I'm going out of Wien till Friday.

John then wrote from Graz where he was staying with a student, Heinz, whom we had met in Vienna.

> Graz
> 23:xii:57

I'm in Graz. Heinz invited me to spend Xmas with him and his family and though I'd had invitations to stay in Vienna I came. It is really delightful. It's a most charming family. Tomorrow we'll look at the town. I wish, he does too, that you were here. The country, for we're a little outside the town, is lovely. I wrote you such a rushed letter this morning. I dashed to the post office, bought an airmail letter and wrote it there. I hope it made a little sense. It just meant, I love you. A lot.

Darling, I don't need any more that grand histrionic gesture. Not at all. Somehow your letter made me come to my senses. Let me explain. These last ten days I've been very busy. Often so busy I've had no time to eat – at all – till late in the evening.

For *you and me* to stay here together it was a blessing and I took it as such. For myself alone it is pretty much a necessary bore. And in my imagination I saw you being given a most select job

and it was glamorous and interesting but just for your own sake
and the furthering of your own ambition – so I thought. I'm
ashamed of those emotional letters. And for being so bloody
selfish and righteous. Suddenly I seem to have become cool and
calm and clear-headed, and even a little happy. You use the phrase
for the first time, it's as simple as that? Of course, it isn't simple.
But I feel as you at the moment. Let's hold on to that. One of
two courses then. I don't mind which. Now. Truly. If you have
no definite job in the offing then come here. It won't be easy. You
know that. But there is work – radio – plays – writing plays. I'm
well in with the radio people – and private lessons in literature,
conversation, polishing translations. It can be exciting here if you
give Vienna a fair chance. Karajan is back at the Opera and the
season is beginning. The countryside is so beautiful now with the
first new snow and the waterfalls frozen and boys skating on the
forest lakes. But this you couldn't rush back to, you would have
to come prepared for $-10°C$ – warmer clothes – and a little
roughing, though nowhere near as much as before.

Or, I'll come back to London. I'm holding some jobs in the air
till the 7th when I commit myself. I could tidy up here and come
back. *You* would have to find us somewhere to stay. We would
have to stand on our own feet. And be prepared for life not to be
lazy but to keep at it even when it gets difficult. Whatever we do,
we've got to do without any bitterness or resentment or feeling
of being caught. I know I won't feel it if I come back to London.
You mustn't feel it if you come here. If we did feel it, then it
would be a lost cause. Somehow I feel very happy. Because,
somehow an end to all this longing and loneliness and incom-
pleteness is in sight. I love you very tenderly and passionately,
darling. Try and forgive any bitterness or bitchiness in any last
letters. Try to understand and forget. It's pretty destroying. It
won't happen again. I know. Whatever happens. Even if you were
now to say you didn't want us to be together at all. I allowed
myself to get hysterical. And I'm ashamed. Whatever we do, don't
let us feel trapped. If you discovered that by going away then all
this pain is worthwhile. We've got to be together. I want to spend
such a lot of time very quietly with you. Getting used to the fact
that we're together again.

This is a crab-handed letter. I had – still have – a lot to say.

And such a short space to write it. Please be happy. And either choice is really not so big really. It is really very simple. For the first time quiet and happy.

All my love,
J.

On Christmas Day we both wrote to each other, admitting that reason had little to do with our decisions. Unfortunately it is only too characteristic of human beings that once they've got what they want, they immediately become understanding and generous. Rereading what John now says about me having a job in London grates somewhat.

Graz
25:xii:57

Today is Xmas day. It's pretty near at an end and I feel I have successfully battled with the various aunts etc. on their annual invasion.

This morning I went to Mass in the cathedral here. I wish you could have been there. It's Gothic with some exciting rococo, altar and pulpit. Towards the end it was unbelievable. The fine featherlight voice floating up in the church, then a sudden explosion of organ and orchestra as the host came down the aisle. At the same time the sun streamed through the windows and a large flock of birds began to circle around the church casting their shadows on to the windows and on to the crowded congregation again and again. And everyone in the pale light grey and only one entity.

We then drove in the country a little. A heavy frost had fallen and where the sun, very warm, had not reached lay long blue white shadows of ice needles on the grass, on the trees, in the furrows of the fields. I have never seen colours sing so much for a long time. This wonderful blue white and the two greens of fields and pines and such a clear blue sky and here the farms are painted in shining oranges and pinks and yellows.

I return to Vienna on Friday. There may be a letter from you.

You know I didn't say in my airletter but I meant to, of course I hope you land soon a good job. Something that will make you *very* happy. I do want you to feel secure if that security is what you want.

My sweet, I hope you had a happy time today. More than anything I wanted us to be together. Perhaps next year.

L. J.

Xmas morning

My Darling – I got your letter late last night. I'm not resentful – I'm not anything any longer, just loving and wanting you so much. I'm still going to catch that train if I possibly can, there is a snag about a dentist as I've had all my teeth out* (I look hideous) and I must get an appointment before I go. A telegram will confirm date and time of arrival *or* if I've been held up.

I think I just know you're right now about us and me. I don't want to stay in England. I don't want the TV job. They wouldn't let me write what I want to write. I get a bit frightened about feeling so *alone* out there, but I must just *tell* you this time and we'll somehow get over the difficulties together. Besides I just know you won't be happy in England.

This month was for me like a journey of self discovery – I found out lots of things I didn't like – besides your letters were so loving and so cruel at the same time. I'm hating today, there is a terrible unpleasant atmosphere here – and I wish I knew where you were. Who you're staying with.

There is just nothing more I can say, except I love you and to touch you and hold you in my arms is going to be the most painfully happy thing I've ever done. O darling.

C.

PS And O God I'm so worried about Australia. Never once did you mention that –

---

*Typical piece of fiction, this. I had had two back teeth pulled because of an abscess.

Darling,
    I heard this sung so beautifully this week it moved me to tears.

Never seek to tell thy love,
Love that never told can be;
For the gentle wind does move
Silently, invisibly.

I told my love, I told my love,
I told her all my heart,
Trembling, cold, in ghastly fears –
Ah, she did depart.

Soon after she was gone from me
A traveller came by
Silently, invisibly –
O, was no deny.
He took her with a sigh.

                    William Blake

4

Living in Vienna

·

Some experiences of rituals become fixed in the mind like an icon. So it was with New Year's Eve 1958 on the streets of Vienna. Ever since, I have been unable to go through that day, much less celebrate and stay up to midnight, without remembering that youthful happiness. No explanation can convey it; it was simple, almost absolute, an evening of fusion between two people who had never loved so much, so deeply before, who walked the street, entwined, hand in hand, or arms around each other, feeling as one, shouting out the New Year's greetings as one, having loved and drunk champagne. It was too perfect to be analysed, pulled apart, scrutinized for motives. There are few times when a love relationship surmounts everything, the trivia and the monstrous egos, to celebrate the reality like a great song soaring above all else. And that is what we were, that night of the celebration of the New Year in 1958.

I had arranged the train times to reach Vienna at around six that evening, there was champagne beneath the bed and a single rose on the pillow. Twenty-nine years later John was to ask me to rearrange my flight times to arrive a day earlier, again on New Year's Eve, 1987, and I did so, but that story ends these pages. It was a thread which wove its way throughout our lives, not always in jubilation, for the following year, 1959, it became a farce.

It was John who introduced me to the romantic touches. The gift of a rose or a flower struck me at first as an appalling cliché – it almost seemed an artificial touch, a little vulgar perhaps. Yet the ardour in which such a gift was given always seduced me. Though conscious of its power, I have seldom used it myself; I think I am still unnerved by the cliché. However, single roses became part of his language of love and no memoir of John would be complete without mentioning them.

From my diary I see that John was true to his word over work for me. At the beginning of the second week of January I was giving private lessons, teaching English literature to students who thought they needed extra tutoring. I was also on Radio Wien acting in short plays in English for children. We had an income.

We found a flat in the Südtiroler Platz. The landlord had been, so John told me, a former member of the Nazi Party. He came once a month for the rent, a small thin creature dressed very neatly as if still in uniform. I surveyed him always with horror, relieved that my lack of German made conversation impossible. I dramatized his presence and imagined his hands stained with blood.

We found the flat in what seems to me now a rather disgraceful manner and I am ashamed of this story. But the book is dedicated to the truth, and tell it I will. John would ask me now and again to charm older men, in order to acquire something or other, a free dinner most commonly, or perhaps seats for a successful play or opera. Poor as we were, with few friends and few contacts, we needed a cheap flat desperately and I was supposed to be part of the bait to get one.

John had heard that a diplomat at the American Embassy, married but a 'closet', had installed a boy-friend in a flat in the Südtiroler Platz, and that the boy-friend was leaving for Rome. The American diplomat, if we charmed him, would tell the landlord that we must have it. Several people were waiting for the flat already. 'But how am I to charm this wretched man?' I asked, utterly bewildered. American diplomats were hardly my favourite brand of humanity. It was then that John told me: the diplomat liked male striptease, and if I put on a show for him we would be sure to get the flat. I looked at John and he laughed and said, 'Go on, you can do it.' The idea was to plant this potential exhibition into the diplomat's mind and we would be asked back to his apartment, where I was to perform.

I asked, 'Do you mean to say that casually, as we are drinking at the bar, you say, Colin happens to love doing a striptease?' John claimed that was roughly what was going to happen. It worked. The three of us late at night were in the American's apartment and John said start now. Cold? No, I must have music,

I insisted. John went to the record player and found Ravel's 'Bolero'. I began. The American sipped his drink and watched avidly. The terrible fact was that neither John nor myself had realized before that evening how long 'Bolero' continues for – twenty minutes, which seemed like an hour. I was down to my black briefs in five minutes and to help me to make it last longer John kept on clutching me to kiss me, so that half a minute might pass without this interminable orgiastic wriggling. I ended the wretched dance at last, flinging the briefs away as the crescendo blared forth. We got the flat. A flat in the end far more difficult to get rid of than it was to acquire. I think I left the American my knickers.

So why is there this element of shame? It is because of the fake femininity involved: I have always liked my own gender and been happy in myself, and I have never worn drag, even as a joke. The thought is so alien to me that it is nauseating. The homosexual man, extremely common when I was young, who is so camp that he indulges in an orgy of exaggerated gesture and mannerism – a travesty of both genders but thought misleadingly to be somehow female – is again something I feel shame for. No one should have to caricature themselves in this gross and pathetic manner.

'Have to' is the key, for I believe this behaviour, which can be taken up when quite young, is the outsider longing to belong to something. Even a minority sect which is despised by the rest of society will do. Children who feel psychologically apart, who do not recognize in adult society any reflection of their inner truth, suffer appalling loneliness, driven by demon visions that they are freaks and monsters. Society heaps coals upon these flames by constant repetition of cosy clichés about the norm, and what is expected, the right thing to do. If the small child cannot see any logic or truth in this then the child is not sure what path to pursue. Better then, sometimes, to be outrageous, show who you are and have that label as some form of defence, because if you can make the straight society laugh at you, they are not, in theory, going to hit you or place you in prison. Mind you, the reality is that they do both. But I believe that camp gestures and tones are taken up in desperation, and that when they are accepted it leaves an alien person inside the disguise.

So I found my striptease objectionable in that it borrowed many of its movements and gestures from every bad night-club act I had ever seen in a film. It was nothing to do with my personality and I still hate the self which complied and went along with the ludicrous scene.

It would be absurd to live in Vienna and not love opera. This was the post-war era of Herbert von Karajan as Director and it was my introduction to many of the great performances such as Elisabeth Schwarzkopf as the Marshaline in *Der Rosenkavalier* and the Countess in *The Marriage of Figaro*, Jean Cocteau as the narrator in *Oedipus Rex*. Like a strange silk-suited spider with a huge silver halo of hair he leapt out from the wings and mesmerized the audience. I saw *Wozzek*, with its picture of the barbarism of the army and its persecution of the individual echoing within me. This man-made monster, I knew instinctively, would still triumph and part us.

Vienna started a lifelong love affair with opera. *Der Rosenkavalier* being the quintessence of romanticism, it naturally deeply affected us both. The last trio is music woven in paradise, drawing together earth and stars and leaving us stunned like idiots. I heard *Così fan tutte* in the small concert house in the Hofburg and the *Requiem* in the Stephansdom, a cathedral sacred to us because on New Year's Eve we had lit candles as part of a loving ritual. In the atmosphere of those cobbled streets below the Stephansplatz, where houses are marked with plaques commemorating where Beethoven, Schubert and Mozart lived and died, I began also to listen to their piano music more attentively and to grow to love the chamber music.

From being, the year before, alienated by Vienna and its culture, now, without being at all remotely aware of what was happening, still on the surface poking fun at the obese cherubs crawling all over the Plague Pillar like flies on jam, I was becoming immersed in certain aspects of it.

I found there were stronger influences than music. On the first visit I had seen an Egon Schiele water-colour in the window of a shop and stunned by its aggressive, bleak beauty I searched for more examples of his work. In 1958 Schiele seemed unknown outside Vienna; his original work was still selling for very little (what a pity we were both so poor), but on finding more examples, I was undoubtedly influenced to make my own pen line more honest and vigorous. The other great painter and draughtsman was undoubtedly Oscar Kokoshka. I could have gone to his school at Salzburg if I had known, and my time in Austria would have been better spent learning from a master. But the power of his portraits was persuasive enough, and in 1959 after my return to England I began to paint work which owed a debt to him. The varied techniques of portrait drawings he had done in 1910 for a Viennese newspaper I borrowed for the Writers of Our Time series in *The Times Literary Supplement*.

I also began to appreciate the baroque. This style at first offends the English in its exuberance and vulgarity, but no architecture incorporates the comical so snidely in its devotional seriousness, and this is very endearing. The rococo is even more enchanting. When in Sicily two years later I encountered Serpotta, I might not have been so entranced if I had not been seduced first in Vienna.

Yet in the end I was too far north for my temperament to be happy. Once I crossed the Alps I would have perked up no end, and the further south the better. Like so many other English throughout history, I am an obsessive lover of Greece. When living there I am never homesick. But this I did not know then, nor had I visited other southern Mediterranean countries which, like Greece, have a similar atavistic pull on my spirit. No, on the second visit to Vienna I was content to absorb the experience, because John was so obviously happy and at home. Before he died, a friend told me that he talked of Austria, but not the time we were there – it was the earlier visit with Kester when he was seventeen and had seen Europe for the first time. I can imagine the effect after growing up in Newcastle, New South Wales, that Austria with its imperial past and its hieratic culture must have had. No wonder the postcard of the Imperial Habsburg crown was sent to me. John must have understood that Vienna was not totally enthralling to me, but like so much else we did not discuss it.

One of the factors in loving that intrigues me is how deeply we believe the loved one understands what is occurring inside ourselves, only to discover through some trivial incident afterwards that this is an illusion. Yet the happiness of love is based upon the idea of perfect understanding between two people. Often in our desperate longing for happiness and for it to continue we go on deluding ourselves that the perfect understanding exists when it has vanished.

John and I achieved the perfect understanding on New Year's Eve, and we knew above all else that we had to be together. But once that occurred we felt naïvely that it would always be there, like an absolute, unchangeable and steadfast, an image of God. Part of his attraction for me was, I now see, his antipodean energy, something quite strange to the caution and control of the English spirit which I had never anyway been very sympathetic to. But this huge reservoir of energy, which was a constant stimulus, disguised much of what was going on beneath the surface. When I had left in November it had appalled us both, but now we did not bestir ourselves to wonder what exactly had caused it. In a sense, throughout that second stay in Vienna I was marking time, feeling I was absorbing aspects of importance yet being still restless and impatient with myself at odd mumblings of discontent. However upon the surface we were, as I have said, happy enough.

We began to make friends – an American girl Sooky, who was studying singing; her friend Jim Harrison, who was studying music with Nadia Boulanger in Paris; and an old friend of Kester's, the Countess Lucie de Bethel, who would give us, in her elegant sitting-room, very strong Italian coffee in fragile china cups. There were others, but I have edited many of the names out of the letters, as now I have no recollection of who they were.

We would go to the bars. There was an equivalent of Brighton's Beach Bar, a basement bar where transvestites would congregate. Many of them were quite dowdy, but most of them made it clear they were gay – unlike today when we are aware that transvestism need have nothing to do with homosexual preference. There was also much drag at the opera. I was always astonished at the finery and the jewels that some middle-aged and rather plump men would arrive in, often unescorted and with such flagrant details as ostrich feather fans and paste coronets. This world was too much like Genet for comfort. Yet the women – this was still European post-war austerity – wore eccentric clothes too. Fur capes, torn lace and faded satin, their faces white with too much powder, they brought with them the overpowering smell of violets and mothballs into the foyer. They were nevertheless an enthusiastic audience, knowledgeable in their music, willing to applaud the fierce discord of Berg as well as the bitter, sweet yearning of Puccini.

We worked hard. John taught at the International School all day. I gave private lessons in English literature, wrote and painted and shopped for the evening meal. My German was adequate for the shopping but little else. I had tried doing as John suggested, half an hour a day, but I hated the ornate print and I could not pronounce a lot of the sounds. The attempt to learn began to be an ordeal so I gradually slipped out of the chore. I tried to time pulling the cork from the first bottle of wine with the sound of John's key in the door. I experimented with Austrian food, but not with great enthusiasm. I tended to look south of the Alps again and we would eat soup and pasta. But it was cheap to eat out and we would do so if we went to the cinema or the opera. We were very alike in our cinematic passions – after all we had both discovered the films of Cocteau at sixteen, and very soon afterwards the work of Eisenstein. I suppose it was inevitable that we should feel so sympathetic to the two most talented homosexual film makers. I was drawn to the incestuous poetic hysteria of the former, but I was more profoundly and politically fired by the Russian. *The Battleship Potempkin* remained my favourite film for many years; the famous shot of the meat crawling with maggots may well have been seminal to my growing dislike of eating corpses. The third figure which made up our trinity was of course Visconti, another homosexual. Our tastes beyond this were fairly trendy, loving the early Fellini and de Sica and the French post-war films; the music from *Les Jeux Interdits* we would sing as we would also attempt to mime Jean-Louis Barrault from *Les Enfants du Paradis*. What we sang – badly and out of tune – was of course mostly Kurt Weill, 'Surabaya Johnny', 'Pirate Jenny', 'The Benares Song' and inevitably 'The Alabama Song'. Forever these songs now call up Vienna and my love affair with John. For years it was difficult to hear them without being stricken with appalling desolation. They were, alas, the perfect music too to bring on bouts of maudlin self-pity.

By the spring we had managed to save a little money and John suggested we visit Italy. We would take the train and stay a few days in Venice, then, if funds would stretch, go on to Florence.

This, I felt, was something more like it. Florence and Venice, I knew, because Billy had whisked me off there. I longed now to show John what I had discovered – the tiny St. George chapel filled with the most exquisite Carpaccios, the Bellinis in the Accademia and in Florence – so much which I longed to see again. I could get drunk on Italian painting and once John had planted the idea I became almost possessed, yet knew it would seem bad manners towards John and Vienna itself if I became too intolerably excited. With some effort I kept my agitation to myself. Then there occurred one of those moments when I was to realize that no understanding existed between us at all, or rather that he did not begin to understand me. It was, alas, mostly John's savings we would be using for the trip, as he had an income from the school while my earnings paid for daily expenses, like the food and the wine. John then called the tune and it went something like this: 'I shan't take you to Italy if you are complaining all the time about *not* staying in the grand hotels. We shall have to rough it. If you put up with that without complaining we shall go.' I stared at him with fury. He didn't realize that I would have slept on a bed of nails in a hailstorm to be back in both Venice and Florence, nor did I care a damn about luxury when I was with John. I agreed, hiding my fury, and that was the end of the discussion.

However, Italy was as much a revelation to John as it had been for me. Venice is a perfect city for young lovers, to stroll through it arm in arm, to sit in squares sipping café and grappa, watching the reflections of water and stone, to smell fungi and garlic, sweetness and dampness; we were almost delirious with happiness. I was content to watch John count farthings and know that we would get to Florence. I longed to show him the Botticellis, the *Birth of Venus* and *Primavera*; these paintings never exhibit their enormous power and elegance in illustrations – unlike most great paintings which do give some semblance of their worth. I wanted also to show him the Michelangelo slaves like seeds writhing out of their husks. We fell in love with the exquisite Donatello David, that lyrical Ganymede. We also bought half a dozen tall green tumblers, which were cheap yet stylish and which became a symbol of our love. I still have four of them, miraculously surviving many moves around the world.

Santa Maria della Salute

In Florence I telephoned Harold Acton. I had met him at
Lehmann's and he had read my short stories and been kind enough
to say how much he had liked them. After I had wrestled in
broken Italian with the butler, Acton came to the telephone and
asked us up the following day for tea. In our horrid way, we had

hoped at least for dinner, one less meal to budget for on our slim resources. We caught a bus out to a spot near his Palladian villa. The entrance was on the road, but the way from there between a line of cypresses seemed to go on for ever and it was raining. We walked up the endless drive, cars kept on passing us, bespattering us with mud. Eventually we rang the bell, the butler opened the door and we found ourselves among a great mass of people who were being escorted around the gardens under umbrellas. We were awed by the beauty outside and in. I seem to remember nearly everyone leaving, and being offered dry Martinis and truffle sandwiches. These were the stuff that paradise is made from. They have stuck clearly in my memory and I have never tasted truffle like it since. The sandwiches were thin white fresh bread, spread with farm butter and then a layer of black truffle, nothing else. I doubt whether I shall ever eat anything as delicious again.

When we returned to Vienna, to mark John's birthday in May we gave a party. I recently found the list of guests but most of them mean nothing now except for Sooky and Jim, Lucie de Bethel and Heinz from Graz. The rest – Dieter, Christoph, Gunter – who were they, I wonder? Our students perhaps. Twenty-three people came, including Sooky wearing a black sack, a fashion which had just come in. There is a note from me for John, written in a parody of my flights of fancy style. John, it would seem, had complained of 'panegyric flights'.

My Love: no panegyric flights here; only facts.
I have *gawn* with the swallows who dip their wings in my blood, only to belief in the cessation of light. I am gawn to pick up, to collect, to receive, or may be to steal a record player, my heart – my cock, my rhythms of introversions, long for the plaintive shriek of twentieth century saxophones.
Your loved one,
bewildered, torn, yet still suffering his sainthood
with a slight air of dismay.
Sooky is coming in a black sack!

All relationships find rituals to identify that complex and almost indefinable union between two people. There was what John called 'Grace before meals' which was a light kiss upon the lips.

Certainly we thought it more potent than prayer. We could have been badly in error there, but there was also a stronger conviction within John that whatever occurred in the day, whatever distance or quarrel, such a break must be mended before sleep. To accompany this, there was a more practical symbol of togetherness. There was no double bed in the flat, only a single bed and a sofa, and every night these had to be placed together and made up as one bed. So the furniture was solemnly moved night and morning. We slept in our sitting-room where there was a wood-burning stove. The bedroom of the flat was piled high with the landlord's furniture. We only used it occasionally, allowing one of the homeless Hungarian refugees to sleep there, huddled in armchairs and covered in dustsheets.

Vienna was full of these lads selling their bodies for food, for the tragic and impotent Revolution had occurred two years before. Much of what was good in those months I poured into my novel *Asylum*. These passages communicate something of the passion. They were written in 1963, five years later. The characters are not specifically John and myself, but the wildness and the loving are authentic enough.

'The flat in Vienna is small, in the main room there is a large black stove – after the thunderstorm, they light it to get dry. Upon one wall, Carl paints a mural of strange organic flowers bursting out of thick and viscid vegetation. The bed, which was once a sofa, is shaped like a wave. Carl wishes to be stated, established, maintained; he consumes Angelo's longing with avid, unending hunger. Angelo wishes to be used, beaten and mortified. But in the urgent threshing of their limbs, in the clawing hot touch of body beating against body they are at last one, these sons of Cleo, laughing behind her back, their secret passion for ever unassuaged for in its depths and excesses it covers her with bile and humiliation. That is why Angelo is Carl's escape and why he tenderly cradles Angelo's head in his arms, stroking his hair, his cheeks, and thinking with love, with concern, of how Cleo, if she observed the scene, would writhe in bitter jealousy.

For one whole summer they stay together, their animal fury takes them across continents and seas. What they say to each other, they say still half immersed in their savage dream; their secret longings grow from out of them, plantlike, flowering and bursting into shape and colour. As yet even their contradictions, their differences cannot go to war, for the very fury of their love and ecstasy is also a kind of blindness and imperception.

These two lovers wish to possess a hundred different names; they move through a vast dance-hall of identities with delight and fervour. Their disjointed words and gestures are ashes scattered to the wind. They never rest for the art of their love is its complete and irrevocable restlessness. They long for each other so much even when they possess each other that they beat the very breath from out of their lungs in their impetuous longing. Time is of no importance, nor place, nor any facet of the changing world about them. They are triumphantly selfish, blind to everything else except each other. Their only peace is the stillness of the night, when they sense, then feel, the other's body in sleep.

Lying together, naked, pinioned in each other's arms, their souls, trapped and chained before, now at last begin to unfold. Or that is the illusion of their love. Desperately they would peel flesh from bone, discarding everything, they thought, yet still their involved and complicated pretences like layers of cheap and tawdry veiling surround every gesture and nuance of their love.'

I was content, more than content, extremely happy to live with John, but I still did not much care for Vienna. I regularly visited the Kunsthistorisches Museum. I admired all the great Brueghels and was mesmerized by the work of Bosch, yet I was too agitated and confused to study them and benefit, as I had from Schiele and Kokoshka.

Now that it was summer, it was warm enough to draw. The baroque made even lamp standards look like sculptures for a royal palace and I had fun with monuments, fountains, ceremonial porches and church façades. Most of these drawings were sold the following year. I was beginning to find a style of my own. The editor of the *Architectural Review*, who reproduced some of the drawings, said, 'You like elegant buildings with fidget on them.' The style I was finding was elegant, but also witty; I liked buildings which erred towards the tasteless. I could do nothing with Inigo Jones or Palladio, for they were far too perfect and complete in themselves. But the crazy excesses of St. Marks, Venice, for example, were a gift from the Gods. The drawing I did took four and a half hours and was a gruelling chore. Several years later I sold it to Lionel Bart for £25. Sadly, his manager of the time, an actor called Peter Arne, went off with all the drawings Bart had bought. Arne was murdered a few years ago. I wonder where that fragile drawing of St. Marks is now? I discovered later that they fade easily, so if put in direct sunlight St. Marks will have vanished like ectoplasm at dawn.

But finding a drawing style which was also admired and quickly purchased gave me only a modicum of satisfaction. The thought of doing nothing else but this kind of drawing to earn a living was an appalling thought, horrible in its unremitting tedium. So staying in Vienna to draw was no compulsion at all. I think John found this puzzling.

So I wrote – each morning between lessons on illuminating the novels of Trollope I attacked a short story or part of a novel. There was no lack of ideas. Lehmann had said that my work reminded him of an open bottle of champagne lying on its side fizzing all over the place. There was more to this metaphor than is apparent at first sight: the bottle lies on its side, there is no one around to plant it upright, and only the first third of the contents will fizz. My ideas were bizarre, tending towards heavy and very obscure metaphysical symbolism, intricate and confused. Unless I wrote a full and detailed précis of the whole saga at once, I would tend to start it, convinced of its profundity, only to find that I had forgotten the theme, the plot and all of its underlying messages. I began at this time about a dozen different novels and possibly thirty different stories, but few of them ever got finished. One that did was 'The Pilgrimage of Miss Prince' whose plot now seems obviously to reflect what was happening between John and me. The story is that of two unmarried women teachers who live together in the London suburbs in a platonic relationship, and who visit Schwarz for a holiday. They go for a walk in the forest above the town and the younger woman notices a young man dressed in rags who follows them. She is not in the least frightened but is, rather, intrigued. A few days later she returns alone. The man lives in the forest, he is deaf and dumb and he touches her on the arm. The two teachers go on the pilgrimage and the younger woman sees the recluse as the wounded dove – religion and sexuality are all entwined. She insists on staying on, they quarrel, the older teacher leaves, then after a few more days returns, finds her friend living in the forest and stabs her in anger.

My recluse is obviously Pan, but it is not clear why the relationship does not work, except that the younger woman is restless and unsatisfied, and is searching for something. That she is murdered for it seems a little unfair and far too melodramatic, throwing the story entirely off balance.

It is undeniable that like the champagne I was on my side. Looking back I see someone psychologically crippled without anyone to advise. For, as all young people, I did not take kindly to any advice, my hackles rising at the arrogance of it all. No, I cannot see how my own crippled state could have been healed; it is only experience and awareness that can achieve this and for that we need time. So like Miss Prince I was restless.

I wanted to move on. I did not want to stay throughout the whole of the summer, yet I was uncertain where I wanted to go, and where it was that I wanted us to live together. The trouble was, we did not dare discuss it at all. I knew that whether we stayed or parted, John must eventually go to Australia, and then the parting would be permanent. Instinctively we both knew it and dreaded it. We did not understand that in talking over fears, they can become surmountable, even vanish; nor did we have any older, wiser counsellor who could have drawn a discussion out from us. Instead we refused to talk, or even think, and the tensions and frustrations, the feeling of the prison coming down around me, the possessiveness of John's love, intensified.

John had written to Kester, and when a reply came he showed me what Kester had written: 'If Colin loves you he would go to Australia, that is an inescapable conclusion,' he wrote, and implied that John's previous lover, G., would have been prepared to go. Appalled at such a simplistic reduction of all our complexities, I wrote to Kester, defending myself against his disbelief in my love for John. I claimed I also had responsibilities to my parents and needed to be elsewhere than Vienna for the furtherance of my own career. In a rage I repeated the story of John's unhappy experience with the false testicle: 'But when I hear about the Christmas before last when John was in intense physical pain with his cock and balls wrapped up in a little bundle of gore and all G. could do was to walk him home swearing at him all the time, you must understand that I feel a little impatient when I hear and read about his love.'

Wisely Kester did not answer this letter. A few weeks later I would meet him for the first time.

One day in early July we were boating on a lake, and I said I wanted to return to London. John answered quickly, 'All right then,' and we never said anything more. How foolish I was, not at least to say why or to explain what I was feeling. But I wanted to feel alone, independent, free. I thought I could dismiss everything that we had been, that such experiences could be rejected without harming them or their natural future.

5

The Second Parting

Without any explanation or even an attempt at a discussion, on the face of it I was being short-sighted and rather tiresome in leaving John and Vienna for the second time. Hindsight says, this was recklessly silly behaviour, but hindsight also sees the panic and the driving compulsion. I believe I was afraid to discuss what led me to act. It was far too dangerous to my equilibrium, always in a most fragile and ill-balanced state. I was a starving creature needing to be fed; I knew what the food was and hated, like all true addicts, the fact that I needed it. I was badly homesick, a homesickness for the cruel psychological knot which made up my parents' marriage. I had to know more about it – unlike other children who may run from such distress, I wanted to explore it, to understand it and make something out of it. It was a very powerful compulsion. I had two years before completed a novel which had used their lives, and was thought unpublishable because of its sexual candour. How could I put my father into a novel without being explicit? I recall the perception of Osyth Leeston at John Murray's who returned the typescript with the words, 'You will use this as source material for other books.' I did – four other novels, in fact.

There seems to be no other explanation for the fact that I chose at that time in my life to live at home for almost a year. The inhumane scene which prompted my finally leaving the following summer (1959) fits into the scenario I now perceive. The reader might well say that being poor I had no choice but to live at home, yet I had left at the age of sixteen, driven away then by the sheer anguish of my parents' marriage. In the intervening years I had had a flat to myself and had lived with John in Vienna, tasting all the freedom of being away from the parental nest. Yet now at the age of twenty-five I returned, using a large Victorian bay-windowed room as a bedsitter and the broken conservatory as a studio. I paid my mother some money each week and started to try and sell the work I had done in Vienna.

My first letter reflects genuine surprise that my family cared enough to celebrate my return. John had given me his gold ring, I had given him a St. Joseph medallion and chain, given to me a couple of years before by Billy.

Croydon
12:vii:58

Darling,

I got back last night: the whole family had been waiting for me the night before with great celebrations till 1.00 in the morning. I never thought they wanted me that much.

I can't bear to think of you alone in Vienna – I'm so confused. I've had abominable headaches since the journey and can't think. The ring makes me happy. This letter will make you angry for it says nothing and it's so inadequate. I somehow feel that only a *book* would satisfy you.

All my love,
Colin

I now know that, not unlike many people, I want breathers from a relationship. Want, in fact, nothing more than to go off for a couple of days on my own. To reflect a little, to feel the pleasure of missing someone and the pleasure of anticipation to be back with them again. If only this simple conclusion had occurred to us. That it was nothing dramatic, merely what most people suffer from at some stage. But relationships change, and we in this parting began to decline, slip down into a low phase. So much of the correspondence deals with small issues, one feels now, which threw us almost needlessly into depression or anger. There can be little doubt that we both missed each other deeply, that we were still in love, yet we seemed hopeless at getting our act together. John's first letter to me sets the tone exactly.

99

My dear Colin,

I wrote you a long hearty letter yesterday which I can't send you, I find now. On rereading it, it sounds so fucking artificial. The only kind of letter I seem to be able to write honestly is a morose one. So I guess correspondence isn't going to be welcome from here.

Darling, I'm so lonely. The flat is a nightmare and I haven't the slightest wish to set it in order. Until this morning Thursday's washing-up was sitting in the kitchen. Wherever I go I expect to see you. Whenever I come back to the flat I can't help but come into this room straight away. I can't believe anything else but that you'll be there.

I'm bewildered by it all. I haven't cried once since you left. Yet it is all as bad as it was last November. I'm getting out of this place, out of Austria as soon as I can. Anywhere but here now. It's not memories of you that upset me, it's memories of us doing innumerable small intimate things here. The air is thick with ghosts.

I love you and I miss you more than I can ever tell.

Oh darling, hold me tightly *now*.

John

John wrote again three days later. His grandeur about London in August I find quite endearing, and his letters are certainly far more perceptive about what is happening than my own.

16:vii:58

Today is the seventh day that you left and more to clarify much that's been in my mind than to tell you something vital, necessary, loving or what, I'm making myself sit and write.

Since you left I haven't cried. I'm not sure why. Before I cried so much that my eyes and throat ached intensely. Perhaps it's because since Thursday there's been a terrifying vacuum which neither tears or spleen could fill or make bearable. I live at half speed, at half awareness, half pleasure. Your letter too seems like this, that there is damn all that can be said or is to say.

I shall most likely return to London about the end of this month. If you want us to be together you had better organize yourself and arrange perhaps that we take the cottage in the Lake District or Christchurch. No one wants to stay in London in August. Or I'll look after it from this end and arrange somewhere to stay in London for myself.

I miss you very much. Every morning I wake up and turn over to find you there beside me. My arms are sore from not holding you. I'm not cold but hungry to have you again.

This makes me feel rather weepy. I guess the best thing would be if you didn't write any more. Darling.

A birthday card had arrived on the day, 17 July. It was loving yet with a grudging edge to it, and listed resolutions for me about money and writing, getting a flat, not drinking and going on a diet. Where the expression 'shittooth' came from I can't remember unless it was our version of 'forsooth'. This letter of mine strikes me as exhausted, as if I'm suffering from 'Tasker love fatigue' and can't understand my own indifference.

Croydon
18:vii:58

Well! After receiving your birthday greetings this morning all I can say is – shittooth!

Not a very exciting day yesterday. Ma and I went shopping in Croydon in the morning, popped into a bar for a drink and who should be there but Roberta Cowell.* Looking indescribably hideous. Ma felt rather weak and ordered a double gin. Most of the resolutions that you've written for me seem so difficult that I don't think I can promise to do many of them. Fruit for a week sounds horrid so does the money one, but I'll try. You don't mention painting and this is what I've been doing since I've got back. I spent five quid on canvases this morning.

*Robert Cowell was a pilot in the RAF, who after the war became one of the first transexuals.

I had dinner last night with Bob* and a girl-friend of his who is a lady journalist on the *Chicago Daily News* and is having a big party on Saturday where lots of people are coming including Ken Tynan (I've decided to tell him my Genet plot). Paul and Jimmy send you lots of love and are looking forward to seeing you. I do want to meet Kester and have written him a note which he should have got four days ago asking him to ring me so we can get in touch and meet, but there is only silence so far.

Yes it was a horrid birthday, very nasty, in fact it didn't feel like anything at all. Even that bugger Billy forgot it and not a word, a deep silence, from Brighton. I somehow feel I'm not wanted in England any more.

Lehmann says he will publish the story if it was two thousand words shorter, but I don't think I can do it. Might, I must see.

Come back soon.

All my love,
Colin

A week went by before I wrote again, this time excited that I had met Kester, who obviously had revived in me those lovable aspects of John that when apart from him I wanted to suppress.

Croydon

My darling, I had hoped to hear from you this morning in answer to my last two letters, but there was nothing, pity. Now to tell you some news. I had a note yesterday from Kester saying he'd been trying to ring me but with no success, so as I was going up to town for lunch (with Chris the clergyman boy-friend of Fred†) I thought I'd go along and find if Kester was at home. He was. I could only stay about an hour and a half but they went like wildfire. I liked him enormously. It was rather painful because I kept on seeing things of yours that somehow had been ours like the black swan/duck, and that nice brown cup which was on top

---

*Bob Haynes, a close friend who became an economic adviser to Lord Beaverbrook and died from a coronary in 1976 at the early age of fifty-two.
†Two ex-clerical conquests of mine.

of the wardrobe in thick dust. But somehow I could understand you far more once I had seen and met him. I think we were both like what the other imagined: there were no surprises, only a filling in of the outlines so that I've laid the ghost for ever now and can see and appreciate how you feel about him. I played my favourite game of imagining you both in each other's arms and somehow you fitted quite beautifully.

I went down to Brighton on Monday to see Billy, and spent a stupid dismal day, but which did end at the theatre to see this first play that Tynan raved about last Sunday, *Chicken Soup with Barley* – it wasn't all that good and in fact some of it was a great big bore. Then on Tuesday I had dinner with Martyn and a publisher and a painter. He has framed a bum view of you which is terribly sexy and hangs just outside the guests' bedroom. Then yesterday was the *pièce de résistance* of my time back. I took Ma to the theatre and chose with some misgivings (thinking of her puritan streak) the new Peter Brook production *Irma la Douce*. I can't tell you what an exciting evening it is. It's terrific fun, the music is rhythmic and waltzy and jazzy, the production has more panache than anything I've seen for a long time and the script is sexily about as salacious as a Restoration comedy. Mum loved it.

Did I tell you how happy I was that you're coming back soon? Well I am, but I wish you'd give me more details. I feel very much in the dark. You wrote to Kester that you might be staying until December. When I hear such conflicting statements I do get a bit muddled.

All my love and lots more if it was there, come back soon and wriggle over my body like a lithe snake.

I luvs yur. Thousands wouldn't.

Colin

I am sorry to see I wasn't much impressed by Arnold Wesker's play. Not true now at all, as I am an admirer of the trilogy. But I think his own autobiographical play in its intense East End Jewishness was too alien to my work, still unborn, which cried out to be written. My suburban English lower-middle-class childhood was culturally worlds apart from his.

Kester and I became close friends. We saw much of each other later when we both lived on Lesbos in the year of the Colonels' coup. A man of great sensitivity, he remained in Greece teaching English in small villages on the islands.

A letter from John refers to a missing letter from me which talks positively of Australia.

Vienna
22:vii:58

Darling,

Your letter in reply to my morose one arrived this morning. So now I've got three letters of yours I've got to answer. The only way is to go through what you've written and answer bit by bit. A scrappy method of work.

I knew you had to get away for a bit from me, that you needed a breathing thinking space. I guess I knew that at least a month before you left.

On Wednesday I was very low in spirits, miserable, wanting and not having you here to take it and feeling that when we come together again it would be again for a short time then another break, more painful than the rest. To be quite frank, I got the shits and that's why you got such an arsehole of a letter.

As for sitting down in the Strand and dreaming of Australia, what the hell can I say?

You say the parting has cleared up your vagueness about Australia. As you're vague about how it's cleared up, I'm none the wiser. Only, don't write carelessly about Australia. You know my habit of reading more into a comment than it can take.

About Kester and G. Kester still hesitates on the brink of a decision. He'll be there still, for the next two weeks if I know him. We might meet up for a few days somewhere. I have offered him the flat if he wants to come to Vienna to *work*.

I wrote yesterday to G. He wrote me half a writing pad of loving thoughts and advice and questions which I was to answer honestly. So I did. I can still quote having written, 'If Colin and I fail then I don't want to, shall be physically unable to, enter into a new relationship or re-enter an old one.' I told him to find someone else and forget me. Kester has already accepted this as true.

Evenings to theatre or musical operettas in Schonbrunn (lovely baroque theatre) Daphne in Belvedere. Operettas at Volksoper (very good ones, better than Theodomaus). Hardly ever do I poke my nose into a bar since the scene I had when Horst got angry at my refusal to take him back home with me. He's a real tart.

Make bookings in September for *My Fair Lady*, Bea Lillie at the Adelphi and *Ghosts* and *Marie Stuart* at the Old Vic. Now! Don't wait. Please.

Think more about how I 'change' you. If I do it's no more than you do me. And I don't mind. It makes me happy.

I love you, a lot, more than I want to. Shittooth!

J.

What drove John mad was not only my lack of decisiveness, but a seeming inability even to book theatre tickets and to make any plans for the future, even a few days ahead. It is a fear, I believe, quite common in people, but of what? Tempting fate, taunting the Gods? That is nonsense, though often the excuse given. Surely it is merely the refusal to commit oneself. Even to give the future undertaking of an evening out with that person seems to me now deeply heartless. Yet in my own way I was husbanding my farthings. I allowed so much for oil paint and canvases, that was the first priority, and my second was wine. Everything else must wait, until a painting or a story was sold – travel, theatre, food and clothes. I began at that time to write more than I painted, for it cost less; though I did do a portrait of John Betjeman for the *London Magazine* and suggested that as E. M. Forster was eighty in the following year I should draw him too.

It was one of my clerics, of course, who had introduced me to Betjeman a couple of years before. Betjeman kindly sent some early short stories of mine to Lehmann who thought at first I must be Betjeman's boy-friend. The idea was alarming, for I had not thought of this plump, convivial man as being gay, or straight for that matter. He seemed then distinctly asexual, but utterly

John Betjeman

lovable and outrageously good company to be with. He gave me a boater of his once and we would walk through the City both wearing boaters, with me confessing the most bizarre incidents of clerical life and Betjeman hooting with laughter. I can hear him now of one eminent bishop: 'My God, he's besotted, absolutely besotted.' And his marvellous assessment of Archbishop Fisher: 'That man is so hard, he'd even boil his potatoes in a widow's tears.'

I wrote to John in a dispirited manner on the 29th. I had stayed in Brighton and found Allan's room 'a sordid messy little hole'; I dreamt that John had had a crew cut a week before he had one. I intended to tour the galleries with my work hoping for an exhibition. But I am not very honest: when I was at Brighton there was a young girl, Honey, living in the room next to Allan, and we slept together. In fact, I seem to remember we screwed most of the weekend. She was on the game, though she said she did it with me free, because she liked it. Why this happened I am not sure, because the girl had an older woman who was her lover and our weekend of fucking caused enormous anguish to this woman. I cannot forget, and it is a scene I am still deeply ashamed of, being in bed with the girl in her room in the midst of frenetic sex, with the woman banging and screaming outside. We could not stop, that was the trouble, the physical impulse once started overrode everything else, and the older woman's pain, her sobs and abuse seemed to be from a distant country.

Honey was the kind of girl my father adored. If he had known he would have been proud of me. I carefully kept it a secret from everyone and next time I saw father I made a point of praising John. Allan knew of this weekend and told me that Honey had started taking *The Times* as she was intent on educating herself. The next time I went down she had vanished with her lover. Behaviour like this from me puzzled people like Allan, who needed to see me as completely gay. I, in fact, didn't think about it much – it was a very physical weekend of effortless sensuality. We just liked each other's bodies – we had nothing else in common.

My next letter to John is bleak. I see myself as a murderer. Lehmann had called me 'cold, callous Colin' and it stuck; I half began to believe there was an 'homme fatal' aspect to my character.

31:vii:58

Darling: I'm sending the enclosed as Kester asked me to. I saw him yesterday, had supper with him and then took him *out* for a drink. I think we get on very well. I've taught him how to fiddle the National Insurance. That was lesson one on the scheme I've worked out, on how to pervert a saint's moral values.

Of course what is fascinating is hearing other sides to stories I already know. I always thought I was the one who either *lied* ever so slightly, or distorted, or simply left out the vital clue which changed the whole meaning of a story. You can guess how delighted I am when I find that you have done the same. What, honest John? I say. Not honest John.

Well now I know: I've been wondering what was happening

to me in the last two weeks. I see now, I've been dying. I'm dead now. First of all we killed off in the last year two upright gentlemen. Poor Billy is dead. Ding dong bell. Poor Edouard died in January. And now we're dead. Or at least I am. What a waste.

C.

(Read this last)

I think black ink makes me pessimistic. I'd better explain. It's simply this. I feel nothing. No reactions, no responses, as dead as a doornail. I haven't missed you. I still don't. Yet I want you to come back, very soon in fact, as fast as you can, because I want to know what has happened, whether we're dead or finished or what.

Odd moments, last night, when the moon was so full in a clear clear sky and I wondered whether you were watching it too, then I imagined us together watching it, and being very close and kissing, very tenderly, my lips on your eyes and nose and cheeks. And then I daren't think any longer because it suddenly brought everything to life in such a way that I thought I'd go mad. So perhaps I haven't died.

John's angry answer arrived several days later, like mine, in two letters. The second letter complains bitterly at my inconsistency. I fear this has been a consistent thread in my nature. Perhaps my Brighton weekend sharpened the difference – the simple but glorious sexuality opposed to all these emotional needs. What could I think? What was the real experience? Both, of course. I had to face it: I loved him, yet I didn't miss him. I have long got used to my own inconsistency and now think it valuable. To deny the validity of some truths just to simplify the picture is irresponsible.

1:viii:58

Dear Colin,

Your letter of Wednesday reached me this morning.

I know what you mean about not missing me. That's how it happens sometimes. It's not that you've died but just fallen out of love maybe. It sounds as simple as that. I hear it happens in the best of families. What all the shit about Billy and Edouard 'dying' is about I don't know, it just sounds hysterical.

About any stories you hear from K. I don't mind at all, if it passes the time for you. But I've been honest with you and never *consciously* lied or left out 'vital details'. You tend to put me on a pedestal sometimes and then throw mud because I'm there.

I've loved you very much these last few days, perhaps because I didn't take up advances to go to bed with people. You now make me feel a fool. I miss you so I dare not look at pictures of you or read your earlier letters.

I'm not being morbid or hysterical when I say don't write any more. When I get back to London I'll get in touch with you straight away. Without feeling the obligation to write to me, you might get your thoughts clearer. And it would be easier for me than letters like these last two I've had.

I want you. Physically, I've one big overwhelming want and need and the only person who could/can fully release it, satisfy it, is you. And when that's done, then maybe I can begin to think.

I hope to leave here in one week. My silly crazy pompous shittooth.

Love,
J.

Go easy on your 'saint perversion' stuff.

Darling,

One other thing that has often been on my mind today. How can you say, don't go off with anyone, all my love etc. etc. Are you crackers? Or, some way are you trying to hurt me? Or are you for the X time going through all the pros and cons of us, are you still unsure of its worth? If you are any of these things, you're fucking crackers indeed and need a good kick up the pants. I'm not going, either by letter now or discussion later, to remind you of what we have been, could be. If you don't know all that now then you never will. And by now, at this stage it would be distressing and degrading for me to do it.

If it can get through the smokescreen of petit tragedy that

enfolds you, remember I love you, that I would give a lot to have you *here* to give you a practical demonstration of what *we* are.

Love,
John

PS See less of Kester. Please.

A letter John had written earlier is full of anxiety about the flat and money. It was a subject I always tried to ignore. My mother said that I was very much like her own mother: I went through life thinking a gold bar was going to hit me on the head. True enough, and it has several times. This attitude is alien to many people who consider it irresponsible, and it was something John longed to change in me.

28:vii:58

Darling,
Your letter came this morning. I think now I even begin to recognize your type, just as before I would have recognized your hand. No one I know has such a worn ribbon, such blunt letters and such a charming way of scattering, like pearls before swine, the address all over the envelope, as you. Sweetheart.

Jane Eyre has been revived across the Platz. It has worn very well really. Welles is an ideal Rochester and the atmospherics are good. I noticed in the credits that Huxley had worked on the scenario. I wish I could say some equally pleasant things about Welles's *Othello* which is on at the moment. For all its excellent photography, it is so pretentious, so artificially artistic. Pretty pictures don't excuse shoddy acting, a bad hacking and resetting (and rewriting) of dialogue and bad production. The wonderful 'Blood Blood ...' was badly fluffed. The only superb thing was the attempted murder of Cassio which was set in a steam bath. No, not clouds of steam everywhere but an exciting impression of a closed labyrinth and the dry gaunt look that wood and walls have, too long exposed to heat.

Sooky has been with me to all these things. I see a little too much of her, but except for her, Lucie and Bill who else is there now? If I go to a bar now it's the old queens I talk to, Erna,* for example, who used to come along in that green skirt but now wears black and very nice too, on my suggestion. Her hair isn't so yellow any more. I am a little taken aback by her compliance to my advice and there's a lot of high compliments. She likes it and it passes the time. There are some others, about equally undesirable but I enjoy talking and listening to them. The woman from the K. asked about you and sends *everyone's* warmest greetings. So there!

Reading: Iris Murdoch's *Under the Net* which is most enjoyable when it isn't being contrived. An example of that is the political meeting at the film studio against a background of Eastern sets (!!) I marked to remind you – 'she would turn her head very slightly with a faint intensification of expression which if produced almost indefinitely might have become a smile'. I've giggled a lot about that. *Dubliners* I've got through again, they are good and the second folio facsimile of *Hamlet*. A most exciting eye-opener. It's the only way to read Shakespeare, I feel now. So have I been bad? I'll get some more out tomorrow. I get through a lot when I sunbathe. Have I been good?

Oh darling, rescue me before I explode or go off the deep end. God, the first time I have you again, you're going to end up with some bones broken. The dots are for you only.

I love you, fucking going mad for you.

J.

The dots John refers to were an outline of his cock, like a paper pattern, as if one was going to make a copy. In my answer I refer to narcissism, not brought about by this pattern, I hasten to say. It is worth observing that young lovers of the same sex often do look like twins, and I think that element is significant. Perhaps it isn't narcissism, so much as a feeling of security being achieved in not straying far from home. It is, I believe, an early stage in sexual development, a bit like the close inspection we all give to our genitals in childhood and puberty. To be able to love oneself is central to loving others. To love and respect oneself and be

*One of the middle-aged men in drag.

on constant, affectionate terms with oneself, is not, as so many superficial religious tracts would have it, selfishness or egocentricity, but the first significant step to loving others. The most destructive people I have been with in my life have all loathed and distrusted themselves and never honestly admitted it. Their self-loathing has then been expressed on the rest of us.

Croydon
2:viii:58

My dear darling, I'm sorry that I've written you such discouraging cold letters lately.

I saw yesterday some old photographs of you and one, it was very strange, which I thought was myself. This of course brought out all my narcissism and I felt horribly lonely away from you.

Your Sun Sex and Dottings letter came yesterday. In a curious way I want you to have someone to sleep with while I'm away. I wouldn't be jealous. I should be interested in your reactions. But perhaps you have and haven't told me.

Of course what is so maddening about you. Is the way you give orders, even a thousand miles away. Stop it. I've no intention of obeying those stern commands and the fact that you'll be angry has no effect at all. I can see you grinding your teeth now.

I have finished the first version of 'The Return'. I'm not sure how good or how bad it is, which is a bad sign in itself. But I can't get back to the novel. One or two ideas for short stories though which I want to work on. Haven't heard a thing from the *Paris Review* so I've written to Jim complaining that I haven't even had a letter of acknowledgement.

Come back very soon. I'm off to Brighton today for the August weekend.

Darling I love you.

Colin

'The Return' was the subject given by the *Observer* for a short story competition and John's next letter is full of fury, complaining of some gossip I had gathered at a party. 'That old twittery Ron, I've always wanted to put a cracker up his well exercised bum.' I had left my diary behind in Vienna, and he was supposed to send it on. He says in this letter that he feared a bulky envelope may have been opened by Customs and its contents thought obscene. This again was not fantasy; our letters if read by Customs or police could have meant arrest and imprisonment. We could not forget our lawlessness or entirely dismiss the potential danger it involved. He says finally in an extended postscript:

Vienna
30:vii:58

The job in September worries me. I know you don't look forward to it. I can easily imagine you being sick about it. The too dreadful thing, not only for us but for you yourself, is that I can too easily imagine you *not* getting one and living off friends and what tomorrow might bring. Why the hell September? Why not get some odd job for two weeks now? Sweetie, you've been a drifter too long now. It's time *you* looked after yourself. Work is absolutely necessary if we live together or *not*! And you fucking well know it. If you're not careful you'll make me feel you regret my return in that it may mean the end of charity at home and free dinners with a pound in your pocket after.

Of course I didn't want to be bullied into doing a job, as he put it. I was intent on getting a novel finished and published and my drawings and paintings seen and sold. It all happened the following year, but it might well have taken longer if I had taken on a job as a ward orderly in the local hospital (I worked for a year at this when I was nineteen) or had rejoined the *Croydon Advertiser* as their art critic, which I had also done a couple of years before. I fear, though, it may have been literary snobbery which made me inactive at pursuing local journalism. I was very conscious that I was published from the age of twenty-one in the foremost literary magazines. The trouble was, my stories were very hit and miss affairs. I worked hard and produced an enormous amount of rubbish and did not have the self-critical faculty to see it. One story out of five would work, have an authentic tone of voice, and I could not tell how it was done.

So John's bossiness and his insistence on a job were deeply resented. But our letters now became side-tracked and immersed in the issue of Robin Maugham's* visit to Vienna and the disposal of the flat. Robin sent a cable at my dictation and it was somehow misunderstood. A letter of mine tries to clarify it.

6:viii:58

About the cable which I suppose is pretty useless now. But I met Robin Maugham on Saturday again with rather a nice companion (Robin as you've gathered has inherited his father's title in our absence) and they were going to Vienna and I told them a few places and said that they must get in touch with you, if you were still there. I thought there would be masses of free food and drink for you. Then Robin asked me if you could help them find somewhere for them and so he sent the cable at my dictation. Could they rent our flat and then sell it when they go? Not possible perhaps.

Now I've re-read one of your letters, the last one. Silly darling, of course I can say all my love and then a week later say I haven't missed you. You write the most fucking damned horrible nasty insults to me and then warble about love in the same letter. There's nothing to choose between us.

Bitching is very exhausting, let's stop it. Come back very soon but let me know when. I guess I shouldn't have come away, I just don't know any more anything.

Colin

PS Next morning: this letter seems to be about the same mixture of yours to me. One side, hatred and resentment, irritation and unhappiness balanced, or not (who knows?) by love/lust, desire, tenderness. O Lord, isn't it understandable that we're so wretched and bewildered? But I'd rather love and resent you here than there. But please don't go on trying to tell me what to do. If I appear to be drifting to you, all well and good, you make matters worse, by storming about it. You said way back last summer: 'Darling, I promise never to try to change you.' There's never been one moment that we've shared together when you haven't tried.

* Novelist and nephew of Somerset Maugham.

But the Robin Maugham episode was threatening to turn into a saga. John wrote a rude postcard to Robin which Robin, puzzled, read to me. I replied to it with irony.

Croydon
8:viii:58

Thank you for your kind help and co-operation with Robin Maugham. He's just read your postcard over the telephone to me.

It might or might not have occurred to you that he would buy the flat for fifty quid as long as we could assure him that he would sell it to a rich American student in September. Which would solve everyone's problem. But you seemed much too busy in feeling that you had been imposed upon for that thought to enter your mind. They'll be there middle of next week, so if nothing is settled you might meditate upon that solution. He's got masses of money. Make use of it – but not obviously. And please don't show yourself as being quite as neurotic and unhelpful as you did in the postcard.

I'm in the middle of another long/short story, I've written 5,000 words in the last two days. Lehmann thinks and so do I that I could make a book of the two which would solve what to do with the other one. Let me know exactly when you're coming back and if you'll allow me to, I'll meet you.

It is strange, I don't feel that I can write or say anything to you any more. Your anger and hatred of me because I've left you for six weeks is something I can only resent, so both together has created this kind of barrier. It seems to me awfully necessary that you come back as soon as possible so that we can get it straight.

Colin

John wrote back about changing people. I quote this paragraph because the subject is basic in all relationships.

11:viii:58

Darling,

Of course you're right. I did really mean it when I said that I never wanted to change you and of course it's true that there's never been a spare moment when I haven't tried my damnedest. I promise very hard to try to stop. God, think how terrible it might be if you did change. Though how I don't know. Though I'm conscious of efforts to change you, how, and in what direction, I'm not at all sure. Haven't the foggiest.

Loving changes all of us; the perfect relationships are ones where the change is so unconscious the couple are not aware of it. But there is another form of loving, another falling in love, where the state of becoming in love is partly the wish to change the beloved. Or to put it in a truer way, 'A' senses that if only 'B' could do this or that, 'B' would be so much happier. I call this the missionary position which 'A' has taken. 'A' wants to convert 'B' to these revelations which will change the way 'B' acts and lives. Such love entanglements are always disastrous. 'B' feels not only resentment but is aware that 'A' does not love the true nature of 'B', but only the potential of what 'B' can be. This is not love at all – the love is all happening inside 'A's head.

I am sure John wanted to change me in a radical way, I don't believe he ever realized how much, nor how tyrannical or moral he seemed at times.

His next letter was in answer to my cold, ironic one.

Monday

Darling I luvs luvs luvs you. And then more and more and more. Your nasty note arrived this morning and instead of making me at all angry only makes me luvs you even more. Sweet. The first part of this letter I wrote Friday. I saw Echels and boy who's taking the flat. It looks as if we've got £35 out of the deal.

This is going to keep me here a week. Then to München for two days and then, if you can bear repentant sinners – bitchiness being the greatest sin – I'm grappling you in a half nelson – a most erotic one – as soon as I arrive in London. Darling, I'm sorry I bitched and sent such a nasty card.

Anyway, Lord M. phoned me yesterday from Salzburg. I was very sweet; he arrives this afternoon and I'm already corralling all the young things to make his visit happy. He and 'the young companion' arrive in S. T. Platz and stay over tonight.

left   John in lederhosen in Austria, probably the hills above Schwarz, taken in the early 1950s

below   John around 1957, in his schoolmaster suit and tie, looking distinctly awkward

above Colin by John: August 1957.
John adored taking photographs. He
posed this with some care: the cotton
polo neck had to be pinned at the
back for a close fit (the gathered
material shows as a bump)

top right Another photograph in the
same session in the Hove flat, 1957.
John can just be seen reflected in the
mirror

right John took great trouble getting
the background right for this sequence
of photographs. They were all of me
swathed in a black cloak that came
from a vicar in Oxford. They were
taken in Schwarz when we first
arrived in Austria, October 1957

My portrait of Father (1959) after a year of soaking up Kokoschka in Vienna. He had sat for me wearing his best suit, which he wore for the Masonic meetings. I had disregarded it and painted him in his fishing clothes. This was a source of some rancour

Me on Brighton beach, August 1957

John that August

above Billy and me on the gondola tour in the summer of 1957. I see that I have my spoilt-brat face on

left Me, taken by Billy at the pool at the Villa Bontoc, Cap Ferrat, June 1957. Billy took a sequence of nude photos by the poolside and then with some difficulty had to learn to develop the negatives, turning the guest loo at the vicarage into a dark room

Mother had this taken in 1916 to send to her brother at the front. He was killed early the next year. Father always used to say of this picture, 'That's how she looked when I first met her'

Father in 1918 in hospital blue

Father in the early 1950s, rowing at Christchurch, where he had a houseboat

Father in Masonic regalia, also taken in the 1950s

My parents with the mayor and mayoress of Croydon on Ladies' Night, when Father was Worshipful Master of his Lodge in the early 1950s

below Considering the rows going on at home over Maisie, this is an uncharacteristic photo, also taken to celebrate Ladies' Night

above Father at the Ladies' Night revue (second from right) in the Bathing Belle sketch

Mother and Father in the garden at Chepstow Road, summer 1957

left Maisie, Father's mistress, in the 1950s

right Father and Maisie at an office party – 1955

A horribly posed studio portrait of me, commissioned and paid for by a devoted and leading churchman, for his study. The same series of pictures ended up in many a vicarage study over the next few years

John, 1959. This photo was taken in Australia immediately he returned, hoping for work as an actor

left John, directing a dress rehearsal in the early 1970s

right John in Sydney directing my play, *Spitting Image*, in 1982

Michael Davidson with Pippo in 1959 in Sicily

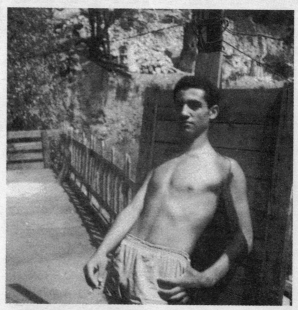

Pippo posing on Michael's terrace in Messina, 1959

John and me in John's garden, Sydney, 1986. Oddly enough, this is
the only picture taken of us together

I've already cancelled a fabulous dinner in order to be here. So don't think the spleen is still running.

Sweet, I feel that suddenly I'm sane. All last week I was a nervous neurotic wreck. Really. Bad dreams, little sleep. Once I went to the K. Someone asked me to dance but I was shaking and trembling so much I made a fool of myself by saying I couldn't finish the dance. I really felt I was going batty. Then Friday evening I had a long talk to Lucie, about me, I went and had a meal out, at the Lusinger and stole the menu to bring back to you and suddenly all my worries were away. The flat was as good as gone. Echels had been *too* sweet for words. And Lucie! By God but she's a woman in a million. I find myself taking her huge bunches of flowers – Vienna is mad with flowers now – and finally she came out to a film with me – *It happened in broad daylight*, a German film, scenario by Dürrenmatt who wrote *The Visit*.

I went to the Kunsthistorisches two days ago. My God, the new stuff. Eight Rembrandts, a lot of Cranach and the fabulous Vermeer, *The Artist in his Studio*. I wanted you so much there. But I am all the time. Darling, shove any bastards out of your bed and make way for me, give me a little room. Don't hate me too much. If I could kiss you now I'd die.

Love,
John

I described the K. in my novel *Asylum*:

'If they left the flat at all, it was late at night, and then they would go to a café which lay at the bottom of a steep flight of steps down an unlit alley that ran from the inner ring near the market. In the room behind the bar there was a juke box, the walls were lined with old tram seats, it had sawdust on the floor and there was one part of the ceiling where the rain came through. It was full of male tarts, some of them wore drag, dancing together. Carl, even under the assumed name, was known and recognized. There were boys, little more than children, refugees from Hungary and Rumania, who lay sleeping upon the seats, who would wake up for gifts of chocolate and sweets, their grubby pointed faces full of grief and longing. There was a fat German industrialist in a tattered crinoline and ringlets. There were deserters from the army and bankrupt aristocrats. There was an American composer who sang his own songs, dressed as a cavalry officer of the time of Franz Joseph. Here, Carl and Angelo danced together.'

Though I was relieved that John was returning, my next letter included in the second paragraph a glimpse of a rather sordid plan that I seem to have fallen in with for the sake of a free fare back to Vienna. Later the flat is mentioned as being possibly used for Robin's pick-ups. The affluent homosexual with strong 'closet' tendencies would often not dare to take a street boy back to the hotel. Some hotels spotting a lad being hurried through the foyer would stop you and refuse to allow it. This happened to me in Athens, four years later. 'Nonsense,' I said, 'this boy is my cousin.' My impudence won the day. Not long ago in Madrid the hotel rang the room because I had a girl-friend there and demanded she leave. It is the rules, they said. Neither argument nor reason prevailed so I left as well.

14:viii:58

Well thank the fucking Lord. That's what I say. Thank the fucking Lord. At last a letter which is loving without a back-kick to it. My dear darling passionate wicked creature, I've read your letter which arrived an hour ago four times and still can't decide whether you mean that you are waiting until 24 August and then spending two days in Munich or whether you are leaving very soon now and will be back middle of next week. I suppose you didn't know when you wrote it, perhaps you do now.

I was made so fucking miserable last night when I rang J. L. at 11.00 and found out that he'd spoken to you. We had tried hard to get through from 3.00 in the afternoon and I hung about waiting and hoping till 7.00. Longing to talk to you. I was so horribly envious that J. had. His idea wasn't a bad one in case you got yourself worked up into a tizz over it, muttering things like, 'well the fuckers, the fucking cheek of it,' etc. He didn't want to have a holiday alone and so suggested that I might come with him (return fare paid of course), he was staying at a hotel and I with you but he wanted to be able to use the flat for boys, stay a few days in Vienna and then all three of us go off to Venice. I thought it sounded fun. But the news that you'll be back very soon is a thousand times better.

I've written about 9,000 on the new story.

I wonder what you thought of the Lord? He is extremely nervous, not much brains but I find him charming and socially amusing. If you are still seeing him, it might be very worthwhile saying things like, 'Ah dear (big sighs) of course it's a terrible problem for Colin and I to find anywhere to live in Brighton when I get back,' etc. He's got two delicious houses, it might be possible to angle for and land one, just think of those packed cellars.

THERE'S NO BASTARDS IN MY BED.

All my love and more if that was possible.

Colin

The new story was 'Nymph and Shepherd', published the following year in the *London Magazine*. It again used Allan and his fantasy life but also his friend, the patient and ever generous Sugar Daddy.

I did not know Robin well at this time. If I had done, I would never have been so naïve as to think he would take pity on us. It is clear from John's next letter that they disliked each other; certainly John was infuriated by Robin.

16:viii:58

The Lord is a silly fucking bore. I got them part of a villa, I've taken them around, will most likely land them a boy servant, have procured for them and got fuck all in return except a lot of 'bless you dear boy' and a load of frankfurters any time we're together near meal times. The only time they're hungry is when I'm not there it seems. Last night I went out to Grinzing where the villa is. We went around but I had to *demand* a meal. And when I finally ordered, then they both found they were hungry. Although it was the second time I'd trammed it out there – you know it takes an hour – there was no offer of a lift into town or a taxi fare. And when I suggested that Keith drop me the Lord assumed his 'Governess of Tooting Bec Reform School for Girls' look and let Good Night slide out from between tight arsehole lips. By God they're mean. They stayed here their first night though why they didn't go to a hotel I don't know. They're rolling in it. I doubt if I show them what I think but I don't want to spend any more of the little time I have left in Vienna with them. I hate going out with mean rich people. And they have shocking manners, I'm embarrassed by the way the waiters treat us.

Recently I read *The Desire and Pursuit of the Whole*. By God it's fascinating and very beautiful and boring and really very nasty all at the one time. The affair with Zildo strikes me as most repellent. The style is so good and so bad too at the one time. I was particularly horrified when I found myself identifying myself with him and his funny twisty reasoning. I do it too. And delude myself as much nearly.

Now I'm into *Wuthering Heights*. God, what a book. In between I read *The Servant*, the banned book by Lord M. What a silly innocuous slick bore. 'The style is similar to de Maupassant,' said Keith, not once but twice when I didn't reply to it the first time. I still didn't have the guts to say yes. So I kept talking about the weather.

There's a lot to tell you. We'll giggle a lot. I luvs you a lot and I'll go mad when I see you again.

Love,
John

John's next letter is full of a court case involving Rudi, a Hungarian lad we had given a bed to. He had been caught stealing, and John was to give evidence in his favour. In the end he was warned to keep out of it altogether. He planned to return within the week, but I was still writing to him on the 23rd.

23:viii:58

My darling, your letter came this morning which was rather a surprise for I thought you were in Munich now and expected any moment to receive a p.c. telling me on what train you'd be arriving Monday or Tuesday ... so I don't know what to expect, next week's arrangements are all left rather higher than in mid air, hoping to get some news from you which is definite. I didn't answer your last letter because I thought you had already gone.

Do you remember my shocked surprise in Vienna when we came across a poster which announced that Gabriel Marcel was

The Desire and Pursuit of the Impossible: E. M. Forster expressed
interest in looking through my portfolio of drawings. He paused at this
drawing and more to fill the silence than anything else, I said: 'I feel like
that a lot of the time.' He glanced at me and asked: 'And is your net
also so small?'

lecturing and you didn't know who he was? But you probably
know he's been over here for the first performance in England of
his play, *Ariadne*. Well, I've been drawing him. Nice old chap,
he's sixty-eight, and a little dotty I think. One would *never* think
that he was probably the most eminent Catholic philosopher in
France. I like drawing old French philosophers who play Chopin
to me rather as I play Liszt.

I've been keeping some nice things to see when you come back.
I'm longing to see the Clouzot, Picasso film. Did I also tell you
that I had lunch next to Simone Signoret in Brighton, and the
Laughtons, who looked astonishingly ugly. Like Beauty and the
two Beasts at the Feast.

Don't forget *Nightwood* – or our Dictionary, which I've missed very much. I'm not asking you what you're going to bring back, for you might not have room for anything, and you'll feel I've got a cheek but you might as well know that you can throw, if you want to, the green glasses at Lord M's head, and just bring yourself back, for I can't hug a green glass and though I did once fuck one with a gammon inside of course, you're much cosier.

Directly I get a date I'll arrange some luncheon and dinner parties and we'll send London sky high.

Not a whimper have I heard from the *Paris Review*.

Of course you silly pusspuss I don't hold anything against you. It's much more likely to be the other way round. Try not to resent the fact that I left and that we've been parted for six weeks.

In the meantime, all my love, and all the other trite things like, can't wait to have you! which hide under their clichés a large throbbing cock which will travel all over your body saying the nicest possible things.

But I write again on the 28th.

Croydon
28:viii:58

I suppose I'm hardened now but I did kinda expect you to be here today.

I'm almost fully concerned in this new story. Which started out as an idea in Vienna, one of those I get on the loo, which I thought might be rather tense and exciting and macabre and would run for about 3,000 words, when I started on it I saw that to make it convincing I had to lengthen it a good deal, to about 10,000 and then I thought no it's going to be much more interesting when I make it 20,000, now it's changed again, I've gone right back to the roots of the story, and I think the first two chapters are deliciously funny, I chuckle like mad over some things. So I think the tone of the thing will be this most of the way through with a vein of the macabre running underneath which may or may not triumph. Perhaps macabre is the wrong word and J. L.'s 'lyrical revoltingness' fits better. I'm also rewriting that story of last year about the two tense people in the room and I'm untensing it.

122

Also, today and tomorrow, I have to rewrite and type out 'My Return', which I fear is not very good, but I shall send it in hoping for a small prize or nothing at all.

I think it's best if I send this note this morning. And then write again tomorrow. Expensive of course, but you must feel starved of news out there.

All my love my darling.

Colin

PS I'm reading the funniest book I've ever read. Anarchic and delightful. *The Good Soldier Schweik*: gives one a vile picture of the military soul in the old Austrian Empire.

I loved *Schweik* and still do. Here at last was a writer who put down with huge gusto and humour all that had horrified and mortified my soul when I was in the midst of National Service. But *Schweik*, I have learnt, has little power to affect people who have not experienced the military machine at its most pedestrian and brutal.

The story that excited me was the germ for my first novel, *An Absurd Affair*. John had joined a camera club in Vienna, in order to borrow their enlarger and printer. We had had this machine in the flat for a few days, until it was collected by a newly-wed American couple. By mistake we had left a negative of a naked man in the machine, a rather artistic back shot John had taken, full of the play of light and shadow. Nothing in the least offensive. But in my story the negative was sexually powerful and enigmatic and the novel became an explanation of the effect this had on the sheltered life of the young wife.

'The Return' (the *Observer* short story competition) was won by that sensitive writer of scrupulous probity and syntax, Diana Athill.

John's last note before returning contained a letter now missing which he describes as unfair and uprighteous. He also wrote:

Dear Darling,

Darling that you've been faithful is very wonderful. It flatters me like your cock, more than words can. But if it's making you miserable, as in the letter, then please go off and find someone pretty. But don't f . . .

I'm going slightly crazy wanting you so much.

J.

All this concern about faithfulness was disguised by mutual lies, common enough, I suppose, with young lovers. But I do not believe this to be a recipe for success or happiness. John had had a mild affair that August in Vienna with an Austrian lad, Woolf. He confessed this some weeks later and showed me a photograph of Woolf posing at the window of what was once our flat. I did not mind in the least or made out I did not, but by the following year Woolf had become a symbol of 'new love' and therefore threatening. Whether John would have cared about my wild weekend with Honey, I do not know; I doubt it. We were back together by then and little else in that euphoria seemed to matter.

In that time long before AIDS, the odd one-night stand or brief fling seemed natural when lovers were parted for any length of time. Sexual experience is necessary in the young, the wider the variety the better. It is informative as few other experiences are, as long as we listen in a sensitive manner to our partners' responses. Nearly all young people are insecure, and loving and being loved generates happiness, far above genital satisfaction, because it gives the illusion of something absolute within that temporal movement which we all find so confusing.

The psychology of sexual satisfaction fascinates me, for when it is achieved between partners, few experiences in our lives can ever be so profoundly fulfilling. Now, I am not sure how John and I ever managed to achieve it, for it occurred without us knowing; with no former acquaintance of how to cultivate this uncommon miracle, we were negligent with its power and mystery.

How casual we were with ourselves, the next few months showed. Issues beyond what we had achieved claimed my attention more than John's, but we were still in a low phase which promised little for our future together.

6

Living in London Apart

I had found a room in Parsons Green where we stayed for a few days. It had a bathroom and loo across the corridor, which was hugely inconvenient for the ardour of young lovers. We were glad to leave but though we talked of taking a place together we had no income. John, impatient with my lack of decision, got a temporary teaching job and found a tiny room below a gay club in Thistle Grove. There was a single bed crammed into an alcove, a small hall, loo and bathroom, and a gas ring for making coffee. Here I often stayed with him, but the fact that I worked from home and took messages there irked him.

So that people would see, and perhaps buy my work, we hung this tiny space with a dozen of my oil paintings. It was the fashion then to have floral wallpaper of bright colour and complexity; my tortured oils clamoured loudly against this background and were to be a source of dissent and farce. Life was not easy and our relationship was stormy. We quarrelled too often. The first undated note from me that autumn is the bleakest I wrote to John.

Darling,

I'm going down to Brighton until Sunday. Please come for the weekend if you want to. Allan has two rooms now so we needn't even sleep together if it makes you unhappy.

I leave it all to you. Expecting you when and if I see you.

All my love,
C.

I wanted to keep John at arm's length. This, I believe, was mutual, yet we both saw how destructive this behaviour was.

Colin, silly,

There's very little I can say after this afternoon. But I must shake us both and we must tell each other to stop acting like silly schoolgirls.

The most I've always – and you know *still* – wanted from us is that we stay together not only to Australia but back and to Europe and see a lot and do a lot together for a long time.

The least is that we remain affectionate and frank – yes you can smile! – with each other and that because of the time we've actually spent together – through that – that we reach a more sympathetic understanding of each other.

If things go as they have these last ten days we'll be hating each other's guts this side of Xmas. And it would stay like that a long time. It would be a complete negation of everything we achieved.

Swallow your pride – and help *me* to – and come down to Brighton. If you've got some cash even better and I hope you've some good connection with a gallery today.

Ring me after you get this. Please. Before 10.30 or I may not be in. And don't hang up; and want to be with me in bed as much as I want to be in bed with you and nothing will stand in your way.

I hope the evening was pleasant. How many times must I tell you I love you before it sticks in that silly head of yours.

John

That autumn we were invited to a party of Robin Maugham's. John overcame his dislike of the Lord for this occasion, for parties were still a source of decent food and free booze. We met there a writer, Michael Davidson, then a foreign reporter for the *Observer*; Michael was to become one of the dearest and greatest friends of my life. He was rather taken by John, who was being highly entertaining, but Michael thought him aged about sixteen, much nearer to the age group Michael himself loved. I registered him as an astonishing gargoyle, made more bizarre by the fact that he was so often in spasms of laughter. It was at our next chance meeting that our friendship began, and it flourished until the day he died.

It was that autumn too when we went to the Paris Pullman to see Visconti's *Senso*, in a cut version titled horrendously *The Wanton Countess*. I still consider it Visconti's best work. This story of intense passion and revenge, from a story by Tennessee Williams, was set in Venice at the time of the Risorgimento, with that city under the domination of Austria. The film had amazing photography by G. R. Aldo. We left the cinema so moved we could not speak. The film became central to part of us, the romantic, manic and doomed part, perhaps. Visconti used the slow movement from Bruckner's Seventh Symphony and so integrated is the music with the film for me that a few bars will summon up the intense evocation of nineteenth-century Venice under military occupation.

In the middle of November I visited King's College, Cambridge, to draw E. M. Forster. His eightieth birthday was on New Year's Day and the *London Magazine* wanted the portrait drawings for their January issue.

A Passage to India and *Howards End* were key novels for me, of great power, beauty and persuasion. They, like works by other writers who deepened my understanding of the world, were introduced to me when I was fourteen by Jill, the girl I was later to marry. Forster's novels in particular helped me to understand England, throwing my own individuality into sharper outline. Though English myself, I confess that I have always found the English puzzling. I am deeply out of sympathy with the nuances of England's class system and more particularly its suppression of truth leading to blatant lies in order to keep up appearances. Such a complex national character cannot be analysed briefly, but Forster helped me to understand what I hated most about the English, and enabled me to live with it up to a certain point.

My first impression was of Forster's smallness and his liveliness; he made little dancing sallies about the room. This leaping and lurching for one his age seemed remarkable, but it was also his mobility of expression that delighted me: his face was full of inquiry and mischief, and he listened attentively. At first he insisted that I must draw him when reading. He had a book to review, the memoirs of Ruth Draper, but it was impossible to draw a head

Caius College – the Gate of Honour, Cambridge

buried in a book and I sat uncomfortably on the floor. He then, obligingly, wrote the review at his desk and still on the floor I managed to do several drawings. They took most of the morning. We then had lunch in College together. His curiosity was endless. I revealed to him most of what was happening between John and me – perhaps I thought I might receive some Forsterian wisdom.

E. M. Forster – 1959

I knew of the existence of *Maurice*, his homosexual novel, but did not inquire. I felt strongly on that first meeting that I was in the presence of a great novelist and, alas, such feelings restrict conversation. When I left I did not expect to see him again. I was wrong – I had forgotten the astonishing capacity for friendship Forster always possessed.

Without Forsterian wisdom John and I were stuck in a morass we could not understand. In the following letter we exchanged roles. I wrote him a letter which was full of the Tasker tone, the bewildered moralist trying to keep young lovers together. No wonder John had found a Sugar Daddy, after suffering mine. However, I was piqued.

*

It seems more or less inevitable that things get emotional when we see each other, not that I'm feeling unemotional now, but at least more able to write why I feel hurt over your reactions to everything since yesterday morning.

It's partly what you used to say that it is so difficult to see someone else doing and giving you things which I should like to be able to give. Money would solve a great deal of our troubles, but as there is no possibility of any it's not much good thinking about it. I find it difficult to appreciate that there is any choice to make at all about tomorrow night. If you really think that you prefer going out to the theatre and having dinner to us being together, it does seem a little ironical that I ever came back to Vienna at all. But as you've admitted that most of the spleen last December was not caused by such high motives as you made out but from honest envy, you go ahead and enjoy yourself now, but just make quite sure whether you're sacrificing anything for it or not. Is there anything left of us worth saving? I think I told you on the last night on Monday that this week had been the happiest I'd spent with you, that was true in a way, getting to know the new John, the reasonable and less tense and neurotic one, was exciting and rather wonderful, it couldn't have been for you at all because I suppose I haven't changed, but it did seem to me that there was a great deal of happiness for us both *still*. But in order for that to happen it seems that still the Sugar Dads have to be buried. I purposely did not resurrect them in July when I came back, I purposely didn't accept the Italian offer, I made it quite clear to everyone that I loved you and that when you came back we would live together until you had to go or we went to Australia. But while you were in Vienna not quite content with having a love affair on the side you also have to resurrect your Sugar Dad and make quite sure he is willing to be there with hospitality and gin and theatre tickets and whisky at bedtime waiting and willing to please you. Is that quite fair to me?

It does seem that this has all happened before. You do seem to treat your former lovers with an alarming casualness.

C.

This is a silly letter scoring unnecessary points. How shameful to be reduced to that. But we could not make up our minds about where as a couple we were going, or indeed if we were going anywhere together at all.

An important aspect of young love seems always to be the drama, scenes, sulks and flouncing off into the night, carrying one's pride head high. It all seems dreadfully silly to me now, for I detect a terrible indulgence in it all, which is such a waste of time and creativity. As if there are not enough real dramas in the world to distress us, without manufacturing them. But I am forgetting that the scenes and the quarrels were all about being in love, about being undecided about going to Australia, and this problem was never discussed in a thorough manner. If it was my roots which made me stay in that Victorian mansion with my parents in Chepstow Road, it was John's roots which called him back to Newcastle, New South Wales, which he had left at sixteen.

We were stuck in limbo because we had not grasped one aspect of homosexual love. In one sense it is the most obvious, and yet it sounds psychologically crude: neither of us had a loving father. When we were young, the adult male in the household was cold, withdrawn and totally unaffectionate. A physical caress from father to baby son, even being picked up or hugged, was unknown. (My own father, in old age, hated being kissed on the cheek by me; he thought it pansy behaviour.) I am sure there are many male children who have unloving fathers and yet become heterosexual lovers. I do not wish to suggest otherwise. All I wish to suggest is that with John and myself this gulf in infant loving was a kind of dark despair we carried around within us, to be forgotten only by being immersed in each other's arms and love. But our limbo now was caused by the fact that we had both turned back to our fathers. I was living in my father's house trying to understand my parents' marriage, my father's life. John was returning to the other side of the world to see his father who, he claimed, was ill and dying. 'I must see him before he dies,' was a cry from him, said often and not given much credence by me.

On 10 December my sister, Paddy, was getting remarried, and John Lehmann was giving a pre-Christmas party. During the previous week my John and I quarrelled badly, and on the following evening I attempted to write a letter which, however, I did not send at once. Exactly a week later John telephoned home, his excuse being that there was a television programme on Duse. I then finished the letter.

Croydon
2:xii:58

I get into a panic when I feel I can't see you because you obviously don't want to see me – I long for us somehow to get over what happened and I'm frightened you won't. I'm frightened that I really did destroy something in that silly tantrum of bewildered frustrated emotion. What happened to the thing we pride ourselves on most – our sense of humour? How could we possibly let such a melodramatic scene occur? And one which was so meaningless?

You have made me come to the edge of fury and irritation many times. At least admit this, that you have a unique capacity for even making the saints furious (Kester?). And there have been issues when I have seen red and somehow managed to control everything. That it should all spill over upon some issueless occasion seems ludicrous. Perhaps it is then that one is most off one's guard. Oh God I was dead tired too, I had very little resistance. These are a few excuses where there should be no excuse at all.

I have never really doubted that I love you, I've tried to when it seemed inconvenient, I think you're doing that now too. What I do question is what we mean to each other now and how far we are prepared to give up things for each other, we seem to be in limbo, an unemotional limbo, with no security around us and little passion inside us. It is the lack of passion since your return that has most worried me, for it was that before that instigated everything, this is why we've stopped moving I think. I suppose the wise men and the sages would say there was something else and it's true that I'm ridiculously happy when I'm with you and more contented and excited than when I'm with anyone else, it's true that your enthusiasm sparks off my own and vice versa, and that when J. L. says 'talk the story over with John', he's talking sound sense. It's true that I've been drifting about doing nothing these last few days feeling bloody, because I knew I couldn't reach you, not with words nor actions certainly not love-making. God how randy I felt that night. It's true that I don't even know whether I shall send this letter to you, whether I'd better disappear for good or just a few weeks. If only we weren't so proud we wouldn't get ourselves into such a mess. Do you know what I'm trying to say? That because we're in limbo we have been living a dog's life, but perhaps our dog's life is better than the life we can live separately. I know this is true for myself, but I'm not convinced about you. I wonder whether you want to use last night as an excuse? That is what it seemed like. That is why this dog is lying low (I was tempted to say doggo).

Monday, the 8th

Just after you'd telephoned.

Now of course I don't know what you want, after that miserable conversation, was Duse an excuse? I hope so. For I know what I want. To be with you. To hold you in my arms. To lie on that bed with you. Last night I didn't go to sleep for ages. I was thinking about Vienna, regretting I ever left it, thinking that there I wasn't nor ever could have been so bloody and miserable as I was last night. I thought, he'll sleep with someone out of revenge this weekend, and again I thought I can bear just plain sex happening but not if they sleep together all night and he has his arms round him curled up in that bed. I'm so afraid that is what has happened. Heaping coals upon my head.

And then an extraordinary thing started to happen, I felt that the part that was us, that was bound together somewhere outside us was being severed by you at that moment maybe even consciously. That it was like an operation and I felt the pain physically so that my whole body for two or three minutes hurt acutely, really hurt I mean, as if I had toothache all over, and with it the sensation all the time of you cutting me away. Eventually I must have fallen asleep and I had one of those horrid John/G. dreams where everybody is hurting everybody else. All this has left me rather bewildered today, feeling as if I'm not unlike a combination of Chucky* and Kester, having psychic experiences.

*A painter, an ex-girl-friend from Brighton, who had psychic experiences.

Did I physically really hurt you the other night? Could it be in some strange way that because I feel so fucking guilty about it, that it came back to me, I would feel reassured if I had had bruises this morning. But I didn't have!!

I'm not going to enjoy seeing you for the first time Wednesday, [Lehmann's party] it will make, on my part, lunch-time much too tense [my sister's wedding]. But I suppose there's nothing I can do about that.

Darling I luv yur, come back to me soon if you can.

Colin

It never occurred to me that John's facility for unreasonable behaviour was intensified by what the cancer had taken from him, for somewhere within him he must have known that his inherent masculinity had been wrested from him. This lack of imagination on my part seems grotesque. Today I would hope that some form of psychological counselling might be given to victims of testicular tumours, but then it was a forbidden subject unless people joked about it.

How restrained we were about my mother! It strikes me as particularly odd in the following letter that John had to make excuses in order to talk to me on the telephone. My mother knew of our relationship, for I had 'come out' with my parents when I was nineteen and had insisted on bringing my first lover, the Polish lad, Jan, back to the home, requesting the same warmth from my parents that they gave to their sons-in-law. My impudence went further as I showered endearments upon Jan at the supper table in front of my father. He ignored it, or pretended to, but somewhere in my soul I must have exulted at the price of my revenge upon him. But here we are in John's first paragraph protecting my mother's sensibilities.

9:xii:58

Darling,

I was so miserable last night after I'd phoned you. Later I phoned again but mama answered the phone and as I couldn't think of a reason – there was no second television programme –

I put the receiver down. All I could have said to you was sorry for seeming such a bugger on the phone.

But I think you can understand how I felt last night. We make so much show still of being together when really we are drifting apart – drifting seems the correct way to describe it. And secondly, when we're sober I think we're a *succès fou* at a party but after a number of drinks we tend to bicker and become too emotional. Look at Ken's party. And tomorrow, both the wedding and the party, is going to be an emotional day for you particularly and don't pretend it isn't. If we don't have a row in the evening I'll be very surprised.

Darling, I luvs you, worse luck.

J.

It interests me faintly now to note that I was asked to do the food for the wedding reception. I don't think I was paid, so they got what talents I had on the cheap. But I did make something out of that wedding as I obtained several boxes of champagne via Edouard and the French Embassy which I thought I could purchase at the wholesale price. Edouard refused to charge me anything, but I charged my new brother-in-law. I suppose I made something like thirty quid and it helped me to live through the next week.

On the same evening John Lehmann gave his party at his house in Egerton Crescent. The Eliots and Dame Edith Sitwell were to be there. John had been asked as my mate. I suppose he feared that I would arrive drunk and pick a scene with him. This was extremely unlikely, as I had been an ardent fan of T. S. Eliot from first reading 'Prufrock'. A school pal and I would recite through the Croydon suburbs, 'I am not Prince Hamlet, nor was meant to be . . .' down to the end of the stanza. Huge wodges of *The Waste Land* were delivered with the same passion amongst the labyrinth of brick workmen's cottages quite likely to have been built by my great-grandfather, responsible for too much of another wasteland, Victorian working-class Croydon. In my late teens I had written blank verse plays of intolerable turgidity and impudently sent them to Eliot. Always a gentleman, he had written back kindly and with great tact, 'I believe your speeches may give the actors

John Ledmann

some difficulty.' I kept his letters folded in my wallet throughout my year of National Service, a kind of talisman of my own inherent authorship which the army machine could not destroy. So meeting Mr Eliot in person for the first time was for me on a par with a student at RADA meeting Dame Peggy Ashcroft. I was unlikely to spoil that meeting with any indulgence in booze or friction with John.

However, I have gathered over the years that a certain radical and volatile spirit within me can make my companions nervous when we have to conform to a social routine, but John was also a great admirer of Eliot; he did not want the party ruined either.

Dame Edith sat in black robes and Tudor head-dress, but behaved as if she were Turandot, or a queen from a distant planet, her heavily beringed right hand visible, the other hidden among the thick folds of the dress. She lifted her right hand slowly in greeting. I clasped it expecting it to weigh a ton. I was nervous of Dame Edith for I knew her penchant for picking up young writers and being the patron of their work. We moved on to the Eliots. The new Mrs Eliot wore a long black velvet dress and a

A Happy Christmas from John Lehmann 1958

single rope of pearls. Her face was very white and overpowdered, her lips a vivid scarlet – she looked absurdly young and seemed an inappropriate partner altogether for the poetic sage. They held hands all the time, sitting very close on a sofa as we all paid court. How strangely artificial this scene seems now.

Eliot himself was solemn and kind. When they wanted to leave, we got them a taxi and escorted them outside. I remember saying how much I loved his work, a sentiment he must have heard a million times. I did not say that a few years previously I had attended St. Stephens, Gloucester Road, several times with one of my clerical conquests, merely so that I could place a few pennies in the collection bag carried by T. S. Eliot in his capacity as a sidesman. So intent was I then on studying his face, which was composed in a kind of morose devotion, that I fumbled the opening of the bag. I wish I had talked to him of Anglo-Catholicism and how I had bedded several of the priests who were his personal friends. I collected the Christmas cards the Eliots sent to these priests for the sake of the signature, which some years later I cut out and pasted into copies of *Possum's Cats* as presents for my nephews and nieces.

The distaste Eliot had for the physical, sex in particular, that we now know of might have caused an interesting collision between us, though I doubt whether he would have believed me – he would probably have considered me a liar and unhinged. I have never understood his Christianity or his Anglo-Catholicism, and for me his earlier poems are greater by far. Christian belief appears to give writers a structure which explains guilt and allows redemption. As a humanist I regard guilt as a self-inflicted wound and a source of terrible misery to human kind, for the people who suffer from guilt seem to work out their redemption destructively through others. In fact, they never work it out, for without guilt they suffer real despair and hopelessness.

One of the great humanists, of course, was E. M. Forster, who had much influenced me. For his eightieth birthday at the beginning of the year I covered a page with drawings of him wearing a laurel wreath. His answer came some weeks later: 'I don't think I was ever intended to wear a laurel wreath, but am very glad to see myself in so many. – Siegfried Sassoon did a picture of me many years ago, being crowned by Edith Sitwell.'

John and I were hardly working out our destiny, certainly not through each other, at this black phase. His letter after Christmas admits in the first lines how we have not been able to discuss 'the biggest things'.

28:xii:58

Darling,

I'm sorry to have to write something and then, like a piece of subterfuge, put it in your pocket, not even with face enough to hand it to you. Then that's because always the biggest things that ever happen to us we dare not really talk about, content to attempt honesty in small things.

It does seem as if November and July are happening again.

With the same gut feeling, the same horror at what seems indifference and even selfishness on your part, and later on, on your side too maybe, the same regret. How can you still love me and still cause me so much unhappiness again and again while you once more expose yourself to whatever else it was you were 'starving' for: money, good contacts, cunts/cocks, mama, papa, etc. etc.? If what was between us now gets on your tits but you're holding out because it's only a matter of weeks to go, then don't, but for God's sake be honest now!

It has not made things any easier, except for my parents, to have secured the berth. It makes me day by day, more distraught and insecure. Now I reach out like some silly gawk for whatever may momentarily steady me. You can't blame me. It's something I've wanted you to do for me. And I doubt if you'll ever think of ways to begin to do it.

I love you. You ought to know how much.

I want you to stay with me here nights. But I dare not let you. Don't ask me to. I just feel dishonest when I do and it takes me the whole day to get over it. But try to understand.

Please,
John

This is a letter I would have given you last night but I foolishly let you come back. I can't believe you even begin to think outside yourself.

By God but I'm beginning to hate you. You simply *use* quite callously what is between us. You make me feel a bloody slut for feeling at all loving towards you. How can you be so completely insensitive?

There is little wonder then that we had the big argument on New Year's Eve that year. We had been asked to a New Year's Eve party given by Charles Osborne, an early expat Aussie like John and then the assistant editor of the *London Magazine*. Diane Cilento was going to bring her new boy-friend, the then unknown Sean Connery. Early that evening John had said something critical about my paintings in his room. I had taken offence and said I would remove them all from his sight. I began to take them off the walls before he stopped me. I said I was fed up and walked out of his small basement into Thistle Grove. John followed me, shouting. The front door slammed behind him. He had no key and the owner of the club, Laon, was at the opera at Covent Garden. What is more, John was barefoot and in singlet and trousers. He was now furious, blaming the predicament upon me. I saw that he had a point and was contrite. I said: 'Don't worry, I'll get back in.' 'How?' he asked. Every small window was barred with anti-burglar devices. 'I'll find a way,' I pleaded. John was adamant, there was nothing for it but for him to go to Covent Garden and to find Laon in the interval and borrow the front door key off him. No sooner had he said this than he disappeared, marching purposefully towards the bus stop. I was now determined to prove I could get into the club.

A little later I found myself on the roof of the Paris Pullman Cinema with the Swedish dialogue of Bergman's *Summer with Monica* emanating from between my feet. I climbed from there on to the roof of the gay club where there was a skylight which miraculously was unlocked. I crawled down beneath it and felt in the darkness for the loft door. I found a bolt and pulled it open, then slowly wrenched the flap upwards. Light from below streamed into the loft, but as I pulled there was a terrible sound of tearing wallpaper. Laon's hall ceiling which had been papered over in blue roses hung in tatters beneath me. I dropped through and lowered the loft door after me. The ceiling looked appalling, with ribbons of blue roses hanging down showing where the loft door had been hidden. I dismissed the destruction and ran down to the basement. There I collected all my paintings and left by the front door. I hailed a cab and landed at Charles's flat, telling him the whole story. He decided to hang the paintings in the room where we were having the party, and we both looked forward to seeing John's expression when he entered the room – foolish and callous creatures that we were. John, of course, was a far better performer than we had given him credit for. He walked into the party expressionless, and we ignored each other for the whole time.

Sean Connery caused a lot of envious glances and was charming. There was another young actor, who was also an ex-Etonian, to amuse Lehmann. When the midnight hour struck, John was at the other side of a crowded room. He pushed his way through to me and kissed me hard for a length of time. I heard the ex-Etonian say something like 'Steady on, it's two chaps,' and Lehmann answer, 'You should have got used to it at Eton.'

John and I were back together again. After last year, we said: How could we be so absurd? But for how long?

Somehow between the two New Year's Eves an act was concluded, a curtain came down. There was still so much to say, still so much left unfinished, not only all the blood, sweat and tears of every real relationship, but so much that he and I did not, and it appeared could not, understand. He was to sail at the beginning of February. One sad isolated little note from John dated 9 January sums up how bleak it was. I had borrowed Allan's room in Brighton and asked him to come down. He wrote saying Allan and L. (Allan's Sugar Daddy) had come to the club and Allan was furious at my inviting him. He adds:

How terrible it is how after straightforwardly and easily writing the simple notation of these facts that the will baulks at saying or admitting the many, many tender things that should appear whenever we have to write to each other.

Then later admits:

My bed is suddenly so big and lonely and my arms open – really as if they'd been cut off and the stubs, up high, are still sore – wanting to hold you – you, I'm afraid; I wish it were otherwise.

A terrible amputation had occurred. It seemed we were prepared for the end. That last year was the final act, after all, perhaps now an epilogue and then the last curtain. But no, though everything pointed towards this, the unexpected occurred.

7

The Voyage Out

Sometime in January Alan Pryce-Jones, the editor of *The Times Literary Supplement*, commissioned a series of drawings from me, to appear weekly and to be called Writers of Our Time. My drawing of E. M. Forster in the January 1959 issue of the *London Magazine* had been the spur to the idea. Stanley Morison, cryptically called the *éminence grise* behind *The Times*, was also enthusiastic and promised to publish a volume of the drawings.

Alan and I decided who the writers were. This, I realized afterwards, was an error of tact. We should have discussed the choice with the assistant editor, Arthur Crook. But no, Alan and I enjoyed selecting an eclectic mixture which mirrored some of my own literary passions. We started with C. P. Snow and Pamela Hansford-Johnson; we had Evelyn Waugh, Graham Greene, L. P. Hartley and T. S. Eliot, as well as less famous poets like Sydney Goodsir Smith and Burns Singer. Our first list was of twenty-four writers. There was, with this commission of a lifetime, no question of my being able to go to Australia for at least six months, or perhaps a year. I did not see John off, but I knew the time of sailing from Southampton, knew the route roughly and had a list of ports to write to, as well as instructions to send the *Observer* each week. Cultural starvation stared John in the face.

The 'unexpected' that I referred to in the previous chapter was in fact an abrupt change in the tone of our relationship. The minute John and I were physically apart, a terrifying desolation descended on both of us. I notice that I wrote at once on the same day, yet in a rather hesitant tone. Obviously I was not sure how any loving message would be received.

My Darling,

As you can see it is only a few hours since you left. And the way I work it out you should soon be in the Bay of B. I feel stunned and enormously tired still. I've slept. That's just about all I have done since you left.

You'll be delighted to know that I've got another cold sore. I'm not surprised, they always appear when we part.

I've painted two gouaches. One tiny one for that tiny frame you gave me which looks a real genuine Sutherland – but it's rather nice.

Darling, I feel so strange and hermit like, all alone. I can't get used to it yet, I have to make myself work otherwise I just drift.

All my love,
Colin

Two days later I wrote again. The card I refer to is lost. Obviously John bought Bells whisky in the Duty Free. He gave me some 45 records of the Paul Dessau music to *Mother Courage*. He had said he would translate a Dürrenmatt play on the voyage out – which one, I have now forgotten. Dürrenmatt was then unknown here. *The Visit* with the Lunts was first performed a few years later.

John, under the influence of Kester, was keen on the daily consumption of health foods, and wheatgerm, fruit, yoghurt and honey were always thrust at me with enthusiastic urgency. I looked at them with vague dislike, but once John had disappeared from my life these foods began to have a sentimental appeal.

My Darling,

Your pretty card came this morning and now looks down at me from the mantelpiece: I'm glad you got the Bells. Hope it was a little material comfort. I, too, feel terribly lonely and miserable. Don't want to eat or drink, or even wank. I feel empty.

I see from the Sunday papers that Bergman is bringing over his Theatre Company in *Faust* very soon, that should be exciting.

I find I'm writing this because I said I must write two sheets, so I'm writing anything, because I feel so shit empty and desolate inside that I can't think of anything. Darling, I hope the sun is shining a nice Big Bright Burning Sun on my boy and turning him the colour of pie crust.

Darling, I can't think. I can only feel, don't feel too desolate, one can't be hopelessly unhappy in the sun. I hope you've started working on Dürrenmatt.

Outside is grey ice cold English February enough to chill all ardour and passion if it was there, which it isn't.

I'll try and see Kester very soon, he seemed so miserable, but I don't feel like seeing anyone.

All my love,
C.

I should not imagine I was off my drink or food for long, though two days later I wrote again, this time to Genoa, saying that my mother had gone down with the same bug. I ended:

I can't feel that we're going to be apart for long. I don't know what to think, but somehow I feel you're still quite near. So I don't feel completely hopeless.

But from Marseilles a postcard of the market arrived with the words 'Je t'aime' written in every available space. John's letter, a cry of despair, followed a few days later from Genoa.

Marseilles

Darling, darling,

What can I say to you? I sent you a postcard today saying all that I can say, can really say.

Darling, what am I doing on this dreadful ship? I'm going barmy and not so slowly either. From Genoa we go straight to Port Said, that's six or seven days and from Aden to Australia is two weeks!! I'm going to be a mental case before then. And I'm not joking. Oh darling what on earth has happened? Were my parents so important or my ever seeing them again? Was it so important that you stay in England and take these crumbs of work?

Whatever was important or not something terrible has happened. It's the end of us.

Together we change together, apart we change in different directions. Remembering what we were both like when we first met and what we are now, it's not difficult to understand.

Darling, it's not sex, it's not that I'm high powered and wanting to go, but I am going mad to have you with me, to kiss me, to touch me, to feel your hand on my skin. Oh what is there to be done? I just can't stand it. The idea of touching anyone else is horrifying. And all this is with me all the time. There's no one to admit it to, no one who could sympathize.

If hell is anything anywhere, it's here day by day and minute by minute. I just feel sick, deep down, all the time. I haven't even got the heart to drink, let alone eat. I'm just smoking countless cigarettes.

I thought I would be able to think of our happy times and that would help. It doesn't. I'm bothered all the time that we're apart and it's not going to be a month or seven weeks, but much longer and most likely not any more.

Darling, do one thing for me. And for yourself. Do this work for the *Lit. Supp.* quickly and in one big go. And then be honest with me and admit how you feel.

Oh it doesn't matter. London will embroil you more and more. My parents won't let me go two months after arriving. We're apart, held apart. Oh darling, my heart is so sore as if it was bursting. I can't bear it, I'm a terrible coward. I can't bear getting letters from you. Soon and more and more they'll be full of day to day news in which I have no part.

Darling, we were the most important thing that has ever happened to us. Will ever, I know. What has happened now? I'm sick to madness.

Oh darling,
J.

Charles Osborne had promised to give John addresses of sympathetic people in Australia. That gap of ten years from sixteen to twenty-six meant he knew no one of his own age with similar enthusiasms. Australia, on that voyage, must have seemed to him a threatening and strange country.

In my next letter I am ill again. I cannot help thinking now that these were psychosomatic reactions. Emotional chaos and schism always go straight to my gut, generally accompanied with cold sores on the lip. John's departure had brought both. My first paragraph expresses a not unfamiliar notion that being in love is, in a sense, being bewitched. I felt it strongly, as this letter tried to say.

I was intrigued to meet Alan's brother Adrian, as he had worked with John Huston on *Moulin Rouge*, a film whose opening sequences so mirrored the Toulouse-Lautrec lithographs that had enthralled me.

Croydon
16:ii:59

Oh Darling,

You're a witch, a special kind of witch. I feel so empty without you, I drift, I can't work, I feel there's nothing nothing to say any more. The play has got to the point when it calls out for a nice enthusiastic but sane criticism from you, and suggestions and hints and everything else, it's somehow lost all the motivating force that it began with. I potter about. I clean out drawers, write letters, smoke cigarettes, anything but get down to work, so that I won't have to face this dreadful emptiness.

19:ii:59

I'm in bed again: with more of this wretched gastric flu.

I had drinks with Alan P. J. and his brother, Adrian, who is an assistant director in films, and lives with a great big film star who looks vaguely like Bill Travers but is Bill something else and has a real genuine cockney accent. The drawings seem to be going on fine, some of the responses are quite enthusiastic it seems, and I shall be starting very soon. There's about a quarter of me here. If that, drifting in a disconsolate manner, really it's all rather high-minded I've discovered. I love you . . . the you inside your body, rather more than the skin outside . . . all, all my love.

C.

But before my ill letter could have reached him, I had received John's depressed *cri de coeur* and I answered it at once.

Croydon
17:ii:59

Darling,

Your screaming letter came this morning. You knew on the boat you would feel like that, I knew you would, it was inevitable. I don't feel so depressed, so discouraged as you about our future, there's no doubt about the worth of it in the past, why should we doubt its durability for the future?

The *Lit. Supp.* thing is moving so slowly I got into a big flap about it. Alan P. J. has given in his notice which takes effect from June, so it has all got to be done by then, shouldn't think *The Times* would do anything off its own bat. Anyway I shall get about twelve of the drawings done in the next six months, that I promise you. I met Arthur Jeffress again at a party of Ken's, and he couldn't have been more snooty, I'd love to push a firework up his arse.

Darling I love you and I cried all through some parts of *Room at the Top* which has an absolutely terrific performance by Simone Signoret. There has never been quite such a realistic English film about sex before. Hermione B. gave a nice pickled performance.

All my love,
C.

Alan Pryce-Jones had implied to me that the series could go on *ad infinitum*, or if not that at least a series of drawings of writers every year. But I was obviously aware that if he were to leave the series might end, and I was too inexperienced to have asked for a contract with *The Times*. I worked hard, more even than I promised John. Almost twice the number of drawings were done in the next six months.

Arthur Jeffress owned a gallery just above Berkeley Square and I must have felt his friendship would be valuable, especially if he liked my work. This was very unlikely – he was a great snob and very precious, and my work and I were far too vulgar for his taste. He was very grand and had a palazzo in Venice, but sadly when he was banned from visiting it by the Italian authorities, who were distressed at his passion for gondoliers, Arthur committed suicide.

I knew Hermione Baddeley from Brighton where she had a flat, and John had met her there too. She had enjoyed looking through all my line drawings of nude men, gasping at the size or shape of their cocks and generally comparing the shape to that of her current boy-friend. I was a huge fan of her acting and a few years later wanted her to appear in my first play, *The Ballad of the False Barman*, but at that time she was working in the States.

My next letter begins when I am fairly drunk on the last train leaving Victoria for East Croydon. Rodney Long was my doctor and remained so for twenty years until I left London for the country. He was a great friend of Dr Eustace Chesser, who had shown much kindness to John and me, and he too became a friend as well as a doctor. Considering this, I am rather surprised I did not discuss with him what these tablets were. They sound like tranquillizers. To dull one's sexual appetite? How odd. To dull missing John? I find that bizarre too.

e. e. cummings was a favourite poet of ours. John had introduced me to 'somewhere I have never travelled', which I still think is the greatest love poem of the century. Good to know, I think now, that it was written to his wife. However, it was little good my renaming Australia 'nothome'. A perfect bury-head-in-the-sand word.

20:ii:59

This is addressed to the most beautiful thing on God's earth and I'm in the *last train* waiting for it to go – darling, I love you, let's make that quite plain first of all. Now, shall I tell you something very silly – they've given me *tablets* to make me not want you! It is a bit ironic isn't it? After all you've taken tablets, or should have – and now I have too! They are supposed to dull that, but I'm not sure that they do. Don't get alarmed darling – it is just that since you went I've had the most awful gastric pains, which have really made me ill, and I thought it was simply gastric flu or something, and then as it continued I thought it must be nervous, psychosomatic (isn't it a nice word, darling, big, big kiss) (read

148

this letter when you're drunk – please). So in desperation I went to Rodney and told him I felt awful and so he gave me some pills – which I think are doing the trick. Darling – everybody is being kind and nice and *distant*, very pro-us. I've just come from a party, odd people were there, that we knew, all asked after you. Somebody whose face was terribly familiar turned out to be somebody you had lunch with in Scotland – a Lord with a castle you told me, but he only had jeans and a string vest on tonight. Central School – I think. Darling, I love you so that in fact you never leave me, that I cannot endure the thought or even vague reality of ever sleeping with anyone else and I left tonight at the height of the party with as you would say in your most extravagant bitchiest manner, 'seven people after me – and not all of them were old queens.'

24:ii:59

My darling, my pet, my honeysuckle rose, you will get this now when you land on the great continent that I've renamed your 'nothome' which is a cummings euphemism for a shitland that takes you away from me. I miss you horribly. I feel rather as if a volcano erupted in the last eighteen months, a great effluvium of spunk which has dried out into a desert where nothing is recognizable any more.

I've just finished working on the short story, 'Nymph One', I'd left it all this time so that I could come back to it freshly, I've cut out the poesy parts, rewritten a whole page of dialogue but have decided to leave most of it as it is. If Lehmann doesn't like it now, it's just too bad, I think it's all right. It's not very funny and I don't intend to make it funny.

Rodney Long is going to write to you. It seems that dear old MacDonald felt concerned about you and wrote to St. George's Hospital and got a report, which is satisfactory. But there could be a recurrence darling and you ought to go on getting a check-up, this is what Rodney will tell you, he has the report for when you come back and are a patient again. I was relieved to know that the old gentleman took the trouble, he wrote a passionately enthusiastic letter about you, he must have been sweet.

All my love,
C.

I was to meet Dr MacDonald later, whose somewhat unprofessional story about John was to shock me. However, his concern was praiseworthy, for it was in St. George's Hospital at Hyde Park that John was operated on for his cancer. I see that I believe here that John will return to be a patient of Rodney's, or is it more likely that I am flying a kite?

My next letter reveals that I have begun work on *The Times*'s commission. I based my technique for the series on a portrait drawing series which Kokoshka had done before the First World War, where he used all the mediums, pen, brush, wash, chalk. For I wanted all the portraits to seem different, to have variety. This perhaps was not as wise as I thought then, for the different mediums sometimes obscured my individual style.

V. S. Naipaul lived, at that time, in one room in Streatham, in a row of two-storeyed terraced houses, the urban squalor of lower-middle-class gentility. This setting was in astonishing contrast to

V. S. Naipaul

most of the other homes I visited on *The Times Literary Supplement* commission. Lord and Lady Snow sat on a sofa together. He was easy to draw except his grossness could easily slip into caricature. Lady Snow was difficult, her features too tight, regular and neat. She wore a large rose made of fabric on her left shoulder, a detail which amused Lehmann, who could not take her seriously. My John had introduced me to the work of William Plomer; we loved his satirical ballads, and I much looked forward to the meeting. Elaine Rawlinson was the second wife of Lord Rawlinson, who became Attorney General. She came twice a week for a sitting in the conservatory with its broken panes. To relax her I used to read *Archy and Mehitabel* poems.

C. P. Snow

Loverboy, I'm worried for I haven't had a letter from you from Aden. What is it? Too miserable to write or what?

I've drawn Naipaul, the two Snows. (You'd like them, the drawings, they're much freer, I've used a brush and ink.) And I'm drawing David Jones tomorrow, and Plomer and Murdoch next week, so things are moving. Also love, started a portrait commission of Elaine Rawlinson, who we met at Mike's party. I picked up a nice selection, second-hand, but first edition, of Plomer poems and of Rimbaud, and a first edition of Isherwood's *Lions and Shadows*. You see what you've taught me. I must get the Plomer signed. All of my love and heart and cock and balls and every part of me that longs to melt, become indefinable, only so that you will make it yours again. Sweetheart.

'Mike' is Mike Richey, a friend who had a tiny flat in Lewes Crescent, Brighton, which I sometimes borrowed. He was also Director of the Institute of Navigation, a sailor, a Roman Catholic, and a close friend of David Jones. In the Brighton flat he had a superb Jones water-colour of a tiger, which the sun tragically bleached.

My Darling,

I haven't heard from you for ages: it is just over a month since you left. It has felt like a year.

David Jones is a poppet. You would love him. Lives in one room in a boarding-house in Harrow, filled with marvellous drawings and paintings of his, lovely singing landscapes, A Gaelic Dufy, and delicious fruity nudes. We got on like a house on fire. He used to come and visit his uncle in Chepstow Road, when a child. And wrote the first book, in a house opposite Tennis Road, the houses on the beach by the canal. He must be about sixty, but he has terrific gusto and animation, debunks a great deal of things. Has kept a kind of childishness, thinks Mike is wonderful.

I rushed away from him and queued in the rain to see *La Terra*

Trema, the cinema was packed to overflowing. I was very, very impressed. I only wish they had given it subtitles, one felt the language must have been so interesting and bawdy. The photography is out of this world. Solemn, sombre black and white, it reminded me of *Que Viva Mexico* in compositions of heads, and boats and rocks.

I'm half-way through the Plomer memoirs, I draw him tomorrow. They're very interesting, I'm sure I shall like him, he sounds so civilized and such fun. There's a lovely passage when he lived in Greece and had a love affair with a boy. They swim out in the bay and an old fisherman picks them up, takes them for a ride and they embrace and kiss their salty lips in the boat, while the fisherman sometimes turns back and smiles.

Kester wrote me a card so I've said that I shall go and see him next week.

My darling I'm sorry this is such a slight abrupt newsy letter. I'm tired. I had to attend a terrible dinner and dance thing with the family last night which has left me lifeless. But I wanted you to get something at Adelaide, I'll write next to home.

All my love,
C.

Many of my letters were missing the pick-up points and being readdressed, so a great deal of what I was saying to John he received much later. At last I received a long letter from him posted at Adelaide.

Adelaide
11:iii:59

Darling,

There were three letters from you at Freemantle, one sent on from Aden, two addressed here. Does that make it I've got all your letters sent along the way?

What a lovely silly letter your drunk one was. I think I prefer you drunk. A little all the time. When you're too much drunk I fear for life and limb – I must tell you about last night – Captain's farewell dinner for us; I did everything you would have recommended, and it got me nowhere. First rule, 'don't go cold stone sober'. So I drank a quarter bottle of Australian sherry (which is really rather good and dry and only 5/- a bottle).

Second rule, 'drink as much as you can'. There was only wine, a too sweet Graves and a fabulous Haut Médoc. Really fab. Soon everyone on my table was giving me their wine and I had less and less time to eat. I told lots of stories, I can't remember – one which has circulated wide apparently concerns my four (!) grandmothers.

Third rule, 'smoke as much as is going'. So that was those cigars.

Fourth rule, 'steal what's left'. So this boy took a huge slice of ham in one mitt eating it rather like a bunch of grapes, Roman style *and* a bottle of fab Médoc. Came back to the cabin, took the cork out – and *flaked* out. When I woke up at 7 a.m. all was gone! The cabin had been invaded by the English bod, his wife, the padre, etc. They'd had a wow of a time, undressed me, put me to bed. I feel today fragile and terribly bitter about the workings of fate.

Darling, not being able to love is unbearable for me. You taunted me sometimes with not creating anything. But I do. Something that I span with my hands. When I'm in love I feel I am creating with every little bone of my body. That it isn't tangible, that it doesn't go down on paper or canvas isn't against that. Don't say all people can do that. They can't and they don't. It's not swellheaded or anything to say that that is why Kester missed me so long, G. waited so long or – well I won't go on. Can you imagine how miserable you would be, deprived of colours and canvas and pen and paper? I've seen you absolutely frantic not being able to get down to work. Well that is how I am. There is so much inside of me and nowhere to direct it. I knew it would be so, that is why I cried so much so often before I left. I dreaded this. And with you somehow I achieved so much in me. I'm afraid of falling in love with someone else, that there must be another Woolf to give me reason and purpose. But must there be someone else? Darling, I can't believe we are finished. There is so much we can do. Of all people we belong together. That old bastard Dodi *was* right when she said we were made for each other. But how long is this break for? How long can you bear it? You'll be horrified but I think of us together for a long time still. I had to go back sometime soon. It seemed only natural to want you to see where I had grown up, my parents, things which are still alive and working and influencing me inside. Was a year spent doing this so wasted? So pointless? It hurt me deep deep down that you didn't of *yourself*, want that.

I wish I could see the play and help you there in some way. Please keep at it darling.

And think all the time of your brown, loving very much wanting boy who loves you,

John

In this letter John pins down that element of creativity that he poured into a relationship. This made loving him such a formidable and exhausting experience if anything in the partnership was flawed, but so amazingly ecstatic and lyrical when we were together. In his long paragraph, I detect the theatre director he was to become very soon. The need to direct other people's lives he could fulfil on stage. The immense frustration he felt in not being able to direct my life sufficiently is clear.

Woolf was the Austrian lad in Vienna. What interests me is the fact that some of us have such deep and inexhaustible energy for loving – or is it such a yawning chasm of need? – that often the object of love and desire is entirely inappropriate, yet it matters not, for as long as the object will take all that emotion, the need is fulfilled. Thus John was aware that in my absence another Woolf would appear. Yet inappropriate objects of love and desire cannot sustain the urgency of so much loving for long.

I am sad that I hurt John in not wanting to see his background or meet his parents, but I think then my distaste for Australia was overwhelming. I feared any interest in John's past, so I suppressed it.

My next letter welcomes him to Australia in an obviously peeved manner.

Darling, poppet,

Welcome again to your doubly nothome in the shitland which takes you away from me.

The two Vienna drawings came out today and look very nice. I have a book jacket to do, one of those publishers I tried a few months ago.

I went all the way down to Oxford to draw our Iris [Murdoch] on Tuesday and she'd disappeared. Wasn't to be seen anywhere. I hunted Oxford, left a rude note, got very drunk on Guinness and started walking in all the Colleges and telling the pretty undergraduates how pretty they were. Until someone in uniform came and chucked me out. I then managed to get into the Epstein Chapel and was found trying to unwind the bandages from Lazarus. 'He's got too much on,' etc. I was furious with Iris. But since then I've had a letter of apology from her full of explanations. The whole day had the ludicrous element of one of her novels. I got back quite safely once the evil fumes (that's what G. would now call them – he's such a bore, dear, I don't know how you stood him for so long) evaporated. I suppose this would be a good time to mention that I'm still as celibate as ever. I extricate myself from situations, I don't like having no sex, but at the same time I don't want to get involved, have to simulate feelings which don't exist, put up with bores before and after. I'd very much like to stay this way, until we were together again – wonder if it's possible?

I have to go to a fucking bore of father's (Ladies' Night tonight ugh!). Spent half a day with William Plomer, drawing him. Told him all about you and our delight in the *Ballads*.

I was asked by Jeremy* to his celebration dinner, ten of them, vaguely interesting. Did I tell you he'd bought a house? And wants me to do a mural on the dining-room wall. The subject, Greek mythology, the *Rape of the Sabine Boys*.

This afternoon I began my big canvas, 6′ × 4′ (those dull blue women were on it) subject – *Cain and Abel*, murder of Abel, very furious, monolithic forms violently fighting.

*Jeremy Kingston, a playwright, later theatre critic, now of *The Times*.

Yesterday, first sitting of Elaine for her portrait. Good handsome head, 30 guineas. I cleared the studio out of everything except my things, and I hung canvases on the wall, including the naked one of you. I talk to you so often, think of you so much. Everybody asks about you and is concerned about *us* being parted. Darling, darling, let's not be too far apart for too long.

Get a job almost at once. A *good* job please. *Save some money*. I am. We shall need it.

All my love, every part of me is all yours.

C.

My father was an enthusiastic Freemason, which is probably the main reason for my own lifetime's indifference to Freemasonry. It was clear in my adolescence that Freemasonry in South London was a collusive tribe of commercialism which veered, in my father's case, towards police corruption and petty larceny. I have no doubt that it had much genuine ideology in it too, but the two never 'connected' and what outsiders saw, what our family saw in particular, was a club of small-time businessmen lining each other's pockets. My appearance at this particular Ladies' Night with my sisters and their husbands proved to be another trauma of filial confusion. There was about these events a certain element of a riotous nature led by my father. Every year he slid down the banisters of the Café Royal. Some years he appeared as part of the cabaret in drag as a bathing belle. Always by the end of the evening he was thoroughly drunk and my mother was in a state of frozen horror, fearing the next vulgarity might be the truly unforgivable one.

In the middle of the evening, amidst much tomfoolery, I moved my father's chair and he sat down hard on the floor. It was clear I had humiliated him in front of everyone. It is also clear to me now that unconsciously that was precisely what I wished to do. I wanted to turn him into the public fool that he played so winningly for most of the time, but for this moment, to lose his act, timing and audience. At the same time he also lost his temper. He turned round and struck me and I, appalled at the humiliation, which a part of me had not intended, sobbed my way to the loo, where the nice new husband of my sister comforted me. It was a time for me of extreme emotionalism, but I see now that something

157

within my relationship with my father was being worked out, at the same time as my relationship with John was reaching a crescendo of choice. A later incident in the summer involving Allan underlined this struggle with my father who was, whether I liked it or not (and most of the time I hated it) my only sexual role model. What a knot of confusion this model was beneath the surface of Rabelaisian womanizer. It was these issues I had to try and work out, balancing them with the demands from my career as an artist and writer which appeared at last to have taken off.

The mural referred to in the letter was done on hardboard and was of Icarus falling upside down back on to some Mediterranean island, littered with nude young lads. When Jeremy sold the flat the mural went to the gay foreman of the furniture removal company who had a house in Spencer Road, Clapham. There it stayed for some years. As the house was of doubtful repute – the stories that came back to me made it out to be almost a gay brothel (though I'm sure the owner, now sadly dead, never made a penny out of it all) – the mural possibly found its rightful place.

William Plomer lived in a bungalow on the south coast beyond Worthing, a curious context for this sensitive writer. He lived with a Hungarian who delighted him by observing on a country walk while gathering fungi that the mushrooms were springing up like bungalows. William was difficult to draw, having regular features and expressing a gentle benevolence out of key completely with the bleak geriatric desert that surrounded him. I admired his Japanese writing set; a pen in a holder with bamboo inkpot complete with crawling ant. Sweetly, he gave it to me. I am still very fond of it.

Though I have said elsewhere that I curse my own insensitivity in not thinking about the effects of John's cancer and subsequent infertility, I did explore one quixotic action. Sometime that spring I wondered whether it was possible to transplant into John one of my own testicles. 'Greater love hath no man,' I think I felt at the time. Yet it seemed worth asking my own doctor what were the chances. I suppose now it might be possible. Then, it certainly was not. He surveyed me sadly, and smiling said more or less that I should forget about it. And so I did, until now. I never wrote to John on the matter. It was far too delicate, so what he would have thought of this rash yet loving gift, I never knew.

8

Spring 1959

There is in my letters the constant repetition of the claim to celibacy and disinterest in sexual activity, so much so that any observer would be bound to be suspicious. They would be right. I do not know why both John and I lied to each other in our separation, when a certain amount of promiscuity certainly occurred. I know that I have always found it difficult to say 'no'. I imagine John did as well. It has always seemed to me that one must have a very good reason indeed for saying 'no'. Sexual pleasure is such a supreme and total delight that to be mean about it seems anti-life itself.

The moralists tell you that you cheapen the experience and that your appreciation of it all grows less, our responses become jaded, we lose the profound awareness of the spiritual qualities in sexual love-making and so on. All this is nonsense. It is usually from fear that the sexual moralists limit their experience. I think the exact opposite is true. The more you love the better it can be, the richer and deeper the experiences. But this knowledge was not mine then – I knew by instinct that rejecting the love of others, even on a momentary basis, was an act of unkindness so I tried not to. But my heart was not in it. I knew too that my companions saw that my heart lay on the other side of the world. Yet I was also aware that desperation leads to strange bedfellows. Novelists are basically curious, and often they get themselves into experimental situations just to find out how it feels. Much of my experience at this time was indeed later used in my novels.

One incident in particular remains in my memory – Wolfgang's visit to London. Wolfgang was the young German lad who had stayed at the Villa Bontoc with his slightly older lover in the summer of 1957 when I had been there with Billy. We had lain on either side of the pool and stared with glowing lust at each other, while Wolfgang's lover glowered with jealous fury and hovered about us like a jailer. Wolfgang was never left alone for a second and all we managed to do by the time one of us left was to exchange addresses. In two years we had sent each other a couple of postcards, and then came a note from Wolfgang announcing that he was arriving in London for a week and would I arrange a hotel for him. Implicit in this command, was a hotel room for *us*. Obedient as ever to the lustful calls of youth and beauty I arranged a room in a hotel near the British Museum and met Wolfgang's train at Victoria. He fulfilled all the requirements of a Teutonic lust object – tall, muscular, sun-tanned and blond – but life and loving are of course about all sorts of other factors than those of appearance. However, I quietened any unease I felt and thought I was in for a few days of the Brighton Honey experience: sex and pleasure untouched by emotional drama. How naïve one always is!

We got to the hotel and were shown the room. We walked in, and Wolfgang threw down his luggage while his hand slammed the door shut. At exactly the same time he fell on me – kissing and clawing. I was pressed against the door by this muscular giant, unable to move with his teeth in my neck and his tongue slobbering all over my face. His hands started to tear at clothing while buttons flew and zips snagged. There seemed no way to quieten the lad down, nothing I could do except endure it until the orgasm, when I surmised he might return to being a quiet, normal student again. Our clothes got thrown all over the place and the physical violence continued. No pleas for him to go a little slower, to relax a bit, had any effect at all.

This was a perfect example of someone carrying around a vast emotional hunger which was off-loaded on to the first possible love object, however inappropriate or unsuited. I was prepared for a cosy, gentle dalliance, some caressing sensuality to the sound of Bach. What I got was a raving lunatic gyrating to the excesses of Wagner.

Wolfgang, of course, returned to the nice quiet creature he had been before, but I viewed him with some reservations. He had said he wanted to see London, and I had been prepared to take him to see a few historical sights, but all he wanted to see was the inside of gay pubs or clubs. So that evening we started off on a tour, Wolfgang's guide being distinctly unenthusiastic. It must have been the first or second pub we visited when I lost him for ever. Every vaguely attractive face he perceived in the bar he addressed, and so was surrounded by a circle of admirers. I walked out and returned to Croydon. I was rather amused. Wolfgang worked for a steel company, J. A. Henckels, and he had given me a present of a paper knife and scissors. I lost the paper knife years ago, but the scissors are still on my desk, beautifully sharp and elegantly designed. A lethal weapon for a sex maniac.

The summer of 1959 was particularly rich in creative work and incident. But my letters to John are self-censored; a pity, as such lack of courage in the truth I now find dispiriting.

17:iii:59

My lovely brown darling,

I do believe you are enjoying life with your drunken banquets and your pretty boys that you pick up on the beach.

John Osborne

Yesterday I began drawing the great Mr Osborne, tall, thin, spectral: in black skin-tight trousers that showed a cute bottom and a huge lunch. And camp, my dear – not 'arf. And the musical, my dear, cor that's a queer dish too, everybody changes their sex half way through and delicious lovely Adrienne Corri grows hair on her chest. Most peculiar: he was moving about so much, it's only the second week of rehearsals, that though I did some lightning things with a brush, it just won't do, so I'm going back after Easter and try some more. He has a curiously camp voice and he appears to stare at one with his teeth.

John Osborne

I saw the Strindberg play with Miss Mai Z: M. Gough, L. Brook: all giving superb macabre performances that chilled one to the bone. But I don't really like Mr S., so terribly earnest, not a ghost of a smile anywhere, so that things that he most wants to say become ludicrous.

I'm going down to Brighton for Easter as a kind of chaperon to mama, she's staying at the Old Ship and I'm having Michael's flat, while he prays at Downside for us all.

All my love,
C.

The John Osborne musical was of course *The World of Paul Slickey*, soon to become the only commercial failure of his early years. Both John and I admired *Look Back in Anger*: our generation felt that Osborne encapsulated the rage we all felt over the limitations of the British theatre. Yet like so much of the later Osborne, the play now seems an hysterical diatribe, the characters thin and invalid, the plot negligible. It was brilliant journalism, I think now, masquerading as theatre.

A few days later I wrote again, delighted to have met Iris Murdoch.

22:iii:59

Darling,

I spent Friday in Oxford again and this time our Iris was there. She is extremely beautiful or rather her face is, one should say her head, but her hair is just like Towzer's tousled coat after a night out, and her body is all dressed in shapeless sweaters and tweed skirt, thick stockings and brogue shoes with a terrific masculine stance and gestures. (You should see her swig a gin.) It's all rather incongruous when you realize this superb head like some hypersensitive Greek prophetess belongs to this ragged body. Her face has that limitless sadness, a kind of internal melancholy that you see in the photographs of Virginia Woolf. She responds readily, far more than she gives, she grins spontaneously at jokes and has a sense of fun that you would expect from the novels, and yet one is tempted to think that without something to spark it off it wouldn't appear, there would be just the sadness. She

Iris Murdoch

seems also intensely curious, asking all sorts of questions about the technique of drawing. 'What did I think of her description of the portrait by Rain in the *Sandcastle*? Was it all right? No it was bad' (going on before I could answer). I've never really made up my mind what kind of painter she was. I told her of my chuckles over the *Net* and *Enchanter* in the tram through Vienna and of your despair at the end of the *Sandcastle* on the boat.

Her room was full of the smell of hyacinths. I'm not a bit satisfied with the drawing. It's sensitive and pretty, has caught a little of the sadness. But she didn't give me enough time. An hour and a half, that's all, we wasted another half hour in talk and gin.

Then things started to happen which she hadn't expected and it was all cut short. I was ambitious perhaps in what I wanted to do.

I find it tiring, travelling and then concentrating on drawings. I was worn out Friday evening. On Tuesday up to Suffolk to draw Angus Wilson.

Monday

I'm rewriting the long Vienna story right from the beginning and making it into a short novel, going on from where I left off before.

It's been the most wonderful spring day here, all the flowers and trees are coming out in bud and flower. Easter in a few days. It makes me sad. To think we were in Italy last year. Let's try and be there next year.

I think I love you and want you more than I ever did.

Colin

On Easter Saturday, I sent John a postcard from Brighton. The message reads:

Here I am thinking of Florence, Masaccio, Angelico, the David, the sun, wine, you, Acton's villa and the cypress trees and wishing one could either go back a year or forward. How about Athens for next Easter? Let's make it a date. Masses of sun here, taking Chucky out to dinner this evening.

What I did not tell John, though it would have amused him, was that after coffee with mama at the Ship Hotel, I popped into the 42 Club, within the same block. Among the crowd there were three men, one of whom was immediately recognizable as Godfrey Winn. He was with two friends, an entourage that was customary, possibly in his mind to help keep the fans at bay. However, there were no fans around him that night as the three of them surveyed the scene. I could tell they had decided to make an advance on me and I was not particularly amused, having a hatred of the Winn prose and persona. On an impulse I decided to be Polish and speak only a few words of English. What they did not know was that I knew only a few words of Polish, and that these would have to be endlessly recycled. A drink was bought. I reacted blankly to most of the things they were saying. Once they gathered I understood little they relaxed and talked about me. It was fun. I found a look of vague puzzlement was best and it was a mistake to appear as if I was listening. Never look at the person who is speaking, stare into the room and look slightly bewildered and lost. They laid plans to drive me back to the Winn establishment. One of Winn's companions was already extolling my physical attributes. It was becoming so hilarious that I had to make strenuous efforts not to laugh. At that, knowing that rising hysteria would spoil it, I rose, stumbled a few thank yous with a heavy Teutonic accent and escaped.

I returned to Croydon to discover a letter from John, to which I replied. His letter is missing.

Croydon
31:iii:59

Sweetheart,

I got back from Brighton this evening to find a letter from you (the first for ages) and the little present from Italy. It's enchanting, a deliciously squiffy heart which made my heart long to see you. A thousand kisses I'm sending you back to cover every inch of that funny brown body to keep you celibate and faithful until you're mine again.

I can't remember whether I've told you all about Angus Wilson. I don't think I have. I was afraid he might not be very nice, but I was quite wrong and I'm completely converted to him. He lives with someone who is younger and a probation officer, they've been together for about ten years and are charming. They're buried in the country in a flint cottage encased in a garden like a parcel. He is wickedly funny telling the most detailed sagas about literary windbags and being marvellously vicious about them. I told them all about you and how wonderful you were, and he gave me a copy which he signed of the last volume of short stories *A Bit off the Map* and bought a drawing I'd done of him. I just love you – till the cows come home 'and the river jumps over the mountain and the salmon sing in the street'.

Colin

Angus Wilson

I was working hard and was enjoying it immensely. *The Times* paid me £25 a drawing, so I was earning a hundred pounds regularly a month: unheard of wealth for me. But I worked quickly, doing many drawings in a session, and I would more often than not also sell a drawing to the sitter. I don't believe I was saving anything though.

Early in April I answered another miserable letter from John, which is also missing. In it, I tried to make plans and begged him to say whether he saw any chance of returning.

My sweet darling,

I got your mizzmizz letter yesterday. A cry from the dark of the Australian bush. I'm crying back from my dark too.

What I really wanted you to write was a very factual letter. Full of facts about jobs (the truth, mind you) and what you think about everything, unbiased by hysteria that is. You see darling, there is so much of me that wants to come out and be and live with you, but I certainly can't for some months anyway, I try to hurry the list of authors on as much as possible, but I've still only done ten and they are talking (because they're very pleased with it all) of extending the number; it's very difficult for me to say 'no' to that.

But at the same time my darling, darling sweetheart, don't put the *possibility out of your mind that you might come back here very soon*.

You see the best thing for me would be to hang on here for about two years, there is almost certainly something coming out of this: the point is could you come back here inside this year, maybe in the autumn, and let us live in London until the end of 1960, and then I should be just that bit more established so that I could afford to leave London and would come to Australia with you for as long as you would like and do anything then. Great big sighs. I know you won't come back. And suppose I never get out there? That would be the end of us wouldn't it?

Darling, please answer this, would you be prepared to come back? This last letter was so raving raving loving, but you never mentioned the fact of *you* doing anything. It was all me again, that had got to move, that had got to come to you etc. etc. etc. *It's true, true, true*. Don't deny it.

You know 'ow jealous you got before you left about Alan P. J. We were supposed to have dinner together, and it kept on being postponed, but at last it happened. My dear, what luxury. I never have been quite so fêted and dined, a dozen oysters and champagne to begin with in this incredible apartment in Albany that looks like something out of a rather bad Cocteau film – all those caryatids. He's an absolute duck, you needn't have worried.

My sweet, do you know what *we* have been offered to 'US' for the summer – a small stone cottage set in an olive grove overlooking the sea in Sicily by a friend of Mike's. Will you get into that oval blockhead of yours that you're missing things as well.

Colin

By chance in Sloane Square I had met Michael Davidson again. We sat down in the pub and the magic of our friendship began. We talked for three hours, laughing endlessly, not noticing anything around us, unaware of time. On that meeting Michael had said he was off to Sicily and that John and I would be welcome to join him.

In my next surviving letter (there are a few missing) I referred to my discovery that John had caught a dose of clap a few months before leaving. I was shocked, not at his infidelity, but that he had allowed some stranger to bugger him, when over that activity in particular we had a tacit understanding to be faithful to each other. I would not penetrate anyone else while he also would not allow it done. Such embargoes are always stupid, because they are always broken. Yet in love they always exist; we need such tokens, perhaps because inevitably they *are* broken.

. Then I wrote again on 18 April. There is a great deal of repetition in this letter, which I hope catches the kind of bizarre hysteria that I was immersed in.

Croydon
18:iv:59

My dear darling,

I thought I'd tell you that I'm coming to Australia that is if you still want me, I thought I'd come right into those delicious arms of yours. I don't care how long we stay in Australia, as long as you like. I'm sorry sweetheart that I'm so doubtful and difficult but don't feel bitter about it and keep on throwing it in my face. I have to find out that I'm only a quarter alive without you. That I yearn for you all the time, and that sex and bed is meaningless when you're not here.

Now the practical things, which is more than you ever write love of my life, I can't see how I could get there before the autumn and I suppose that's your spring. I really have to finish this series,

(i) Because I said so. (ii) Because I shall need the money. Alan P. J. is inclined to be slow and has to be pushed all the time. But he's also reasonable and from what I remember of this drunken champagne dinner was very pro my going to Australia and will advance the cash, I think, so money is no problem. Could I fly out there?

I want work. Broadcast my coming, exaggerate all my talents, tell them any amount of lies beginning from the truth about what I've done. Yes and please a nice flat such as you 'ave said not in the bush I think but overlooking the harbour.

I know your first reaction to this letter will be *unbelief*. He'll never come, etc. just talking about it! Darling, I've said I'm coming and I will if you'll *still* have me.

C.

I now realize that this letter must have come as a shock to John. He wanted me out there but feared the reality. He was just about to make his own name in Australia, as I was in London. Would my being there complicate his life and, more particularly, could he believe that I would stay?

But there was no reply from John to my letter saying I would come out to him. There was also then no telephone number to contact him with. Instead came a letter from John (now missing) asking me to design a play for children he was directing, *The Snow Queen*. It was a totally mad idea, asking for failure – costumes and scenery, all of which had to be done quickly, but without my being there to oversee the designs.

Croydon
24:iv:59

My dearest: your long newsy letter arrived two hours ago, I'm still *reeling* and will for the next few days. I'm terribly happy for you. And terribly miserable for us. In fact I feel dazed. It's strange but you end your letter in the same way that I ended my last letter to you. 'I know you've found someone . . .' etc.

It's *quite quite* untrue. I haven't slept with anyone or *even* kissed anyone. I'm dried up. I don't want anyone except *YOU*. Do you think it's possible for us to be faithful until we're together again?

Yes. I'll certainly design *The Snow Queen*. But you must give me details *at once* of the stage. How long is it? What resources has it? Can I fly anything?

Everything somehow seems so simple now, my coming over and us living together again. Do give me the shipping company that you used.

I feel so tired and wretched and miserable, and lonely that I can't with anyone but I love you, love you with every particle of nerve and flesh that ever is.

My sweet sweet darling what a fool I am to ever let you go.

C.

In my next letter I was certain that as I hadn't heard, John had fallen in love with someone else. Certainly his slowness in answering must have made me feel he had serious reasons for not wanting me there.

Croydon
7:v:59

Now my darling I think you've left me. I think you've gone and fallen in love with some stardust boy who presses your cock between his buttocks and sighs.
Pity!
Shame.
I hate it.

Yet somehow, silly of me maybe, but darling sometimes when I look at the three best drawings I ever did of you and see that glorious body of yours there and see in those thin fragile tenuous lines all my love and fervour for you, then, when I look at that I feel we can last out everything, seas, sun, moons, Australia, Europe, the States, cancer, ambition and hate. Darling, these are the things, maybe I ought to add, distrust, resentment, self will – which part us. Lord, what do you want me to do? Kill myself? Or maybe just cry on our grave. WHY HAVEN'T YOU WRITTEN????

I haven't heard from you for two weeks. It is three weeks since you got the most loving letter I ever wrote to you. What am I to think?

I had sent off the designs for *The Snow Queen*. They had been done in something like seven days and the sets must have been totally inadequate.

John still had not answered in any satisfactory way my first letter saying that I was coming. Obviously, he did not believe it.

Croydon
14:V:59

My own sweet darling, today is Whit Saturday. Two years ago we quoted Eliot to each other in a revolting sweaty crowded bar and I began to love you with every nerve and shade of emotion I possess. Next week it is your birthday. We're parted this year from both celebrations. We won't be *next* year.

I'm frantically busy, as busy or more so than you are and only time for such a short note. The drawings are all a great success. I'm being paid very well and earn other things on the side. I have freedom at last from horrid sugar poppas and take myself to the opera to hear Callas (nobody I want to take with me. I'm terribly alone, think of you continually, every moment and long to share every moment with you, but so frantically busy I've hardly the time to realize I am alone, no sex, no love, my body and mind filled simply with thought and feelings for you). Of course I will telephone on your birthday, at Australian time 10.00 a.m. your 25th at V.M. 7296.

I'm sorry the sets were so scrappy. But you told me you wanted them for the first week of May so I rushed everything. Do *use* them.

Darling, I love you till the *end of time* and further if possible. The next few months will rush away if *we* both work hard.

C.

That afternoon I left Olivia Manning, failing to draw her. She had bought a nude drawing of John. Twenty-five years later she complained to me that the drawing was not the investment she thought it was.

My next subject was Evelyn Waugh. I had received a postcard from him giving me directions by road from East Croydon to

Combe Florey, but in the end I travelled by train. It was a Friday and I had lunch with the whole family. Seated at Waugh's right, I was presented with a platter by the manservant. 'Fish,' Waugh bellowed in my ear, 'we're Papists you know.'

After lunch we retired to his study. He was genial and witty, showing me his own early drawings and making the pertinent observation that he had a small face inside a larger one. I left in the late afternoon to catch a train to Bath where I was to have dinner with L. P. Hartley. In the hall Waugh looked down at my small grip and boomed, 'Is that all your luggage?' I nodded. 'But where are your dress clothes?' he asked in a tone of interrogation, 'Leslie is bound to have a couple of duchesses at dinner to meet you.' This was a wonderful leg pull, a fragment of fiction on Waugh's part.

L. P. Hartley's house was a few miles outside Bath with a garden going down to the river. He was looked after by a couple, a manservant who was both butler and chauffeur and his wife who was cook/housekeeper. It seemed a totally Edwardian atmosphere. At dinner, without duchesses, the telephone rang. Hartley answered it and I heard the puzzled tone of his voice. After a few moments he came back muttering, 'That was the William Hickey column. They wanted to know what duchess I had invited to dinner to meet you.'

I told Hartley of the Waugh spoof. He didn't seem entirely convinced, as if no gentleman would be capable of a practical joke which involved the British aristocracy. He checked up on the William Hickey column and discovered that the girl who had telephoned him worked for it. This to Hartley seemed to be proof that the call was genuine. I tried to tell him that I was of public insignificance and not worth centimetres in the Hickey column. But Hartley was not persuaded.

In the morning he sat on a sofa while I drew him. I asked him to look at the clock on the mantelpiece. Above it there was an oil portrait of a Venetian gondolier, a great love of Hartley's life. He would stare at the clock for three seconds then slowly his head would turn and he would stare at me. 'The clock please, Mr Hartley, the clock.' 'Ah yes,' he muttered his apologies. His head returned to the position I wanted to draw him in, then a few seconds later back it came. It was no good. Hartley seemed to be mesmerized by me. I drew him in this dazed state, staring at me with a kind of frozen longing.

I left without one drawing either of us could be pleased with. Hartley began writing to me about three times a week.

Often my letters to John reflected and parodied bits of Auden, especially one of our favourite poems, 'As I Walked Out One Evening'.

Croydon
16:v:59

Please write soon – just a postcard. Did you get my little birthday present? You didn't say.

My Dear Sweet Darling, at last a half hour to spare so I put a record of Callas on the turntable and start writing to you.

It's just over a week since your last letter came, the confused miserable one, which I answered at once. It had a strange effect upon me, for the days following it, it slowly sank in and I began sometimes to think you were right and that we'd never live together again or love each other again (a thought that put cold icy terror inside me): and then slowly I began to get my balance again. I know I've got to come out to see you. I can't rest until I do.

Yesterday I was at the dress rehearsal at Covent Garden of *Medea* with Callas. What a woman. I was doing drawings of her for *The Times*. An extraordinary opera, very fierce and beautiful and she breathtaking for sheer frenzy and power.

You never ever said how pleased you were about *Nymph and Shepherd*, should be in the August issue. I have no time for writing at all now, which is a pity.

Have I told you about L. P. Hartley or Evelyn Waugh? And my two days in Somerset drawing them?

It's been mooted that I do a talk for the Third on it all. This could be used perhaps for Sydney too. You *must* advertise me. And exaggerate the snob angle. Talented promising young writer and painter angle who, as Lehmann says, is beginning to know more about the background of literary life than anyone else. He is coming to dinner with Bob and Harry tomorrow. Do you know he had the cheek to ask me to go with him to Vienna this year.

The High Priestess gets more and more egocentric. I explained that I should find it more than upsetting and that I'd probably be suicidal. 'Pity,' he said, 'you know it so well.'

Oh darling, darling, I'll love you till the ocean is folded and hung up to dry and Australia gets squashed into the English Channel.

C.

A letter from John which has survived shows how hard he was working at this time. It is remarkable that within two months of returning to Australia he was immersed in so much and especially in the work he wanted to do – directing plays.

Sydney
17:v:59

My dear dear Darling,

What a silly foolish little boy you are in your last letter epistle. After writing off that you were sure I had a stardust boy I hope my letter arrived the next day to show you how groundless all of your concern was. Now I am sure that *you've* gone off on a mad boy-binge just because I'm supposed to be doing that. Darling, I haven't touched a boy since I arrived. There are a couple of bits of stardust floating around the place. But I let them float.

Darling, I have such a full week. If you were here you'd see nothing of me. I go to work between 9.30–10.00, stay at work, except for odd breaks till 5.

6.30–11.00 are rehearsals of German play, four week nights.

7.00–11.00 remaining week night *Snow Queen*.

Saturday, Sunday 12.00–5.00 rehearsals for German play.

Saturday evening, like tonight, I'm either quiet in the flat here working or writing to you or drinking good cheap whisky like now – half the price as in England – or I'm at home in bed asleep alone.

The designs have arrived!!!! For the most part they are exciting to an extreme. A couple of them leave me cold at the moment, simply I think while I'd imagined them definitely some quite different way. I'm giving them a few days to grow on me. I'll not write in any more detail about them now, but the next letter I shall. Quite a number of people have seen them, liked them. Mum was down on the floor the other night ecstatic about them, excitedly going from one design to another.

Keep your fingers crossed on 24 May for me. First night of German play. I'll write more soon. This is essentially to assure you quickly that I love you and only you – more and more and more.

Love love love
J.

The next letters deal with the telephone call on John's birthday.

Croydon
20:v:59

My darling, my love,

I've arranged to telephone you on the morning of your birthday but it will be 9.30 a.m. *not* 10.00. That's ten hours before here, which makes it 12.30 at night for me.

I've never been so busy in all my life. I need a secretary and can afford one! But I think maybe that's going too far. All my love darling and more and more if that were possible. The world is empty without you.

I go to draw Auden and Eliot and Graham Greene in the next few weeks. I'll give Auden our love!

C.

27:v:59

My own my very sweet darling, I'm so dazed after last night it was all so depressing but terribly worth it in a way. I shan't be able to forget your funny crackly voice, but I can't remember what I said and I could hardly hear you anyway. I thought we would be able to talk (people always told me it was like talking to your aunt in Twickenham) and so all the things I wanted to tell you and ask you I must now write.

In the first place love, do you really want me to come out there? You waited so long before answering the letter which said I was going to that I thought you must be having serious doubts. Tell me. Be honest.

I'm doing extraordinary portraits in oils, great swirling ones, Bob says that they're as exciting as those early Kokoshka ones, one of father, Harry Fainlight looking very intense, and Allan looking spiteful. I want to paint your bum.

What work could I get? If you produce anything else let me know in good time, so that there's no need to rush it all.

Of course the designs are your birthday present. And so is every painting and drawing I ever do, every sentence of my novel belongs to you: because I think if you didn't exist and I didn't love and believe you love me in the same way, I would stop painting and writing, stop living, stop caring,

Yours etc.
Colin

On 20 March I wrote a letter, claiming I was not going to send it. It seems, however, that I did post it after all. John's despair was the spur. As a piece of prophecy it was not that accurate, yet what I say in the last paragraph is true enough. If only we could have stood outside ourselves, but we were not good at it. We both needed perspective on our lives and on our love, but we did not know how to gain that advantage, even momentarily. We were both at this stage immersed so completely in our work, it was difficult to surface and think clearly on any issue.

20:iii:59

My darling,

This is the letter I'm going to write now but which I'm not going to send. I'm not going to send it to you because I'm going to try to prophesy and if you read what I think you're going to do you might not do exactly that, and that would muddle everything.

You're going to find Australia exciting and what is more in the kind of drama art world you'll get into you will be someone, maybe a small someone at first but somebody who will quickly and ably become a big someone. You'll enjoy that. But all the same in the midst of this readjustment you will still want me.

Now I'm going to tell you that you will use all these things as sticks to belabour my shoulders with and bruise me into submission. Your need to be at home or near there for the next few years to help them, make life easier for them, your poor old mum act. The work and chances for us out there, you've met so and so who buys pictures just like mine that sell like hot cakes. The wonderful flat overlooking the harbour which you had the chance of getting.

You see I think there's a certain pattern with you and me. You're the one who's bullying, using any kind of means however unpleasant, however monstrously untrue for your end. I'm the one who is cowered and pummelled into submission. I don't want to reverse these roles. Impossible anyway. I would just like us to step outside them. To forget about them. You will see there is enough of us which is true and certain and worthwhile which can stand a certain amount of battering. We've been thrown back upon that now. It's all we have. I wonder with the help of that whether we can just work out a plan of the quickest way to live together again, not violating too much the duties we have to do outside it.

What are they exactly, I wonder? My necessity is to be in London at the moment. I can't really think of anything else.

Sydney
13:vi:59

Dear darling,

Your serious letter – rather earnest maybe – arrived the other day. It made me so mad and angry with you that I couldn't write back. Now I feel cooler and perhaps a little more calm and collected. Do you really misunderstand me and us so much? Do you really have to psychoanalyse us in such a way to make things palatable?

My parents don't need me to make their life easier. I need them. I feel now that I am suddenly discovering so much that is vital and important. Financially, they're quite comfortable. Home I find has lots of expensive gadgets it never had before. And it was my father who put up the £500 for my sister's car. They live simply, and well within their means. I need not return the passage money and may not.

I suppose you're right when you say I bullied you. But equally right is that unfortunately it was often necessary. From that bullying came Vienna – twice for you – and us. Why, oh why, it was so necessary that I had to bully you shamelessly into realizing how important we were, I'll never know.

An earlier letter from John attempts to answer some of the practical queries, but it is also depressed about our future. It sees clearly that our professional lives are lived on separate continents.

Sydney
2:vi:59

My dear darling Pussyfoot,

It is now a week since you phoned me. And every day I've wanted to write to you.

Darling, I was so miz on the 25th when your call couldn't get through. Then the whole day was hard work. But in the evening was a mad mad party. About forty people, mainly from TV and *Snow Queen* and German play. Madly normal, I seemed to spend most of the time pouring out drinks and listening to people pour out their heart's woes. I *didn't* get drunk. Someone gave me a wonderful native sarong which I wore a bit. It was a wow party. Next morning when you phoned I was still recovering. Had a bit of a hangover. I couldn't hear very well. You sounded pissed (were you?) and terribly like some field major. It made you seem so close. Afterwards I went and cried myself to sleep for a couple of hours.

The roll of designs has arrived. The road scene is marvellous. So is the horse. But darling, the poster and programme come over wickedly bad.

The portraits I found very interesting but they left me strangely cold. Maybe because I'm away from you and don't know what you're trying for. The relationship between the heavy brush and fine pen work seems non-existent. To my mind they don't jell. Excepting the David Jones which is very very fine indeed.

I liked the line in the Osborne one but it seemed pointless. It didn't tell me anything about the man or about what you thought of him. But there's a lot in the David Jones.

I have just had the chance of this flat in a modern block. Absolutely self-contained, two bedrooms, lounge, kitchen, bathroom, phone, fridge, etc. etc. all for £2.12s a week. The block is characterless but it's cheaper and self-contained. Spare bedroom could be studio. Double bed! Closer to city. Can do what I like to the flat. It's wonderful good luck. I'll let you have the address as soon as I move in. You can even see Botany Bay from the sitting-room window.

You're not flying? When sweet are you coming? August? In time for spring here? Or late English autumn, i.e. November, December or January?

Darling, I can't wait that long. How can you even? I'll be a year older. You too, since we last were together. Darling, I love you, in fact, you exercise so much influence on me that now I think I'm impotent. Not ever ever a horn up now. I've got a dead cock. And a locked bottom I should add.

Darling, I don't trust us any more. I don't think we would be happy. I doubt us and your coming out here all along the way, even though I want you so very much desperately. I sometimes think we're fools in trying to keep what was between us alive. I can't, honestly, take it much longer, this love by airmail. I feel dead and useless emotionally with life slipping through my fingers. I don't want a whole year lost. It's four months today since I left England, four months dead and useless. I need, darling, and so do you, to love someone with me, not on the other side of the world. I can't go on like this for another six months.

And I think we are already much changed. We are each in love with the person we once knew. We haven't got this power of adjustment we would need.

I think to stay here some time. So much can be accomplished here.

Darling, your life is in England. The future you want is there and from the sound of things it seems you're on the way to getting it. I can't bring you out here, on the chance we can 'meet' again emotionally and intellectually. I want you to be good so much. And I automatically put myself in the position of someone who can help you do it. But many can.

Darling, my whole being and body tonight is wrenched apart. When I'm alone – and I make sure with work that is as seldom as possible – I am so empty inside and then I cry – oh darling, I plan my whole life here on you joining me and I dread it so much – and the time we must wait. I find myself seriously considering marriage – I think essentially as an escape from you and how much I need you.

I love you, darling, but we're finished and if you were absolutely honest with yourself you would admit it too.

John

Before I received this letter, I had written again to John reiterating my intention to go out to Australia.

Croydon
3:vi:59

My sweet darling, there's a hundred things I should do but I can't for I must write to you. I still am constantly amazed how much of my life you share, all of it, in fact. I feel raging sexy at the moment but the rage and the sex is entirely devoted to you. I think of no one else.

This is an anniversary letter for it was 8 June, 9.30 p.m. two years ago: not the 5th as you said on the telephone.

I want *us* to do so much together in Australia, where we must save and plan to go eventually to the States. You see, I really do plan, that we might even be away from England five years. So you mustn't mind a *few* months delay. A few months which has taught me in a curious kind of way as much as I learnt when I was with you. Or rather being parted from you has deepened and widened the awareness of what it all was and how it adds up.

All of my love,
Colin

I replied to John's long, bleak letter on 8 June.

Croydon
8:vi:59

I'm amazed: I've got your letter which you must have written when you were very tired, it's confused, despairing and crazy, upside down, and I fear darling, quite, quite unrealistic. You end up by saying we're finished, if only I was honest with myself I would admit it too. Well I don't admit it because all the facts prove to the contrary. I think of no one but you. I want no one but you. My whole life is centred about you. It's not just only a memory of you or us, it's something living which stops me from going to bed with other people. Darling look at it like this: if when I come out we find it's a mistake, then it's just too bad. I shan't make a fuss, I'll stay there for a little while, and then come back. I think it's very important that we see things like that. It's not going to be one big wonderful union of two souls and two cocks, but I'm just coming out to see you, to look around, to see the other side of the world. How's that? It would be terrible and I would hate it if you felt you had to make a go of it. I shan't feel like that. We'll just relax and enjoy life and see what's happening.

It didn't hurt me. When I reached the end, about 'we are finished' – I laughed. It seemed such a funny, melodramatic thing to say. Don't worry about waiting so long. You're working hard and so am I. The time flashes past. I know this is what you hate. You have this feeling all the time of being cheated by time, of wasting time, but love, even being apart teaches us something about each other and about love. It won't be six months. I can get to you in three. How's that? You say you need to love someone with you and you can't stand this love by airmail. I'm sorry. It is inevitable at the moment. But do try and hang on a little. If you get impatient and have a thing about someone, you will, I believe, be wasting us. Throwing us away.

> All my love and more if possible,
> Colin

John's black mood did not last long, yet it seemed always near, just below the skin. His new flat cheered him and as he referred to it as 'ours' I was at last convinced that he believed I should arrive.

My dear dear Darling,

I'm whizzing along in an express train, home for the weekend. That's why my writing is all over the place. There is just no time anywhere else to write any letters at all! I'm sorry my last letter was such a long, unhappy moan. It was cock moan, heart moan, empty arms moan.

I have now moved into *our* flat. It's huge. Big double bed for *us* (and no one else), spare room with lots of sun for your studio. All self-contained and central. Big view with Botany Bay in the distance. Am selling you left, right and centre. I wake now every day randy for *you*. And am still virgin. How long darling, how long? If you come in August you'll be here in spring and can see *The Snow Queen*. We'll go off to a little isolated house I know on a bay, for a couple of weeks as soon as you arrive. And make love and love and love.

I'll try to be good and write to you often, if you don't mind scrappy notes like this. Darling, the train just now is going through rugged bush and mountains and bays of sea way down below. If only you were here with me!

I love you, darling, darling.

J.

The day before this letter was written, I wrote to John.

Croydon
21:vi:59

Darling, the more I think about everything (and by 'everything' I mean 'us' and by 'us' I mean everything) I come back to one or two *facts*. And the big fact, of course, is the depth and nature of the relationship which is above and beyond words but which is, I believe, signified in certain symbolic gifts that we gave each other. The ring you gave me and the medallion I gave you. My heart I brought back from Italy and gave you, and your heart that you sent back from Italy and gave me. Now, sweet darling, this is not just sentiment. We live in a world of symbols and these particular symbols have a wealth of significance for me and I hope for you. You see darling, I do feel married to you!! I can't help it – because the ring signifies just that. So if you want to break this very real *union* the only way is to send back the medallion. Then I shall know all is finished and in the sight of Heaven, etc... poor God will have a fit of course because you know he did rather favour us, bless his cotton socks and yours too.

All my love,
Colin

The last letter of June which John wrote to me reveals his own desperation and vulnerability. The silence from me continued until the middle of July.

Randwick
30:vi:59

Darling sweet,

I went home a week yesterday and your rather sane and calming letter was waiting there. On the train up to Newcastle I scribbled you a little love on an airletter, you must have got it by now. I haven't heard from you in more than a week and feel terribly miserable and cut off because of it. But then I often callously leave you without word for longer than that.

Darling, thank you for your letter and for not rounding on me. It was written late at night and terribly alone. Darling my sweetie, it's awful being alone. Last night in our big double bed I tossed and turned in all its lovely wilderness. Come and fill it beside me. It is so empty and big.

Your letter hit the nail right on the head. That 'monstrous ego' of mine has collapsed – absolutely. I am left deflated, bewildered. I'm no longer sure of anyone, thing I do, or of my ability to take any strain or override difficulties. I would hate you to see me like this. It's pathetic. I guess often my letters weren't directed at you, 'passion of complete desolation' sums it all up. I no longer have any point to anchor myself, I flounder in a sea of half-baked personal relations with people, longing for something more durable than the superficial contact I make. If I wasn't so busy

I'd be a goner. If my life had any free time, I'd be a good catch for anything pretty and well baited.

Darling, we *are* being cheated by time, we are wasting time. You say in one part of your letter *three* months. In another more unguarded moment *six* months! Why must it be *three months* even? Are you cautious of leaving someone or must you be there now? Can't the work be hurried up? You've been at it four months now. Darling, at times like this, when I think of it, I begin to panic. I ask myself why you're not out here now. You said in one letter that you could, with an easy happy heart, come out here now, while you couldn't have before. Darling, that means it doesn't matter about how unhappy I felt, simply *you* must be content absolutely about something before you undertake it. No matter how much misery that entails for someone else.

Darling, I feel I'm going to pieces. I just can't cope with *us* any more. I want you here so much my whole body cries out. You want to come out, for God's sake come. Soon. Before it all does collapse. What is, was 'us' is collapsing and crumbling. And it panics me.

Sweet, read love into all this. Darling, come now and end all this pain and loneliness.

John

9

To Australia ...?

Sometime late in June, I had gone down for a weekend to a country house near Henley owned by Ken Villiers. It had a huge garden which he was landscaping and on the Saturday it was his birthday party. About a hundred friends drove over, the sun shone, it was the height of summer and Ken's boy-friend parachuted down into the garden party as a surprise birthday present. As this was happening I saw Godfrey Winn and his entourage coming towards me, prepared to greet the young Pole, while my host with a firm grip on my arm steered me towards them and introduced me. There was nothing for it but to behave as if I had no idea who my *Doppelgänger* might be. I expressed a great deal of lascivious interest in his whereabouts and escaped to linger in more congenial company. Sadly, I did not take them in for a moment.

There was a small swimming pool with a gazebo built at the side which Ken had designed in the mode of an Oliver Messel set. The gazebo was used as a changing room, and in the summer became an extra bedroom. It was decorated within in the grand manner, with gold cupids, drapes and chandeliers, absurdly camp in fact for its purpose but therefore quite beguiling. It was there I slept and, the following morning, awoke to the sound of a huge splash. I shot up in bed, staring through the open double doors at the pool, and watched as a perfectly formed naked young man arose from the water. We spent the next two hours together. The bed got very wet.

Looking back, I now discern that I was desperately trying to find reasons and people to stop me from going to Australia and continuing the relationship with John. There were reasons and people enough, but there was no great love, for John was there, even though I did not then appreciate how rare was the love between him and me. The young man, let us call him M., was handsome and intelligent; my unconscious decided he would do as the great love substitute. So I set my heart on M. and for the next three weeks attempted to create a relationship where no possibility of one existed.

John wrote, jealous of my life in England. 'Nymph and Shepherd' (another story using Allan Sills as a character) was my third short story to be published in the *London Magazine*.

Randwick
8:vii:59

My dear darling Colin,

I don't know what to say. I was a raging lunatic after reading your letter, it upset me so much. I wish I wasn't so involved with you – then I could read your adventures and be pleased and happy for you. As it is, although I am pleased, a bit of me – most of me is frustrated and angry – none of what you write about can I *share* with you – drawing Madame Callas, Somerset with Waugh and Hartley etc.

I guess a part of me is envious too, but mostly it is anger that all these things are not 'ours' but 'yours', I can't bear to read all about them.

I'm going to be interviewed on national television shortly concerning what I've done overseas and the coming production of *Snow Queen*. I'll be showing some of the more finished designs. I'll do a boost for you there. I already have boosted you around town. The poster's been pinned up for three weeks and still seems bad to me. It's a pity we can't use it. When you see it again I think you'll agree with me.

I was so upset this evening reading your letter that I took off the medallion to send it back to you. It's been on me all the time since you put it there. I've calmed down a bit now, but I think I won't put it on till you're here to do it for me.

Darling, if you're coming out soon – in two months now, I can wait. But I just can't keep on waiting and keeping myself to myself – battling rape and seduction and temptation. I expect you less day by day.

I love you and I want you. And I'm going batty alone without you. Tell me it's all over or come. Either is better than this empty waiting.

Ever,
John

John was right, of course, in that my social life seemed engrossing and exciting, and up to a point it was a substitute. But it could hardly fulfil the depths of my being which were still starved and made their desolate presence felt. However, his next note apologized for what he had felt and said.

14:vii:59

My dearest sweetest Darling,

In just three days' time it's your birthday. For the third time we're not together. First you were in Venice, then you returned too soon from Vienna and this time we're even further apart on other sides of the world.

Forgive me my own sweetie whenever I'm bitchy. I'm just lonely and longing and terribly suspicious. I guess whatever happens I can't stop loving you and wanting you. My mind and body pivot on that moment when with a bottle of champagne in my mitts, my face white and my hands trembling, that moment when I lean forward towards you and take your arm and say 'hello'.

I feel quiet and strong at the moment. Deep down assured that everything is going to be well for us – and soon.

And no Woolf is in the background to make me feel like that! And none of this girl business you've heard in a garbled version from Kester.

I luvs yur. An orful lot!

Happy birthday darling,

John

His next letter divined the reason for my silence. It had to be someone – woman or man? But at last, with sweetness and desperation, he confessed to the same need to find someone, anyone, as a substitute for our relationship.

Sydney
19:vii:59

My dear dear Darling,

It's now two days since your birthday. In between racing around doing six jobs at once, I wondered what you were doing. I hope it was a happy day.

It's now a month since I had a letter from you. A whole month. I've gone to the letter box every day this last week looking for one. I'm at home this weekend. First thing I did as I came in the door was to ask if there were any letters. Weren't any here either. I feel depressed and lonely now – feel that you are beginning to forget – feel that you have found someone. I felt that so strongly the other day – suddenly from nowhere – I don't think I even had you in my mind, I felt an awful pain inside of me – an awful tearing pain as if someone was wrenching something out of me, away from me. And then I vividly thought of you. No darling it wasn't gastric. And then after that, you have never been out of my mind and everywhere I see you, feel you and nearly hear your voice. I feel it so surely that I can write quite sanely what I want to say, have wanted to say, directly to you these last few days. I'm envious of him or her. I'm envious that they can fulfil all the needs I want to fulfil. I'm jealous that their arms don't ache empty wanting you in them. I'm jealous of all the times they joke or smile or please you to make you happy.

But on top of all that, apart from it, a part of me feels happy for you, that you feel more complete now, more sane and quietened. Is it a boy or a girl? I well know it could be either. Do you see him or her often?

I guess I don't want to know very much – as you often pointed out, I'm a coward in many ways, but I would like to know if it's a boy or a girl, if they're important, if you're happy and how it affects us. That girl of Alise's that you mentioned and that your informant bungled in giving details. It's not Alise's daughter but the daughter of a friend. Alise will be over there soon and can tell you more about Cynthia. I did fall in love with her – or was it an infatuation? When you meet her – as I hope, and, as she hopes, soon – you'll understand. She is marvellously beautiful in every way. You know, haunted, intelligent, zany, arty, dry, sympathetic, etc. etc.

It fell through for a number of reasons and very quickly. One of them, the biggest one, was that you were always there and she sensed it (I had told her all about us). So for the most part I was bloody impotent and moody and depressed. We're still friends, still see a lot of each other – well, coffee once a week – but it's just that and nothing more.

You warned me not to go to parties etc., well knowing what I'm like when I'm high etc. Well, some weeks ago I went to a couple. Got involved with someone at each. Went to bed with them – that old 'physical need' you used to excuse so much with – and couldn't do a damn thing. Of course I didn't let them have me. So all there was was a frustrated evening for them and embarrassment for me the next morning.

You see darling, that idealism and ideas of faithfulness don't even enter into it for me. You are constantly there. I have only to begin to think of you and the barest dregs of passion die away. You haunt me, your body barricades mine from others. And yet alone I'm so randy for you I nearly go mad, stark mad with desire and frustration and a cock aching and pining for your body.

And that's all that's been near me. In one way this might seem a confession of misdeed, essentially it is a testament of how much I long for you, love you and keep myself for you.

Darling, are you coming out here still? Honestly? One other reason why I wanted to, still do want to, keep myself for you was I wanted to spare you the hurt of meeting people whom you felt, and rightly, had known me.

First night of *Snow Queen* is now 14 August. Very early in August I'm appearing on TV talking about the play. I'll be talking about you too and showing some of the designs.

I thought I could escape you and I find myself yet more enmeshed in you.

Yours, and only yours,
John

Before I received this last letter I wrote to him. I had dumped all idea of M. some days before, realizing my own idiocy.

Oh my Darling,

I love you, I love you, I love you and I haven't written for over three weeks I know because I've been in a frightful nasty desperate emotional panic about just about everything with you in the heart of it all and Australia and us, and only this morning am of head and shoulders out of it: but if I was seeing you with a bottle of champagne in your mitt, I'd simply cry and cry and cry and cry with relief, with fury, with *anguish* at having to do without my other half for so long. Darling I'm no good without you. I miss you beyond everything. I miss your passion, I miss our dottiness.

The shipping company are booking me in a cargo boat for middle September so I should be with you late October, maybe sooner. I have two murals to do for people before that, as well as the series to finish and a new one of politicians which I shall say I can't do or else I'd still be here at Xmas.

My cock has shrivelled up through non-use. I am dead sexually. Horrified at the thought of one night stands with ephemeral camp lads. I am pursued by Furies. I don't sleep very well. I'm thinner. I'm browner.

Darling, let me try and explain a little why I've been so panicky. 1. Papa discovered Allan doing some typing and chucked him out of the house in a white hot raging neurotic fury, which brought on a family row on a vast scale. 2. I'm going crazy not having sex and not wanting it but wanting something like us and knowing it doesn't happen except twice in sixty years. 3. I was hurt deeply – oh love, more than I can say, by discovering for certain that you were fucked by some shit who gave you clap. I'll tell you how I found out. I never knew before at all, the business of saying I'd met the man was a red herring to see what your reaction was, the fact you didn't answer it made me suspicious, but I buried the suspicion again. You see the awful thing is that I love you so much that I trust you implicitly and if you actually say 'no' there wasn't anyone, I believe you, just like that, even if I realize it is against common sense. You remember the spot on my bum, it grew bigger and started bleeding so I went to Rodney Long who sent me to MacDonald who cut it off. He talked about you. He's still dotty about you and sends his love. And quite indiscreetly and gaily, he said how amused you were because the man had such a small cock you didn't think there could be any harm in it. That was three weeks ago and I left the hospital crying like mad, all through Stratford, it must have been a pretty sight. I could have taken you having sex with someone, but you used to say all the time that I was the only one who fucked you, that your bum was mine, that you hated being fucked except by someone you loved. Even if it did happen six months ago, it happened a month before we last made love together – and darling, that fact took some taking. I know you were unhappy then and I suppose I can see how something like that could happen but oh God it *hurt*.

Don't be humiliated now by the fact that I do know. But remember darling, I could have taken it much easier then if you'd told me, and it caused me a lot of unnecessary suffering and unrest when it needn't have done. We're quite strong enough to take things like that. It's not even that it's big enough to make the slightest difference. I just can't bear you lying in your teeth, you lying in my arms. But you know I've done it as well so what's the difference. Five candles to be lit and ten prayers to be said that in future we *won't* repeat *won't* lie to each other.

Darling, I love you, I love you, I love you and I'm joining you very soon in that huge double bed.

C.

The scene with my father was crucial to what happened that year. I had reached a stage in the writing of my novel, which was set in Vienna, where I needed a clean typed copy. Allan was a touch typist and offered to do it, as well as various letters to do with *The Times Literary Supplement* commission. He came to Croydon and worked in the large study-bedroom I had on the ground floor. Father returned for lunch and saw him through the open window typing away. My father's spirit, I always considered, was of great liberality, but like so many others he had never thought it through, and I must have seen him to some extent in a fictional guise. For a few moments Allan became for father everything loathsome in me. He could hate and rant against Allan, when he suppressed those feelings about me. Within seconds he had become a towering, hysterical tyrant screaming out for Allan's immediate dismissal from *his* house. In my room we heard the noise as he stormed at my mother, then the door flew open and he said it all again to us.

It is odd how at such moments, high in hysteria and therefore drama, we all seem to fall back on clichés of gesture and speech patterns. He stamped his foot and pointed to the door. I heard myself say, 'If Allan goes, I go too.' And out we went. I was shaking with fury and indignation and swore never to return again. Of course I did, after a few days (my work was there) but I knew that I could not stay there for long.

John had sent me an LP of Lotte Lenya singing Berlin theatre songs by Kurt Weill, which was then difficult to buy here. The record sleeve had a highly theatrical portrait of her by Saul Bolasni; we were already Lenya groupies. Accompanying it was a photograph of John modelling clothes in some back alley in Sydney which struck me as both absurd and unflattering.

John had introduced me to Stevie Smith, her one novel and the poems. He had first editions of two of her early collections, which I possessed and took along to my meeting with her. Stevie went through the books correcting all the printer's errors and scribbling more lines of poetry.

Croydon
22:vii:59

My own Darling,

The anniversary present has just arrived and is playing now. It's marvellous. I couldn't be better pleased or more excited. It's a record I've wanted and meant to buy for myself. It brings back Vienna. You, Sooky, that flat of Sooky's – everything. Thank you very much. I know how much you must have wanted to keep it. But I'll bring it (with other records, I've got 14 now, including Cranks!) so we can share it.

I've just written to Stevie Smith, who I'm having lunch with next week and then drawing. I'm reading the *Yellow Paper* novel which I love – must get the others.

This is merely to say – thank you. Thank you. And all my love.

C.

My next letter expresses no surprise at John's feelings for Cynthia. What he had told me struck too many similar notes within myself. I am not particularly honest though. M. is moved back in time and I seem to recall that our sexual gymnastics in the gazebo were hardly a failure. But my heart was not in it and that, after all, is inherently what sexual pleasure is about.

Croydon

24:viii:59

My dear Darling,

I'm sorry you had to think and feel that I found someone else. Your long honest letter came this morning. I'm happy to tell you that I haven't. Neither a boy or a girl. No one.

My love for you has eaten me up whole. Like you, in these long months, I've been to bed with someone only once and it was a complete failure and that was some months ago. I don't want sex with anyone except you. For sex now is completely bound up with love, and that you have.

I'm terribly tired of thinking and feeling and thrashing everything out, but I'll be with you very soon.

All my love,

C.

Sydney

27:vii:59

My dear dear Darling,

Oh thank God for a loving letter from you. I would hate to tell you what awful thoughts were going through my mind and when I complained bitterly to those here who know of us, what they said must have happened. I recently wrote two letters to you I couldn't dare post, they were so full of anguish and doubt and suspicion and self-pity. Darling, I was going mad not hearing from you. For days and days I would go to the letter box and there'd be nothing from you and then all day such a keen pain inside me as if from the other side of the world you were mutilating me, physically mutilating me. It was so sharp and hurting that I still believe you have found someone, that you are making love to someone and that every time you do this hurts and pains me, so close we are.

Of course I am wearing the medallion again, I couldn't bear to be without it, it so comforts me when I miss you most.

Darling, don't doubt us, trust us, we shall find ourselves again quickly. We'll lie in bed for days together when you arrive here, the bedside stacked with drink and goodies and KY and the sheets sweet-smelling and your boy more loving and wanting you than ever before. My life has no meaning without you, no fixed straight line, no real happiness.

Sweetheart, come sooner rather than later, October. Can't you finish the series and the murals very quickly and then fly out or at least catch a quick passenger ship?

Hugh Hunt, I finally got to a rehearsal. He was impressed – and by the way, liked the costume designs a lot, I saw him going through them more than once.

I'll try to get you into designing for the National Theatre, the Elizabethan. You can help yourself your end. Anthony Quayle is going to be the next boss when Hunt leaves in October or sooner. Quayle will have a lot of power to employ you. Get yourself an introduction to see him now, tell him – true too – that theatre design is shocking here and that you'd like to do some work. He's anti camp and anti David Webster, I hear, so be careful. Name of theatre is Elizabethan Theatre. I'll help you this end in this and other ways. I thought I might not have heard from you because you had gone on to the Continent for a holiday, that made me most upset. Darling, get this work over and rest on the boat or plane. Then too, as soon as you arrive if you like, I'll plan for us to have a little cottage on the water away from everyone.

I'm not bedding with anyone. My God but that's the truth. I can understand how you must have been hurt about that silly indiscreet fool MacDonald. Darling, my bum is yours and only yours. Here in Australia it's not been touched let alone anything more.

Darling, make this last time apart as short as you can. Please please please.

Darling oh darling,
John

In fact, this loving letter from John arrived just before the last act began. Little did I know what I was doing, but in my search for something, *anything*, to call a halt to the relationship I had to go further back into my own depths and what had helped to create my own identity.

When I was fourteen I had met, through a school chum, a family with bookcases stacked with literature and classical music, with children winning scholarships to Cambridge, and I fell in love with the idea of the family as much as with any single person within it. However, these concepts nearly always gather around one individual and the daughter, Jill, who was two years older than me, became the centre of my adolescent being. We wrote long letters to each other, and hers became part of how I saw the world. It was all, as these relationships tend to be, vividly real and unreal at the same time.

It is naïve of us always to underestimate the competitiveness in relationships, especially when we are young. I see this drive as part of the creative impetus and our basic familial competitiveness is perhaps the most powerful. A spark of showing off then made me send a letter to Jill, suggesting we see each other again and mentioning my friendship with E. M. Forster. Our relationship had come to an abrupt halt six years before when I had my first passionate, though short-lived, affair with Jan, the Polish man I had met when working as a ward orderly.

I took Jill to the Hungaria restaurant for dinner. We ate early as she had to catch a train and we were the only ones there. A violinist serenaded us, to Jill's embarrassment. I remember her making gestures above her head as if swatting a fly to get rid of him. We came from totally different worlds, and our lives now were further apart than they had ever been. But none of that seemed to matter. The past, and all its symbolism, was far stronger than anything else. Besides, I was to be used in the unconscious battle that Jill had with her mother. We arranged to have ten days

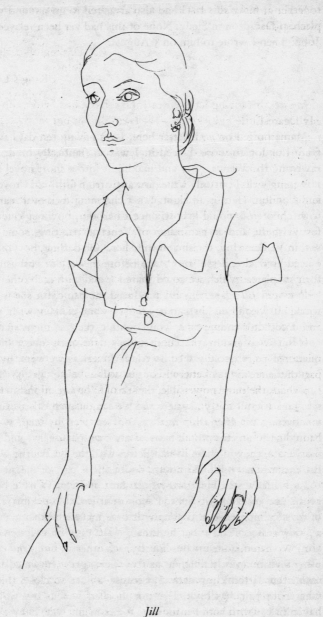

Jill

together at King's Lynn. I had also arranged to go out and visit Michael Davidson in Sicily. None of this had yet been relayed to John. Then I wrote to him on 5 August.

King's Lynn
5:viii:59

My Dearest,

Mama posted on your letter here, I am having ten days away from London to write. I need it. I was so frantically tired. I'm rewriting the Vienna story and making it into a short novel and it is going well, I can only write now away from filthy old Croydon and London. Here is all right. It's a charming medieval market town, how you would love it, once a harbour, now neglected, a festival here, and an exhibition of Venetian painting, some we saw in Venice. How I wish you were here. Oh darling, how much I need your closeness – our grace before meals, our enthusiasm for new places, which we could share for and with each other.

I've seen *Jill* again, this has produced the panic, for she is my roots, but I don't understand it. I must try and explain; when you left, I couldn't endure it, as you couldn't, the one night stands, couldn't even endure the cheap glossy nauseating queer life – queers to be bearable had to be young lovers as we were, living together and faithful, otherwise it was waste, waste, waste.

Unendurable and impossible, there had to be a relationship that was creative, all this you knew and we taught each other except you were a *lot wiser* than me: so you see, step by step, I was brought back to the whole basis of my own personality and the whole concept of loving, which began with the gentle, the wise, the extraordinary Jill. Without a doubt she is part of me, at my roots I am twisted inextricably into hers and always have been ever since you've known me. I suppose it isn't merely just a lot of mystical nonsense, it is simply that we met each other at such a *formative* period, 14 to 19, and that (as the case with Kester and you) we shared, quite unconsciously, each other's vision, and each other's vision (vastly different as they were) grew entwined into each other. I think my darling, because we are so close, this is what your pain has been. I've not violated you in any way, I haven't slept with her or made love to her in any way, but maybe

198

you've felt a usurper in that closeness that we have. The fact that I write and paint is bound up in those roots as they are in the roots that we have. My panic has been the necessity to make a decision. I don't want to live with her but maybe I should marry her? And yet when I am with her I am constantly reminded of you and forced back to the kind of electric ecstatic happiness we shared. If you blockade my senses and my body in this way, aren't I really deceiving myself with a kind of mystical hocus-pocus and vaguely trying to make a brother/sister relationship into something it cannot be? Life is hell without sex and sensuality being bound up with the deeper issues, while a part of that is the shared enthused intimacies, then and only then come the electric ecstasies. Aren't I right?

And my sweet darling, it is rare, isn't it rare? Aren't we both funny individual odd people, who suddenly struck, not a spark, but a great big bonfire, in each other, and if so *who are we to leave it blazing* and do nothing about it?

Sweetheart, I saw Eustace Chesser the other day and had lunch with him, he's very fond of you and admires you greatly, he told me *not* to come out. He said that if it was so perfect in Vienna, that was a moment of truth which cannot be repeated. But we're not going to live in Vienna, I said. And we both know so much more and value each other more, now. I think he's wrong, don't you? I'm sure. I'm convinced he's wrong.

Don't despair. Because of the panic I've also got myself into a financial mess. But darling I mean to come to you and so nothing can stop it. Maybe I can fly out in middle September.

Then Faber & Faber want to publish the three short stories and another if I've got it, in a volume of six new writers, who each give three or four stories, as a way of launching them. They are also interested in the Vienna story – which really has quite funny patches now. But all this has got to be done by the end of August as poor James MacGibbon has waited since January for the Vienna story.

No one is in London in August anyway who I can draw. Oh my goodness, I shall bring with me your two Stevie Smith books, in which she has written very curious things like – 'publisher's mistake, silly ass, S.S.!!' She was so delicious. And for my anniversary present to you, you are getting a drawing of her, by me.

The one the T. L. S. will do is very *outré*. I'm quite won over by her and her work.

So darling, in my panic I said to myself I've got to get away not only to here but to some sun, so forgive me and don't mind too much, but I have taken this flat in Sicily for three weeks, and go on your gala night the 15th to the 5th September, I just want to write and paint in the sun and rest, I shall be lonely and I shall want you, but darling I didn't know what to do. Everyone says how much they are pro us, but everyone says, don't go to Australia. I don't listen to them, but they are worrying. Forgive me sweetheart for going to Sicily. Maybe I'll just catch a boat from Sicily, I may do that, and never come back here at all, it's one way. Don't be horribly angry with this letter and write me a stinker. I do hate your stinkers. They make me cry. So do your loving letters anyway – sometimes I can't tell the difference. And Darling, do know that I love you beyond everything, and inside me, I'm quite certain, that what I feel is the true and only thing, the fact of just having you naked in my arms is the only satisfactory conclusion to this useless stupid parting.

All my love,
Colin

I have noticed within myself many conflicts, one being the urge to tell the truth and, in contrast to it, a longing for secrecy or privacy. This strife leads inevitably to seeming to be devious or just being found out in barefaced lies: a failing in others I have always disliked intensely, while having to recognize how culpable I am myself. Too late in life I have adopted Bertrand Russell's wise observation that it is pointless to lie as you will always be found out.

For the life of me I cannot understand why I did not tell John that I was going to stay with Michael Davidson. The flat I was supposedly renting, Michael already had. Was it because there was a further complication still? Michael had promised me the love of a Sicilian lad throughout this stay. Whether one can call it that seems debatable. Others might say I was buying the sexual services of a young lad and Michael was a pimp. I found this notion erotic and alluring, as have many Northern Europeans who are drawn to the Mediterranean countries. This certainly was not confessed to either John or Jill.

10

... or Marriage?

·

My challenge from King's Lynn was met magnificently. John wrote back on the day he received my letter, his second attempt being calm and sensible. Before leaving for King's Lynn I had said to my mother, 'I am either leaving for Australia or marrying Jill.' She replied at once, 'For God's sake go to Australia.' Being naturally perverse I was inclined to ignore her advice. My distaste for living at home under father's roof was driving me to Norfolk, to Sicily, perhaps to Australia. Odd that I didn't just rent a room in London, but there is something deep within me which retreats from looking for homes for myself, a distaste so strong it can lead to inaction, living out of a suitcase, a car or shabby hotel rooms.

10:viii:59

My dear dear Darling,

I'm sorry you feel in such a mess. It does seem so from your letter which came this morning. I can well understand how upsetting it must be to meet Jill again. I remember how upsetting it was to meet G. again and the terrific pull there was to restart the affair again. In some ways G. came along at what was for me a more formative period than when I was with Kester. There were a number of times when I found myself on the edge of asking him to start again, times when he sensed it and was most frantic. Yet one can't go back. I'm glad the words could never form on my lips – you stopped them. One just can't go back. Or if you do then you live in a half coloured sundown world, each drawing hard on past memories and experiences to cover and hide the gaps that have formed. And this no matter how much you are still fond

202

of each other, still entwined and influenced. This is one of the things that disturb me now about us. If a big affair for either of us came up, then there would be no more of us. Of that I would make sure. I'd insist rather than be witness to painful efforts on each other's part to adjust. Of course at such times one does go mad with money. I spend foolishly and recklessly when I'm in a mess. It's a pity though when we both need money.

In some ways it must be wonderful meeting Jill again. It is some time I know. Is she much changed? I wish I had met her. Why didn't you arrange it? I know how much of you originates in her. And I like to think the parts of you I love. Don't feel unhappy or messed up about it. Give it a try if you want. Become her lover again if need be. I think that it wouldn't be very satisfactory but I might be wrong.

Darling, you are right about us. There was – and I hope will be – something electric about our relationship. Life becomes full and meaningful and exciting and even surprising. If you can experience that with anyone else you're a lucky dog, luckier than I am. Don't darling, marry Jill just yet. Don't dash into it as a solution. We've tried these 'solutions' before and as yet they haven't worked. It would just be hysteria to up and marry her, even if she wouldn't mind being 'another Madame Gide'. It does sound like a lot of mystic hocus-pocus with regard to Jill, but then others might think the same with regard to what has been between us.

Darling, you've got to make your mind up and not dither, either make all arrangements tidy and come out, or don't and tell me so. There is a time limit to us, not one that we impose but one that is there in the course of things. A point is approaching, past which we cannot be together as we were before. And if we are together again then it must be as it was before, nothing less would do.

And what hurt, and still does, is that you could go to Italy, that we both love, without me, and that by doing that you lengthen this parting by at least a month.

I have for your birthday present a beautiful opal shot with darkest richest turquoise and emerald. It's like fire. Shall I ever be able to give it to you?

Darling, don't get mixed up. I love you and shall always. You are my flesh and my blood and I am yours. Darling, don't let us waste away. Give me that that I have such hunger for.

J.

This letter of John's went by express to Croydon. I found out its existence when I telephoned my mother from Heathrow. She sent it on to Sicily. Whether she made a comment on my decision to marry Jill, I cannot recall. Probably she made an utterance like 'Oh dear', or 'Crummy lorum'. Neither my family nor Jill's were much pleased at our plans. I wrote from Messina and told John.

Darling,
    The following letter is clumsy and cruel. So prepare yourself. I have tried to explain for I should hate you to misunderstand. As always I am torn in two. But I have come to a decision, through which no one or anything influenced me except, I think, the most essential things. So darling, we are forced to abide by it and you must trust me enough and believe that somehow it is the right one. If you can, write to me here. If you want to that is. But don't send it express. There is always such a pantomime getting it. It should get back inside the 5th.

Sicily
20:viii:59

My sweet Darling,
    I missed your express letter by three minutes last Saturday night, I rang mama from the air terminal and she told me it had arrived, so she sent it on, and I got it yesterday. Almost immediately I found a bottle of the cheapest nastiest foulest vino in my hand which never left me the whole day, pissed in Sicilian back streets, I fell over goats, hens and lizards.
    I'm marrying Jill very soon, in about six weeks. In one sense I have always been married to her. We didn't see each other for five years at all, and the last year before that was a screamingly unhappy one because Jan had turned up. My darling, the ironic thing is that it was you that led me back to her. It was because we belonged so completely to each other. And you with your bullying insistence on digging down to the essential roots of a

relationship. We found these together and I rediscovered that this was oxygen to the desperately ill. You see sweetheart, I could not bear another queer affair; you fulfilled and completed this longing so perfectly that now it no longer exists, not in any way; emotionally, physically, sexually. But there is a great longing and that is simply for roots, for closeness, it is only in that, that I feel I can work, and this you taught me, or we taught ourselves. And she is an essence of exactly that; she is at the heart of me, at the centre where we lived so closely. So you see I feel I have no choice at all. I have thrashed and thrashed the matter out; I have, as far as one can, dug down into my own motives for this action, and though inevitably one uses other people in love (that is always a factor and can't be helped) I can see it essentially and ultimately only as legally and spiritually recognizing a fact that already exists. In your letter you gave a lot of space to this business of going back to a relationship and how wrong it is. I quite agree if the relationship is exhausted but Jill and I never got going, on my side it was pure spirit, from the age of fourteen when I met her to when I was nineteen when I met Jan, it was simply a very profound (as it seemed to us, then) intellectual, spiritual relationship, on her side to that was added emotion. But with me, as you know, then all the emotion and sex was directed to boys. It now has only just caught up and become bound up with love and the whole thing for the first time is a whole, so in fact it is a new relationship altogether.

This roots thing for want of a better word is the only consideration, a kind of observance of the truth. I think darling disaster comes if you don't, it is angering the Gods for it is going against the few clues that they've been kind enough to leave around. You gave it to me, and I think we could still give it to each other, but for how long? O God what a fucking world; I have been in such a panic because of the effect all this might have on you; darling, you must try and forgive me for not coming out and for saying I would for so long which has led you to stay in Sydney, won't you stay there now? I was sincere and honest about this because I longed for it for so long and because of this I kept Jill locked out for I believed and rightly so that all my responsibilities were with you. I have never loved any boy as deeply and as hugely as I love you, you must know this, and believe it, for I am certain, things as large as this don't just stop.

O my darling my darling, if I could only have you in my arms now.

Colin

But before this reached him, he had written to me again – a slightly drunken letter, carefully avoiding the shadows that were beginning to close in on us.

Sydney
23:viii:59

My dear dear Sweetie,

Don't mind this pink paper – it's from work and it's all that's to hand. It's Sunday evening and I've got Italian songs on the radio, some Gauloises, a big slog of VAT ... and I'm sitting in my pretty sitting-room. Bruno, who's my stage manager – he's Austrian and terribly butch and normal and fond of me – and I have been painting all day. It's so lovely now I don't want to go out of the room. Our sitting-room – yours and mine – has got two white walls, white ceiling and one gorgeous Tibetan Gold wall and another prepared for bronze metal paint. It looks bright and terribly smart. With a turquoise carpet I've got my eye on it will be very pleasant. Before, in the dark ages, it was all greys and dirty blues. I've got a fine Dufy print well framed and what with a couple of your gouaches and my blue and gold sarong, it is going to be so very pretty. I wish you were here to tell me what colours you wanted. The spare room I'm going to paint all white, and have special daylight globes so that you can paint away to your heart's content.

Darling, I need love again, I need it so much that if I can't have yours then I must find someone else and soon. Even if it wasn't so deep and soul shaking as ours. Ours was like some savage tropical flower, brilliant and savage and rare. Forgive me the terrible image, but I'd make do with a garden variety of love. I need someone – God I need *you* – just to be silly with, to flout my body in front of them and be so deep deep happy to be wanted and to be full of want, to know that half I feel need not be said, to wake in the morning and reach over and kiss, to tart up and go on a razzle dazzle through town, to work together and feel that it had all borne worthwhile fruit, to again go to a play or a film with 'myself' in someone else, to fall through and through space in that rapture that comes in bed, to know that *honest* passion again.

Darling, this is no ultimatum. It is just to say how I feel now after six months, half a year, a one hundredth or less of a lifetime without any of all that. I want you by me darling, for the biggest most vital adventure of our lives. I want you to fill this emptiness. I love you and long for your arms, your pot belly and knobbly knees and shopping bag balls and that cock that has yet to have an ode and you and you and you. Darling, my heart feels as if it bursts out towards you. At this moment I know right now, you will be aware of it.

J.

His next letter, a cry of pain, of anger and bewilderment, arrived in Sicily. I was working each day on my novel, *An Absurd Affair*, the first to be published. As true as his word Michael had presented me with a sixteen-year-old Sicilian lad, Pippo, with dark glossy curls and the look of a Caravaggio about him. He enjoyed hugs and kisses and a little daily adolescent sexuality. His friend, Angelo, was Michael's lad and the four of us would lunch together after my morning's work. I felt relaxed and happy, beneath the Sicilian sun, the dramas I had engendered seemed not of my world. John's pain hurt and confused me, but I felt I could do nothing about it. Everything he said had no effect on me any more. I find this now a terrible confession, as if I had become some other creature, and I do not pretend to understand it. It is, of course, true of human nature that when terror and cruelty have been caused by ourselves, we distance ourselves from the result. It is the Mozart concert in the concentration camp syndrome. As T. S. Eliot put it, 'Human kind can bear very little reality.'

25:viii:59

My dear Colin,

I got your letter about one hour ago. I guess I was very hysterical, fortunately I bumped into Carle Cross, a pleasant gay

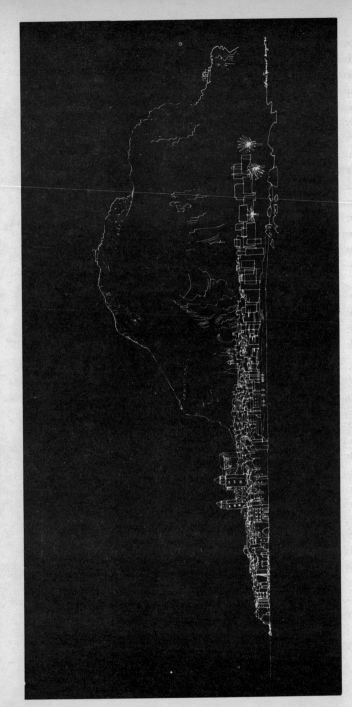

Cefalu – Sicily. A drawing by Colin Spencer

boy here and he's loaded me up with three double Scotches. It deadens the pain and lets me write you the semblance of a sane letter. I don't know what to say. My whole body and mind and spirit are numb. There's nothing left after all the tears and pain.

Darling, if you want to marry Jill how can you write 'if only you were in my arms'? How could you have written the last time 'when I'm with her there is none of that electric vitality between us'? Isn't it the most rash thing to race into a marriage with her? It does seem like that, no, it is that, racing head over heels to be tied to her, to have her with you. If it was as important as we are you would wait a few months. Darling, you asked me not to fall in love with anyone soon after leaving you. Now you want to *marry* Jill. It is all so terribly irretrievable, irrevocable. If you love me at all, if you have ever really loved me, then please give yourself and her and me some little breathing space.

Darling, it is madness, pure and utter madness, to marry so soon. She's not going to fade away unless you catch her in the next few weeks. Please darling, do *not* marry her just now. Not this side of Christmas. Live with her, make love to her but love, *do not marry her*.

Darling, when I met Cynthia I wanted to marry her. There's a charming girl who's very fond of me and who wants to marry me now. I too am very tempted because I too want to escape this useless wasteful camp world. But darling, *that* is no reason to marry someone; to escape from unhappiness which one should solve oneself. I too don't want another queer affair, not after us. But that for me is no reason for marriage. It is a reason for battling for us to be together, to hold what we still have. Darling, it could last as long as we wanted it to last, our whole life through if we wanted. And leave us happy and contented at the end of it.

You are responsible for me. Now you rush into this and think to throw that responsibility away. Darling, to marry so soon now will kill me. I mean it. And for that death, physical or spiritual, you are responsible. Do you know how much I love you? How can you know? We have let it grow, we've built it up carefully and lovingly between us. It is utter vandalism to pull it down, to break it.

I think in all this you have considered yourself too much. How about Jill? Can you take that with courage and honesty? And how about me? Can you love me and do this in a few weeks? If you do I shall believe there was *no* love in you for me, it would be so callous.

I want either to fly to England to see you, or to send you the money to come out here for a couple of months. I'll give up work here and come to you in a matter of days. Just for you to see me, to talk to me for a few hours. It is a big thing yet a small thing when I think of what is at stake. Then when I've seen you, I'll go, or you could come with me. In some ways it would be the only thing to do to show you how important *we* are. Or come out here for a few weeks. I'll pay the air fare. Please darling. This so vitally involves us that we must see each other beforehand. You can't be so heartless to marry and end us without us seeing each other. If Jill has waited so long for you, if it is so vitally important then wait a little longer. For all that was between us.

I intend to make tentative bookings on a plane. I could be in England before the middle of September. Today I'll discuss with my boss if he'll take me back after I've come back. For I shan't stay in England if you do marry.

Or darling, come out here if only for a month. Think of it as a holiday. Think of it as the sanest thing you could do at the moment to the three of us.

If you want me, say and I'll come immediately. It is so easy to have me in your arms again to renew, even better, those drawings lost, to do everything better and happier than before. *Give us a chance of survival.*

J.

The letters from John arrived fast and furiously. Michael and I left Messina and visited Taomina and Noto for a few days. There, enchanted by such classical symmetry quietly decaying beneath a surface mould of ferns and fungi, I drew some of the buildings. I could not have transmuted them into pure line if it had not been for John: the fact that I now saw architecture with his sense of what was fruitful for my drawings, I owed to my time with him.

When we returned, three letters awaited me.

Colin Colin my dear dear Darling,

If I don't keep writing to you I'll go round the bend. Oh sweetheart, I couldn't go to sleep at all last night, I lay there thinking of you and you married and the end of everything we stood for and I writhed and tossed in bed the whole night. Somewhere about dawn I must have finally gone to sleep for an hour.

Sweetheart, what what what is happening to us? Darling, time and time again you've written that you wanted to come out here, that this would be a big adventure, that the last anniversary would be the last one apart and then this letter, this terrible one that burns a hole in my pocket, and that like some crazy hypnotized thing I must read and read again.

Darling, your decision – can I really call it a decision? – affects us tremendously, nullifies what I hoped would be a fruition of two years together, would be recompense for all this intense pain and longing and loneliness.

Darling, could you really love me and still rush into this? You've been seeing Jill how long now again? Is it so urgent that you must marry immediately? If only for me, for the barest peace of mind I can have, please delay it a little. Please. These roots you speak of, that you need. What are they essentially? Security? Love? Understanding? Belonging? These you had with me. Surely you don't want to *settle* down already, a married man with a house and all the attendant pulls that castrate work? You know that with me you did your best work, that it came to a kind of fruition with me. All that exciting vital life we'd planned – Australia, the islands, the States, Europe, Italy. Does that come to nothing? For us both those few days in Italy meant so much because *we* were together. We give things meaning. Jill can too I'm sure, but can she give you that deep meaning *and* coat everything done and seen and touched with that glaze of *fire* that we did? You said that you didn't find that bonfire with her. You said we had lit one which shouldn't go out. Darling, don't let it go out. We lit a fire which illumined everything and, oddly enough, was a guiding light to others. There is so much to be done and now you are the only person I can do it with. How can you be so cruel as to qualify us;

I am the only *boy* you have ever loved so deeply. Only *boy*! But not counting girls? Not counting Jill? Darling, that is an untruth. A terrible blatant untruth. Be honest. What was *is* – yes is still – vivid and savage is between us, joining us. And darling, it is not to be found again. I hate this nether region, neither dark, nor light. Living and half living it certainly is. Darling, you can't suddenly not be in love with me. Did you lie or exaggerate in those loving letters that came so recently?

Please darling, come here to see me. If only for two weeks. I've already set things in motion so that you can easily come for the shortest time. Darling, this you owe to me. Please have enough sensibility to wait and to try to see me. Darling, how hurt you were about Woolf. Can you imagine how hurt I am now? And have you no responsibility towards me? To me who is as much a part of your body as your arms, as much a part of your being as the air you breathe? Darling, do not let me go mad.

27:viii:59

My dear Darling,

I sent the earlier letter express. I didn't realize you meant letters to Sicily, I thought you meant to home. I hope it wasn't too much of a pantomime.

Darling, darling, I can't co-ordinate anything. Today I haven't been able to do any work. All day those words jumping and careering, 'so I'll marry Jill in a few weeks very soon' in my mind. Oh darling, how how how could you be so cruel? If I was drowning would you refuse to rescue me, if I was hungry wouldn't you succour me, if I was thirsty wouldn't you give me drink? How then darling, when I feel annihilated will you do nothing to save me, to keep me whole?

Oh darling darling,

J.

31:viii:59

My dear Darling,

I go every hour it seems to the post box to see if there's another letter from you, one this time to make me a little happier, I don't think any letter could make me more miserable and frantic than I am now.

My dear it is like a death sentence hanging over my head, nowhere in it can I find any place of rest. I don't know what to say to you.

Oh sweetheart, as you love me wait wait wait, put off if only for a little time this marriage. Just so that I don't feel this sudden terrible pain inside of me that it is rash and wrong.

Try, you have often said that you were married to me. Use all those memories of me now to grasp what it is you give up. Darling, you are still so much in love with me. You can't hide that from yourself.

Can you bear to think of our happiness together? I can't bear to. It would send me mad.

J.

I find my reply sincere but utterly nauseating. Jill, at that time, was inexperienced in relationships. The quotation from her letter, repeated by me to John, shows that she lived in an ideological fantasy world and I had somehow been infected with it. My lofty tone is unbearable. If John had appeared, it would have vanished amongst tears and laughter.

Sicily
Tuesday

I arrived back in this town late last night to find your two letters waiting for me, the third one arrived this morning. I spent most of the night and all of today trying carefully to think clearly. At first I was prepared to cable Jill and to tell her to stop the banns being read out in Church this Sunday when they begin. But now I have decided that it would do no good at all. I'm quite certain seeing each other wouldn't either. By now I know exactly what would happen if we did. I could not bear to see you so unhappy and would do anything in my power to stop it, which means that we'd live anywhere in the world together again, but it would only be temporary for I would still end up by marrying Jill even if it was five or ten years time, that is as inevitable as Aristophanes' two halves.

You said not more than six letters ago that all you cared about was my happiness and that if I found anyone else you could in the end be happy about it. That was very noble, it is understandable that in practice it doesn't work. I have not stopped loving you; I would like, if it were possible, for you to understand that people who have really loved each other don't suddenly stop. I never stopped loving Jill in those five years; it was simply that its nature changed, that certain aspects went underground, changed their course. If we accept Auden's view, which I do, that love is based upon mutual need, it is simply that at this moment I need Jill more than I do you. I cannot help this and in the end, however badly you feel ill treated and to an outsider it looks as if I'm a rotten bastard, I can't be blamed for this, for it's not within my control.

These three letters are more hysterical than any letters I've ever had from you, things are more distorted than ever. I can't argue with you.

When I reread your letters all my sanity goes; you seduce me by words, and I cry for your suffering and I think in the end of my own. Oh why the hell did you ever have to go away, and then none of this could have happened. Of course to a certain extent you're right in a lot of things you say. We did; still have maybe; so much that was good and necessary and vital for us, it was just that in my wilderness of this six months I had to dig deeper still, beyond you and me, and there I found Jill. It is very very far away from being anything near a brother/sister relationship; let me make that quite clear – carnal, in fact.

My darling, you plead with me for a chance of survival of our love; my darling, it would be very easily done to just come out to Australia, but I don't think any longer I could give you enough love, and I think in the end I would be committing a worse crime. You see my darling, I think the tragedy is that though we were enormously strong and our love and our living together seemed, was, wholly happy and profound, the very core and centre of me remained untouched because it wasn't there, years and years before I had given it to Jill, and I had not myself to give. This is something I have only recently known; to come out to you knowing this seems to me a crime first of all to myself and certainly to you and Jill. I don't know how you feel about her but I would like you to know what she feels about you; in a letter last week she said, 'I told you I would like to say something unsayable to John, which is I love him because you have and because he loved you. Even now if you feel his claims are stronger, you must go. I've told you that I would not stop you.'

I cannot and will not phone you, think what a farce it was last time, we could do nothing but sob over the whole Pacific Ocean. And it would be ridiculous for you to come to England and spend that amount of money when I know I cannot change my mind. Of course the thought of you coming terrifies me for you know very well how much you bully me and I know how weak I feel. John, you've got to somehow face this and try to understand it and try not to blame me too much.

I have purposely made this letter cold and firm.

Colin

I return to Croydon on the 6th.

John wrote to Croydon several letters to await my return before he had received my last Sicilian letter. This is one which has survived.

Sydney
1:ix:59

Darling,

I want this letter to be waiting for you when you get back home. I try to imagine when you'll read it, if Jill will be with you, and oh so many other terribly depressing things.

Darling, I can't do anything but believe that these last days have been a nightmare, a terrible terrible dream that haunts you even when you're awake. I dream of you consistently, you being cool to me, refusing to recognize me in the street, being caught in some terrible machine and calling out to you and then last night something very wonderful and still very vivid that I was lying on a very furry floor naked in the most impossible positions and you were drawing me and then you came over and we made the most marvellous love. I woke up with a horn up still and feeling miserable and happy all at the one time.

Darling, I once wrote about marriage and you'd said that you would come and kidnap me and then more seriously you advised me not to. I have urgently wanted to marry out here, but I know, know, know that no matter how keen I was on the girl that it was an *escape*. Darling, that there is such a rush makes me think it is an escape you now want.

Darling, oh that letter was so very different from all your other letters, that when you saw me again you would cry with the futility and waste of this parting, that you found you had grown to love me more than ever before. You are terrifyingly a part of me. You are the very sinews and muscles of my body, your heart is in me and mine in you. How can you give your heart to someone else? It lodges in me. Even as we exchanged those token hearts, ring and medallion, you yourself called them symbols of us and of our 'marriage'. What a silly word that looks too when it's written down so boldly.

Darling, if we are not to be together again, send me back my ring for that was a big symbol of us. And then tell me how I am to take the medallion off. It has never been off my neck, no matter what I may have written earlier. With whose hands am I to take it off? I dread to do it. Tell me how.

Tell me how you were able to take off my ring. Maybe it will be easier for you now. But if we are over – and that in the definite logical sense – then these we must return. You always told me to send you back your medallion if we were over as a sign. Send me the ring then and somehow I shall send you your medallion. But, darling, as you love me, do not, please, do not marry till we have done that, till we each have returned to the other what should never have been returned – what we never meant to return.

J.

Then his answer to my Sicilian letter arrived in two successive airmails. The second letter's last paragraph haunted me. There were many prophecies in John's letters at this time, and they all came true. But this paragraph most of all, and perhaps now, after his death, with renewed vigour.

My dear Colin,

What I suppose will be your last letter from Sicily arrived this morning. I can't understand it. Are you so insecure, so unsure of what you are doing that you must be so cold and ruthless? What I needed was something a little human and instead I get this.

The thing I asked you repeatedly was just to wait a little. Surely from all the hysteria you got that! Just to wait, not to marry while the body of what was us is still warm. Did those letters amaze you really? Couldn't you understand what I was and am still feeling?

You shall have no more hysterical letters. But in return I ask you for no letters as callous and hard and afraid as this last one. Yes darling, afraid it is, afraid of me, afraid of what you do, afraid of our ties.

One day you might understand why I was so frantic. It is all bound up with 'at my back I always hear Time's winged chariot drawing near'.

That terrifying sense of time nearly spent already, that old man button-moulder being so close now that he walks in my shadow. It serves me right, I asked too much from those Gods who were already more than generous.

J.

I know those letters were hysterical. Darling, I don't want you to argue with me. But how can I bridge this gap that now seems to separate us? You have no snivelling boy crying his eyes out on your doorstep now, it is a man who stands and demands that you open your heart a little, not a queer boy upset at a loss of a cock but a lover who is an integral part of you. If I plumb down, down, down, down deep, there was nothing queer about us. That word just doesn't enter into it. I am not, my dear, trying to coerce you back into the terrifying queer world. I am just wanting you to remember those times when we gave each other more than our bodies, our hearts, our memories or our souls.

Jill might have always been there just as Kester and G. were always there. Much of me was formed by them, much of you by Jill. This is no new discovery of yours. I unpack Kester's books and cry for the past and what it meant and what it still means. Now darling much of you is from me. Never think to escape that, when you are again in Florence, Venice or Vienna, sometimes when you swim at night, when you lie in a forest, when you fuss in a kitchen over something special or when snow lies on your window-sill. Or reading a poem 'somewhere my heart has never travelled', then suddenly you will know that I am there, you will smell that slight earthiness of my body or touch something which transforms itself into my body, or hear my laugh and see my eyes. We neither can escape. This is the love of my very life and I suspect deeper than all roses the core of yours. And then you will cry as I fear I do now, tears salt with longing and regret.

J.

Here is my inadequate reply. I cannot understand why I continued to lie about staying with Michael, nor why I was against taking advice from anyone older and more experienced. I had just spent three weeks with Michael with plenty of time for us to discuss what I was doing; he would no doubt have been deeply sympathetic to John. Yet I did not broach the subject. I remember once passing over to Michael one of John's letters and he sighed deeply and murmured, 'Poor chap, what pain he is suffering.' But I never once asked him whether he thought I was doing right. To ask for such counsel was then not in my nature. Was it just the arrogance of youth? Not completely; I can remember feeling driven to marry Jill by a compulsion beyond reason which I could not fathom at the time.

Croydon
14:ix:59

My own darling, who isn't my own darling I suppose any more because there is a wretched thing that I suppose the Gods have got called Time and I would like to scream across the gulf of Time and would also like not to be complicated at all nor have several parts of me that insist all at the same time to be fulfilled so there is very little I can do. Been back a week. Got three letters I think from you in the first two days. I took the ring off, vomited, and put the ring back on, that has been the pattern. I've tried three times to take it off, each time my sides have caved in and I felt sick as an inebriated dog. But I suppose it's got to be done.

I do think of what is to happen to you and even myself. I do think, but my sweet darling what is the good, what is the good? If I send you my love or my wretchedness you cannot now believe in its worth.

Love,
C.

Somehow I will take it off before. But I don't know how.

At least this answer told him honestly how afraid I was of his power over me. If he had flown to England I imagine the marriage would have been delayed if not broken off for ever. There is also creeping into both our letters a distaste for the gay world and its inhabitants. I don't think now that is very fair: I think on reflection that what we disliked was what the straight world did to gays, but unhappily we confused the two. While being immersed in society it is difficult to extract oneself and look coolly at the pressures we coped with. Being gay is, after all, a joke in society's eyes. Many sorts of entertainers, from comics to Wogan, still extract derisory laughter from the smallest aside which makes out that being gay means you are less than a complete person, somehow obscurely crippled and inadequate. When the majority of people believe this is a source of hilarity, it needs an effort of will in a gay person to insist that the rest of the world is wrong. Such an effort of will can be an exhausting process.

Croydon
16:ix:59

I was thankful to get your letter in two sections, I know the one I wrote from Sicily was callous, it was meant to be and I told you it was meant to be, for I thought that was the only way to stop your hysteria which I felt only *confused* an issue already complicated.

I am still certainly afraid of *us*, of the power we still seem to possess and you *do* of course, as I suppose you meant to, terrify me when you talk of dying. John, John, my darling, is that fair to me, or if it is true and not some crazy romantic idea shouldn't you go to the doctors now? Of course the whole world is full of you, everything or almost brings you constantly back, and I think, in a way, you are right when you say there was nothing queer about us. I shall never be able to go back to Vienna, ever. But you know, I do wonder now why you ever went away? Yes, I know all the old reasons. Why we wasted those six months in London. It wasn't *only* my fault. We, both of us, mismanaged this last year grossly and I am forced to think that there must have been a particular reason, cause. That through the smokescreen of love letters and the emotions and longings that produce them, beneath that, we, both of us, just didn't want to go on as we had done in Vienna. My darling, I'm sure somehow that is true, for otherwise, *we would have done*. Don't you see? I'm a frightful fatalist and I think the deeply important things happen in spite of oneself, they happen, as it were, beyond oneself. This happened when we first knew each other, it happened when it made me go back to Vienna, and again with a terrifying inexorableness it is happening to me now.

I am ready to believe in the Devil or Angels. My nerves are naked to your pain but I am made helpless my darling, there is nothing I can do! Allow me to wear the ring until the very last moment.

C.

John's next letter also seems to have become infected with this fantasy ideology. The terrible thing about human beings when they are struck down by immense psychological pain, is this urge to take it well, to be good about it, to think only the best of the person who has done us wrong. I am quite sure we would be happier if we behaved truthfully, stormed, cried, wept and cursed. The idea of John loving Jill seems gross, even bizarre, quite as much as she loving him. How could all three of us have pulled the wool over our eyes so willingly?

My dear Colin,

It is difficult to write now. It is rather like shouting into a vacuum, no sound, not even an echo. But I do want to write just this letter for two reasons.

I finally saw *Room at the Top* last night. It moved me tremendously, I think because one of the problems seemed our problem. And then what had been in the back of my mind materialized into a clear thought. That most likely Jill is already expecting a child. Tell her please that I don't feel there is anything unsayable. Tell her – I would if I knew where to write – that I love her and that never have I resented her in any way. I always wanted to meet her and now I'm sorry you never let it come about. I love her and I bear not the slightest grudge against her.

And the second thing. Since that first terrifying letter I have been trying to arrange an air ticket for you to come out here for a few days. I just wanted to be able to offer you the opportunity of coming out here to see me for a very little time. It would have been easy to arrange and the slightest token action I could do, so far away, to show you how important we are. And now I'm afraid it will be too late, or not even wanted.

No hysteria now darling. Just one big nothing. And the inability to do as you ask me, to accept it all. An inability to accept that you could cast off our love like last year's skin.

J.

Two more letters arrived from John, the first quoting my letters back at me. I have to admit that being in love with two people at the same time does not seem odd to me in the least. The reason for this is, as one would expect, complex, but I do not think it that uncommon. Most of us have the capacity to give and receive love from several people at once; it is just that we would find it intolerably confusing to live in such entanglement. Such a state cannot be endured for long, as my own life has shown. Yet we have this compulsion to love more than one person. The obvious reason is a fear of total commitment to just one person, and I would not deny it, though I also distrust that fear in myself and consider it a major stumbling block to any real fulfilment.

My dear Darling,

I seem to write to you so much and you now write so infrequently.

I read some of your letters last night. Darling, I was amazed to read that so late as 5 August, just on the eve of your leaving Sicily, just five weeks ago, *5 weeks*, you wrote what you did. Is it any wonder that that letter from Sicily threw me into a panic – a panic that you said you couldn't understand?

Darling, I'm not throwing words back in your face. I'm not saying please explain. Just that two weeks after this letter you write telling me we're through, that Jill is the only one. No amount of thrashing it out, unless it was the most callous cold reasoning of personal advantage, could make you change so quickly and so violently. Did you really mean all that you wrote before you left. Or was it a romantic literary exercise?

I'll not write again unless you ask me to.

Goodbye
Darling

Sydney
21:ix:59

My dear,

Your letters came this morning, just a day after I said I'd not write again.

Please, darling, if I can read your letter aright, do not rush into this. For God's sake give it a few more weeks. If you love her so then a few weeks is nothing in a lifetime, if it is not so important you might find out what it is all really about.

Doesn't it say something that it so upsets you to take off the ring that symbolizes so much? I have been sick and wretched a long time now. How am *I* to take off the medallion?!!

John

The next letter from John is the last one I have. It was a week later when I wrote to him and explained how my proposal came about. I must say now that a gay bar full of GIs in the middle of

King's Lynn seems so improbable I must have been dreaming, or perhaps seeing what I wanted to see. That it bore any relationship to the K., the drag and sawdust bar of Vienna, now seems also somewhat unlikely.

24:ix:59

My dear Colin,

Marry, murder, kill, do whatever you want to do but *do not*, to ease your conscience, belittle us. I shall hate you for it.

I do doubt you now, because of this turnabout, this rush – that would have hurt you savagely if the position were reversed. Stop, for Christ's sake, telling me how helpless you are. This marriage for you is not something you can step into in one day. All the preparations depend *on you*! You put them into motion, darling, forget about us. Just think! Think not what you want at this moment. Give all this a little time. *For the three of us!!*

Things do not happen in spite of us!! They happen *because we want them*! I want us to be together. We are parting because you *want* it. Don't blame fate! It is in *our* hands! If you *want* me to come over there I shall. If you *want* to come out here I can arrange it in a few days. But I doubt if you will take any of this up. You seem so frightened of us.

I wasn't being romantic about death and I didn't intend to scare you. It's just a fact.

I'm frightened darling, I'm frightened.

J.

Croydon
27:ix:59

My Dear, thank you for your letters, the last one of which I received yesterday when I got back from Saffron Walden at 2 a.m. with a letter from the Wien Radio – which of course I can't make out, haven't a clue why they are writing.

I know it must seem extraordinary to you this sudden change, and as you have quoted extensively from that letter I wrote to you in early August from a King's Lynn hotel, I must try and explain the events of that day for it does throw some light on everything. I was staying there with Jill in separate rooms and most of the day working on the short Vienna novel *A Negative Man** – on that Tuesday, Mama had sent on a letter from you, a great screaming cock-loving letter, one of your best, full of your own very precious darling self which disturbed and upset me greatly – I mooched around in the morning in a thoroughly unstable tearful state, had an almost silent lunch with Jill, and then decided in the afternoon that I must deal strongly with myself, be severe, try and understand what I really wanted and so I wrote you the truth as I knew it then, and knew as genuinely as anyone could know that the only solution was us, and had to come out to you for in a strange way you needed as a person that kind of demonstration of love. Okay, it was all decided. I had some whisky, wrote a little, had dinner. Then told Jill I wanted a drink alone, and discovered to my surprise the other side of the market square a queer bar full of GIs and a juke box that was terribly reminiscent of the K. I stayed there an hour, then went back pretty well pissed on double whiskies, a bottle of wine, and beer, went to Jill's room to say goodnight and instead just cried and cried. I then, in between the tears, told her about you, I had never wanted to before. I wanted to keep you to myself, not share you with anyone; the strange thing was that in telling her it released something in me and that night I slept with her which had never before happened to us. Next day I asked her to marry me.

How do I go on from here in this letter, I wonder. You are wrong about Jill having a child. We want to marry because for us it is impossible to do anything else. All through those six months I had thought my responsibilities were with you, as indeed they were. I fear that one night changed everything. Jill had never ever slept with anyone else, for those five years we were parted. She went on loving me, and though it was a great deal more diverse, I, her, you brought me back in our love, forced me back to the essential things.

But the important things which are beyond us, or beneath us, have this way of persistently inexorably going on from the realities where once we were securely loved, and it seems to me there is little we can do to try and impede that kind of movement, I can't call it progress, for it might well not be.

* To be retitled *An Absurd Affair*.

You have persistently asked me to wait, but John my darling, I cannot see how waiting could alter a situation that is absolutely fixed, besides it is not only me you will have to ask but Jill also. Of course I long to see you, to come to Australia, there is very little that I would like better, of course, I long to hold you in my arms, to make love to that delicate fragile sparrow-chested body with the baroque legs and the Modigliani bottom – such paradoxes all the time exist, it does not mean that its contradiction is untrue or not real, it does not or ever should mean that something in the past that seemed true now is no longer valid. That would be a ridiculously naïve conclusion to come to. But I do think what does happen is that one has to, at some time, make a choice, as to which ultimately is more important. I suppose quite unknowingly, I made that choice the night I've described to you and now nothing can unchange it.

I have purposely not told you the date of the wedding, which is simply with two witnesses and in a church, but it is now a matter of a few days. I promise to take the ring off the day before. Perhaps in many ways it would be a great deal easier for both of us if we could see each other, for this letter sounds consistently cruel when it really still is considerably loving.

Colin

I was married to Jill on 2 October. I sent John's ring back with the following letter, written a few days later.

Saffron Walden
7:x:59

My Dear, I send you this back in great misery as I know now I have lost you utterly and it is my own doing, but I also know that I had to do it.

Don't feel too bitter about it. I could not bear it if you decided to hate me for ever after amen. If we could have talked maybe you would have understood, as it is, the understanding part has been disastrous.

My dear, I'm sorry you had to fall in love with someone so complicated, I can do little about it.

Colin

I am aware that I come out of this story badly, untrustworthy and unlikeable. If I stumbled on myself and saw what I see now I would avoid myself like the plague. But however dishonourable the events and the part I play in them appear, there have to be some revelations surely, now that thirty years have passed.

I cannot, of course, reread these letters without feeling deeply disturbed and shaken. My first, almost involuntary reaction is that I do not understand why I did not go to Australia, even for only a year. I do not think John and I would have lasted for longer, though I have no way of really telling. One of the factors I hate in my past self is the fatalism. How could I reject any notion of free will? How could I not go out to Australia on a short visit, as John begged me to do? Though when I pause and look below the surface, I see the decision to marry Jill as not only tying the sacred knot of an adolescent influence (which it rightly appeared then) but as my rebellion against what society did to gay people. Sadly, I fought it with a conventional weapon. I can remember clearly wanting John, but clearly not wanting us as a gay relationship living in Sydney. This inability in myself to accept the responsibility of what I was, of what we were, is of course immature. But I could not work it out then, or see, with any objectivity, how society was pressurizing me into one mode of behaviour, rather than another.

There were also deeper compulsions driving me towards marriage: the longing for children and a family, and, most of all, the longing for a son, so that I could create a relationship of love and trust different from the tortured relationship I had with my own father.

But we decide on certain actions also because of a mass of small details which come together in a kind of assembly vaguely pointing the way. Like interpreting the chicken's entrails, it may be that we extract the meaning we want. Nevertheless, that summer my work for *The Times Literary Supplement* also had a part to play in the decisions. It was too good a commission to ignore, as I have stressed, but at that time in the height of summer it looked as if it might go on for ever. Alan Pryce-Jones first asked for twenty-four drawings, then said he would do thirty-six, then thought we might have one every week *ad infinitum*. My indecisiveness was partly caused by this change of mind from the editor, whom in my inexperience I never pinned down to a letter or a contract. A letter from me written a year later complains about *The Times*. By May I had done eighteen drawings of a sequence of twenty-four which then was changed to thirty-six. I knew that would take me to September. But I ignored the fact that Alan was leaving and that without a contract the series might easily end. If I had fully appreciated that, I would have left for Australia in June. This would have been before the meeting with Jill, before even the incident at Henley – staying on in that first week of June was fatal. It was as fragile as that. In the end *The Times Literary Supplement* only used the first eighteen drawings; the other ten that I had completed were never published or paid for, and finally all the originals were lost.

However much I now analyse my motives I am still left with the vile suspicion that I murdered a love that should have been nurtured, that I destroyed that which should never have been destroyed. I had the youthful temerity to think such a fiery and intense relationship could occur again, grow perhaps even more powerful through the years; but nothing like John ever did appear again, or had any chance, for if Gods exist I had shown myself to be a wastrel and could not be trusted. But all this is perhaps just jaded romanticism. I was too complicated, I wanted fierce intimate relationships with men and women. I feared any single commitment. Though that autumn of 1959 I promised this faithfully within the marriage ceremony, I did so partly to balance my psyche, needing now a close, fierce, intense relationship with a woman. I was consuming everything too fast.

A novel would end now. Indeed, I had intended to relate my visit to Australia and the events of the last New Year's Eve John and I spent together, and to say no more. However, there are too many threads left undone and some at least can be tied or unravelled a little more before the story closes.

John quickly, almost instantly, became a very successful theatre director in Australia, possibly the most successful in the sixties, referred to then as the Tyrone Guthrie of Down Under. The range of work he did – Brecht, Genet, Sartre, the Greeks and Shakespeare to begin with – reflected our own passions which we had enthused over in Vienna. He never cracked success over here as he wanted to. He never lived with anyone again. We had known

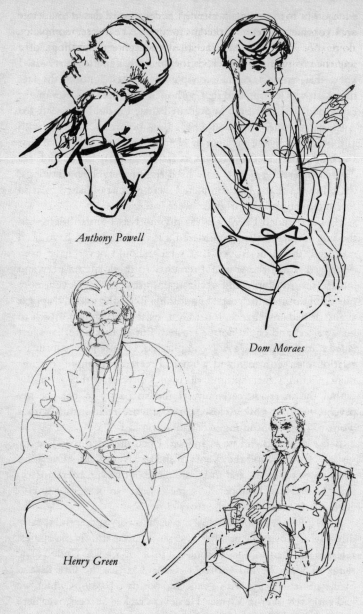

Anthony Powell

Dom Moraes

Henry Green

Graham Greene

each other for twenty-six months and for only ten of those did we live together, yet it marked us for ever. As a war scars a soldier, no relationship I have had since then has been without the shadow and the stimulus of some aspect of this early experience.

I I

On Men and Women

·

What, in essence, shattered the relationship? We were both complicated, but what split us apart stemmed from two sources, the
nature within us and the cultural society we wanted to join and
influence.

In 1959 Australia was the place you left, with no notion of
returning and conquering it. The country then had little to appeal
to me, though later it was a different story. John, as it happened
for him, returned at the right time, for he was one of those
pioneers who helped Australia to find its cultural identity. In the
early sixties in Sydney when he was directing the contemporary
European classics, people like Germaine Greer were in the audience. Yet this cultural flowering, so vital and necessary to him,
was completely alien to my life and needs.

I knew that in order to understand myself I had to explore and
grasp the nature of those very bourgeois British roots which both
troubled and delighted me so intensely. To begin with, this process
took at least ten years and five novels. But that would not have
been possible in Australia. I needed to stay, at least throughout
the sixties, in Britain. These cultural instincts we were both aware
of, but at the time we, of course, could not understand how deeply
they threatened our living together.

These were the cultural pressures. I do not regard our natures
as so great a threat, though I think John was as bisexual as myself.
In order to understand John's life, it is necessary to appreciate the
significance of his early testicular cancer. To have undergone this
experience at any time is no doubt bad enough, but thirty years
ago it also engendered smirks and ribald laughter, even perhaps
a verse of the Hitler General's song. So John was a double victim,

driven into silence and secrecy over his infertility. It is only recently when celebrities like Bob Champion have publicly admitted suffering from testicular cancer, and a national newspaper like the *Guardian* has devoted an article to it on its Health Page that the public is coming to accept it seriously. Now of the thousand men who develop testicular cancer every year in the UK between the ages of twenty and twenty-four (John was twenty-two) over 90 per cent are cured and recover their fertility after chemotherapy.

This book hopes to avoid conjecture, but I think it likely that if the early cancer had not occurred he would have become a happily married family man, giving to his wife and children the immense passion, concern and kindness that were always within him but were, alas, for long periods of his life deeply frustrated. His anger and emotional tirades were about that often, more than anything else.

Bisexuality seems to me to be one of the most commonly misunderstood and reviled conditions that exist. It is obvious why it is a threatening position. Gay society does not much care for bisexuals: you are either gay or not, and if you are gay, you come out of the closet and are proud of it. Quite right too. Straight society finds bisexuality either immoral, evil, irresponsible or dangerous, as at the present time when AIDS has made us all radically change our sexual behaviour. Society does not want to know, persists in fact in disbelieving that such a state exists, and if it exists it cannot be natural. The American distributors of the film *Pascali's Island* in 1988 insisted that all hint of bisexuality be removed from the eponymous hero as the average American viewer would not understand it.

It may be somewhat trite to say that to some degree or other we are all bisexual, or have the potential within us to be so, yet Jung's theory of the anima and animus in all of us is not one that rational people disagree with. And it is, of course, our psychological needs and nature which dictate how we act physically. We are somehow firmly of the mind that our sexual nature is given, never acquired, and is always inflexible. Yet one of the most challenging revelations to arrive at is the amount of freedom we all have in choosing our sexual behaviour. The majority of us deny this, for there is something strong within us that demands limits, prison walls, a tight encirclement – psychological freedom is terrifying to most of us. We are inclined to say that ever since childhood we have known, without doubt, what gender we are attracted to. But a moment's reflection will reveal the psychological programming from birth which steered us towards one gender or another, or none at all.

Our society, like most, is geared towards matching male to female, almost to a hysterical degree. The smallest deviation from a simple biological twinning of genders is searched for, scrutinized and reviled. Men in particular are made to feel inadequate if they do not score enough macho marks; this merely, as we know, makes them take it out on women, whom they unconsciously resent. Many men (my father was one of them) take the easy way out for them and divide women into mothers and whores. The wife then somehow becomes holy, and sexual activity, if it exists at all, is low key and takes place solely to produce children, while the real sexuality occurs with women who are controlled by money. This is a horrible division for all concerned, producing a spiritual desert. The woman artificially raised on a pedestal by the male is then resented and reviled by that male. He never wanted to marry a saint anyway.

It is easy to turn to homosexuality in order to get out of the social pressure, though homosexuality is programmed too. I think some kind of Orphic complex is at work here. One interpretation of the Orpheus myth is that he loved Eurydice so passionately that when he lost her the second time, he forswore womankind altogether and introduced homosexual love into Greece. The Orphic complex can be innate, when it is the mother who bitterly disappoints or rejects, or it can be experienced later, as in my own case, when the rejection* was so bitter and so powerful it became almost an emasculating force. The thought that an unfortunate occurrence with one woman could trigger off a choice of sexual partners in the future may seem to be too superficial an analysis. But there is a strong case to be made that all homosexuals are frustrated woman lovers, though I do not believe that statement negates the positive factors of man loving. A digression into the Orpheus myth is not questioning why homosexuality exists, but merely noting what can sometimes make it flourish.

* An episode not referred to in this memoir.

The central enigma of our sexual identity is that it always remains a mysterious force. For much of our early life we are not in control of the source, nor do we understand where it stems from, yet we are driven by it. But once we have partly understood its nature, it is possible to choose what to be, when or where. Other events can dictate it to us, being in a single gender society for a length of time is the obvious one, and society even accepts this as a pedestrian matter, an unfortunate but inevitable occurrence. What marked myself and my relationship with John was the pathological fear within society of homosexuality itself. What was fundamental to my own psychological health, happiness and fulfilment was to understand why society chooses to emasculate itself by self-afflicted wounds, by negating whole areas of emotional sexual knowledge.

Society, in order to confuse, divides. Take affection, which in some areas must never lead to sex. It is almost as if society would prefer to have its sex cold and without emotion because it can be controlled more expertly then. There is in western man a theme of buddy-love that I find particularly nauseating. My father, again, had it to the nth degree, some pals in the pub being elevated to the position of his being prepared to go through fire and water for them if necessary. I think buddy-love fills a real emotional need for men to be close and affectionate. Men, after all, are nicer creatures if they are allowed to express tenderness and be sentimental. But the intimacy of buddy-love always stops at physical affection; the most modest embrace of an arm around a shoulder is allowable but the continental hug or kiss is taboo in the British male. My father always had to make a derogatory comment when I kissed his cheek in greeting, to cover his embarrassment. Think what a caress means. That your friend is a poofter. How ugly this attitude is, which halts affection and chains it to an evil slur. If men could learn tenderness from other men (or indeed from women) it would then infiltrate their relationships with women. There can be a form of macho-homosexuality which has little to do with buddy-love, which I observed in the army and which treats a vulnerable male as a sex object to be violated and raped. This is the only form of gay sex which is openly bragged about.

There is a common myth that men are more sexual than women, that men can divorce sex from emotions more easily than women, that because of all this, men are more promiscuous than women. I have found from experience and observation that all these generalizations are nonsense. All suppositions about sex generally are. As it is the most powerful instinct within us after we have satiated our hunger, society through law, religion and myth has spun lies and misconceptions around the subject so as to confuse and mislead us. It is the fear of this powerful instinct within society which turns simple and strong emotions into monstrous perversions. We live in an age where sex is twinned with one word only. It is not love, not tenderness, not spouse nor children. No, sex is united only with violence. Sex and violence, they say, is what has destroyed the moral climate of our time and which promotes new monsters to unnerve us all. It is almost as if we do not want the responsibility of sex as part of gentle, loving concern because that concept is too alarming; better to banish sex from the civilized compound, to behind the walls where it is linked only with violence. It is almost as if we want to be ashamed of sex, to alienate ourselves from it, to fashion it always into shapes of satanic danger, so that we do not have to accept it as a source of comfort and joy. It is almost as if we fear sex so much we are certain that if we allow it into our lives it will drain us of all other will, dominate reason and sensibility and turn us all into gibbering, masturbating idiots.

Real and truthful sexual freedom must to some degree include elements of bisexuality, for it is natural for us to love all people regardless of gender and loving has no necessary circumscribed limits. My defence of bisexuality rests finally on the concept of the wholeness of the natural being. From the pre-Socratics through to Neoplatonism and early Christianity, the idea persists of divisive man, of human nature as both sacred and profane. The profane part, from the Ancient Greeks onwards, has always been sexual expression, and – particularly to Romans like Philo – has taken the form of homosexuality. To them even marital love, sacred to the Hebrews, was not above criticism. Read Seneca on marital sex and it is like hearing a Victorian patriarch speak: 'Let him control his impulses and not be borne headlong into copulation. Nothing is fouler than to love a wife like an adulteress.'

It would seem that in the urgency of the spirit's longing to be fused with a timeless essence, the Platonic Ideal, the grossness of sexual pleasure had to be controlled, tamed and finally sacrificed. I have always taken the opposite view: that the world of ideas is enriched by physical love and that so-called sacred and profane loves must be indissolubly fused and our human nature made whole again. To observe, recognize and accept our bisexual natures seems to me part of our salvation as compassionate human beings.

Is There a Difference?

Dr Miriam Stoppard once asked me in front of a television audience, with middle-aged women from Leeds behind me and glue-sniffing lads with their mums in front of me, 'What is the difference?' 'One has a cunt and the other has a cock,' I replied. This brought from the glue sniffers howls of hilarity, from the Leeds housewives acknowledgement that unless the discussion starts from fact and practical application you are stuck in a sea of waffle. Needless to add, the television company cut this statement, and then decided to cut the whole interview as bisexuality was too shocking for a family audience. The TV audience itself had thought otherwise.

There is, of course, a world of difference between loving a man and loving a woman, and again there is no difference at all. Love is love, and the same comfort and ecstasy, the same fusion of close opposites occur in both gay and straight relationships. Yet if we start from the practical application, it might be interesting to note what the differences are. If sex includes penetration, it is somewhat easier in straight couples; it is always slightly annoying to have to stop fondling and unscrew a tube of massage lotion. However, it is a small pause and of little consequence. And oral sex is, after all, much the same.

The penis is a great deal more than its physical parts. It is also a phallus which deep within the psyche is a religious symbol of awe, power and fecundity. Not only deeply embedded in the atavistic consciousness, it is blatantly used in contemporary times. Barely disguised as the microphone, no pop singer is without it close to the lips, held tightly, caressed and fondled. Yet, of course, the act of fellatio itself is still frowned on. Far safer, society seems to say, if we harness it to commercialism and merely use the phallus subliminally. It is another example of our fear of sex, for the penis/phallus is felt to be too threatening. Why should all illustrations of the organ erect be automatically considered obscene or pornographic?

There is something deeply mysterious and magical in the way a flaccid piece of skin becomes charged, erect and proud. Eric Gill put it well: 'What marvellous thing was this that suddenly transformed a mere water-tap into a pillar of fire?' I must admit that I find it odd that all men do not enjoy fellatio, though gymnasts and dancers often perform fellatio upon themselves – a wall being necessary to support the torso. Men, after all, experience this miraculous transformation in their bodies. Why not with other men in their own mouths? Placing this modest soft organ between the lips, feeling its velvet mushroom-like form on the tongue and then experiencing its slow swelling to something rigid yet still precariously vulnerable, is for women an amazing and beautiful experience. It is for me also, and it is for some heterosexual men. Again it was for Eric Gill – an astonishingly truthful and strongly heterosexual man – 'The shape of the head of a man's erect penis is very excellent in the mouth. There is no doubt about this. I have often wondered – now I know.'

There is a myth about homosexuality, the idea that same sex loving has a clearer understanding of the mysteries of the orgasm. I am sure this is not necessarily true. For this appreciation relies on how close, relaxed and deeply loving the couple are rather more than anything else. If there are differences, they occur mostly in the psychology of the loving, not in the physical acts.

The anima and animus in all of us fluctuate in a relationship. A girl I lived with once said to me, 'The trouble with our relationship is that either there are two men in the house, or two women, and there is never at the same time a man and a woman.' All straight and gay relationships I have noticed have the male and female attitudes changing by the hour, and this I believe is the secret of a rich and truthful relationship. Neither men nor women should be afraid of showing their vulnerability and frailty as long as they are also strong, protective and decisive. We are all, of whatever gender, mixtures of these factors and we should not allow our gender to be labelled by society as one or the other.

The difference is not so much in whether the relationship is gay or straight, but in the relationship itself. Some gay couples appear as rigid in their behaviour, observing all the social proprieties, as might newlyweds from Cheam, while many straight couples are more anarchic to society's normal criteria than gay couples would be. Of course, it is natural that if you start off as an outsider you are more inclined to conform, while if born within the established order you are often going to fight to get out, and this confuses what we see. Yet, as a bisexual, I have certainly observed some differences myself between loving men and women. This has nothing to do with society's traditional notions of what male loving entails, like protectiveness. Husbands are supposed to protect their wives and families, but I have felt enormous protectiveness towards both younger and older men, and I have also felt vulnerable in a heterosexual relationship and known the tender protectiveness of a woman.

When I was young, there was undoubtedly an awareness of security in being loved by a man (a factor which John sensed accurately) but this stemmed from the lack of a loving and kind father in childhood: certainly an absent or unloving father can trigger off the need to be loved by men in adult life. However, this need to feel secure gradually lessened as I discovered a growing security in myself, where after all, if such a psychological state exists, it has been there all the time.

Does the difference lie in single sex loving being somehow more equal? On the surface possessing the same genitalia should help, yet it doesn't, for the attitudes that create an equal relationship are in the head not the crotch. There is only one difference between the sexes, which really counts, and that is the fecundity of a woman and the fact that she carries within her the new foetus, a fact which gives the female gender a superiority and also a secret atavistic awareness of truth which men can so easily miss entirely. Women are far more deeply in touch with those unspecified rhythms within the unconscious world, far more in touch with race memory and something which perhaps can best be summed up as the aboriginal dreamtime. I think there are many heterosexual men who sense this strongly in women and in their loving of them become closer to it. However, it is not always so. Just as there are plenty of women who deny this darkness within themselves, there are also men who can appreciate it and will discover that the wisdom of all things is to listen within the silence. But men cannot become pregnant and carry a growing embryo within themselves.

How then does this creative power in the woman change a relationship? I think the act of love is made more profound, more revelatory when it is also an act of creation of a human being, or an attempt to create a new human being. For me, there was something wholly miraculous, sublimely beautiful in that orgasm and discharge of sperm which is missing from other love-making whether gay or straight. This fact of human loving, of course, reinforces Catholic doctrine and it goes some way to explain the Church's power.

If I had managed to talk in depth to Dr Stoppard, that must have been the inescapable conclusion I would have come to. When a man and a woman make love to produce children the act is enhanced to something far greater than the two lovers themselves, as if in the attempt to create a third human being they become not only fused as one but also with that third potential spirit which hovers between the void and life.

This explains my earlier statement that there is both a world of difference and yet no difference at all between straight and gay love. The latter is infertile and this circumscribes the limits and areas by which that love can go, and of course for many heterosexual lovers for long periods in life their love too is infertile, and the same limits are prescribed. This does not mean that I consider gay love to be inferior, for I attach no value judgements whatsoever to the categories, but in this profound sense gay love has to differ.

It was in defiance of this that in 1967 I wrote my play *Spitting Image*, where two gay men in love discover that one of them is showing signs of pregnancy. A son is born to them. The play, a comedy with serious intentions, tries to explore, firstly, whether a gay couple plus child are just the same as a heterosexual couple. (The child takes to distinguishing his two Daddies by numbers, Daddy One and Daddy Two.) And secondly, society's homophobic reactions to the situation. Ironically, it was this play, out of my six plays produced, that was put on in Australia.

It was not by chance then that the only relationship that could sunder the love I had for John was the one I carried within me for a woman I had known earlier, with whom I would then create a child. No other relationship could have torn me away from John. But at the same time I was aware that our physical love-making in the marriage was going to go further than the spiritual elements I had experienced with John, and that I needed this urgently. It was an awareness that the infertility, made more ironic by John's sterility, had cornered and somehow trapped our lives. It was a vague awareness that this was reducing our potential in ways which unnerved me and in a manner I could not quite rationally understand.

This attempt to probe into the nature of what difference there is between homosexual and heterosexual love has taken me all of half a lifetime. After my marriage I returned to men, after the men to women, and so it goes. George Melly, in an interview with John Creedy for *Gay Times* (June 1988), said: 'I was gay in the '50s mostly, certainly in the '40s. I became bisexual towards the end of the '50s, then heterosexual. That's no moral judgement, just a plain statement of fact.'

I see in my past little fluctuation at all, though I am aware that possibly many of my friends and society in general might have always considered me gay, but that impression owes more to social values than to reality. As far as I can detect, I have always felt bisexual, strongly and equally attracted to both men and women. At certain stages in my life, for psychological reasons, I have felt impelled to love and be loved by a man instead of a woman and vice versa. When I was young, because of my relation-ship with my father I felt more emotional about men than I did about women. Now, that too is fairly equal. It is the human being which first intrigues and attracts; what gender the human being is is a quite secondary consideration and should not intrude too much at first into the exchange.

What I strongly emphasize again – knowing most people will disagree with me – is that there is a huge area of choice in what we become. I was inclined to say in the above paragraph that like Melly, I detect too as I grow older a much greater heterosexuality. Yet I think the truth is that I choose now to be heterosexual, choose also to be faithful and loyal (in the world of AIDS it would be dangerously irresponsible to do otherwise). This choice is a culmination of many factors. As soon as my father died, I was aware that there was no need to appear homosexual for his sake.

At the same time, I was being counselled and discovering various points of programming which my mother quite unwittingly had committed on her small male child. The two realizations together released me from any emotional propulsion towards being gay, so powerful at times in my life that it had erased all other loves, duties and responsibilities. Thus relaxing into my own nature, without commitment to any particular notion, allowed me to know myself with greater serenity.

The minute society detects gay behaviour in what was previously thought of as a heterosexual man, he is automatically labelled homosexual. Even if the man continues to live with and to love women, our society likes to stick to the gay label, rather than the bisexual. I have said that society rejects bisexuality, even as a concept. In a serious news report in the *Observer* and the *Guardian* on the incidence of homosexuality in the American male, bisexuality was never mentioned. Even though the incidence of gay episodes in married heterosexual men were alluded to in the report, these men were counted as homosexual and not bisexual. Only a very deep-rooted fear of bisexuality can distort the facts in this way. Either one or the other, but not both, society appears to say. So in my life, I think, society and even friends have seen me nearly always as gay, which is a pity because it is an inaccurate and frivolous assumption.

There are some women (quite sensibly, the reader might conclude) who dismiss men whom they think of as gay or bisexual, though there are always other women who are attracted to the challenge, perhaps asking to be humiliated? These women I have observed, but not known. The women whom I love are the women who view homosexuality as part of the pattern, as neither here nor there, as about as interesting as any other feature of a character, who are neither threatened by it, nor challenged by it, who merely see it as part of the fabric of human nature. They would say that the bisexual male at least understands something of what it is like to be a woman and tends to treat women with more sensitive understanding than other males. These are the wise and beautiful women, and I salute them.

I 2

Finally, to Australia

.

It was early in 1980 that I eventually reached Sydney and was astonished, becoming spellbound by its beauty. To have once refused the chance of living in an apartment with a view over that harbour struck me then as a form of aesthetic sacrilege. With the irony that should only occur in novels, but which I suspect permeates all lives, John was directing *The Threepenny Opera* in Canberra. I attended a rehearsal and watched him direct the actress in the lead-up to the song, 'Pirate Jenny'. Together we had last sung it walking – or perhaps staggering – down the Graben.

In that same year John directed my own play, *Spitting Image*, in Sydney, but I had left Australia by then, so I never saw the production. It had been, of course, one of our youthful dreams that I would design the plays John directed. We had never dreamt then that John would direct a play I had written. He had tried to get the Australian rights ten years before, some time after its short run in London's West End. The actor who now played the lead had been born in Thornton Heath, near Croydon, a fact that John took as a good omen. But it wasn't; the play did not run in Sydney any more than it had done in London. The only city in the world where it was a rave success, running for two and a half years, was oddly enough Vienna.

I returned to Australia on New Year's Eve 1987, and was to stay for a couple of weeks at John's home in Sydney. He met me at the airport. I was shocked at how he had aged: he was not only grey haired but lined. Patrick White, with whom he had had in the preceding ten years a bitter and distant relationship, after having had great success directing the White plays, saw John at a première and called out, 'I see you've joined the wrinklies.' This great change over seven years worried me but I kept such anxiety to myself.

We had first met almost exactly thirty years before, but we almost never talked about the past. Occasionally in company a story would be told, and then I noticed that John's version would be quite different from mine. For example, the time he told the story of how we had become locked out from the basement of the gay club in Thistle Grove and how to get the key he had had to go to the Royal Opera House, Covent Garden, and confront Laon Maybanke in the interval, asking to borrow the key. In John's version he was dressed only in pyjamas, in mine he wore trousers and singlet. I stick with my version as we never owned any pyjamas, sleeping naked. And then, to catch the bus or tube to Covent Garden he had to have some small change, which he would have had in his trousers but not in his pyjamas! It fascinates me how subjectivity distorts memory. I never quarrelled with John's versions, knowing that, like everyone else, my own must be subject to fiction also.

On this visit to Australia I had left my girl-friend in England and she telephoned me several times at John's. She noticed I was on edge when I spoke to her. I could not but be conscious that when she rang the atmosphere grew suddenly cold, even though John never inquired who she was or what was happening to my life. (I had explained to her what the problem was.) It was as if thirty years had vanished, yet here we were aged fifty-three, having spent those thirty years apart. How was it that I could so easily fall back into the role of a betrayer and John could emanate such jealousy?

It was true that on this visit, staying at his house, I found John difficult to be with, tetchy, querulous, hypersensitive about my reactions to Australia. It was as if the new secure golden era of Australian culture had not given him an iron faith in it at all, as if he was still fearful that I would think the place philistine. I was researching into the illegal killing of kangaroos for an article for the *Guardian*, and I was also following up stories on AIDS. Some of the statistics I returned with offended him and at one point he told me aggressively I was writing it in the wrong way. I wish I had reread the correspondence in this book then, for I would have detected the old John, the domineering director, and laughed, but I grew angry too and we had a short quarrel.

If I had read these letters then I would have asked him what happened to him after I got married; what he eventually felt, whether he could forgive me or understand what I had done and why I had done it. If I had reread the letters I would have engineered an in-depth probe, an analysis, a discussion in which we could have dissected our past lives, thoughts and emotions. Did we love each other? Or was it an illusion? Was this, for both of us, our youthful great love, or was it so temporary that it counted in the end for little? I would have wanted to know whether he had loved or been as happy with anyone else in those thirty years. I would have wanted to tell him what he had given me, how he had shown me the immense tenderness of loving and how I had forgotten it again and again. That an incident which invoked him would remind me with revelatory and traumatic power, bring it all back, the sweetness of being gentle. That now, after half a lifetime, I would swear never to forget again.

But I had not reread his letters for twenty-five years and I had forgotten mine completely, never supposing for a moment that I would see them again. So our past love remained shrouded in time, never referred to or questioned. Yet not quite, for on my first visit to Australia he had said, 'It was only in 1967 when I read *Asylum* that I realized how much you had loved me.'

It was also important when I arrived in Canberra that he and he alone (and no other Australian friends) met me at the airport. There was something ritualistic about my feet on the soil with him, as if its significance was marked by the soul and not commented upon. It was important then that I saw his work. I was whisked into a car driven by an ASM, and whirled into dusty industrial suburbs to find backdrapes or bits of scenery. I remember feeling that I could have been, in this anonymous scrub with shanty garages and piles of rubble and cement, anywhere in the world, yet I was acutely conscious of John beside me silently exultant. Aware of him feeling that at last I was in his land, his continent, that he so loved.

At the last visit in 1987 I should have asked about this meeting and what he had really thought when a little drunkenly, after we had had dinner together, I had confessed how unhappy my own life was then, imprisoned, I mistakenly thought, in a sterile, fraught relationship with a man I felt immense pity for but no love, where not one iota of tenderness was ever expressed. Usually, we kept our own private lives to ourselves. On this occasion he made comforting noises but did not comment. Did he think that this was what I deserved after I had rejected him? There was nothing private in those thirty years that I can remember him telling me, nothing in his letters, when inevitably they began to arrive again.

After my marriage I heard nothing for a year, nor did I expect to hear anything ever again. But then a letter came, planned to arrive on my birthday, but with the novelist's irony – again – it arrived on my wife's birthday. Then it seemed to us that nothing in that year had changed, except that we had not written to each other. Jill, with customary pertinence, drew the shrewd conclusion that I had opted for love and not passion. But it has never been the intention of this memoir to detail the thirty years apart, simply to note that intimacy had gone leaving raw emotion, like some leviathan thrashing about in the dark. Our lives diverged, we were, alas, always to some degree in competition. I would send him rave reviews of my novels, but never the dismissive ones, while he sent me rave reviews of his plays with notes on ambitious offers of commissions for work in New York or California which crossed with notes from me that said much the same. Carefully, we eschewed all talk of our inner selves, while raising our professional voices in noisy clamour.

Somewhere, a distant voice within me wanted to know the significance of this early relationship, which was the main reason why I visited Sydney on this last occasion. I was checking up, re-evaluating, hoping the middle-aged self could now look back and assess what it was all about. Yet, as one does, I hid this factor from myself, did not care to probe into it too deeply. Which is why when I left Australia I felt, without bothering to scrutinize too carefully, to some extent that that had been done, that the whole episode was foolish and rash, a youthful and intemperate passion which had lit bonfires, which had burnt furiously but left nothing of any singular importance. In some way I felt I had tied up the relationship with John, because I had found it now so irritating to be with him for long. On parting, he had told me not to forget his observation on raspberries for inclusion in a possible

Guardian article. John's ego was still supreme, I remember thinking. What I find curious is that even then, on the flight to New Zealand with a book from John on my lap, *The Secrets of Pulcinella*, with the inscription 'It's been wonderful to have you visit my Sydney. Let's make Pulcinella the first visit on your return', I was still anxiously protecting myself from any commitment to him. Even my diary is silent and inexpressive on the one significant incident that took place. I wrote in the diary of New Year's Eve:

JT opened a bottle of Australian bubbly and we drank it in his garden, then coffee, then to a beach, Neilson Park and I am swimming in part of the Bay but which is, after all, the Pacific Ocean, then sitting in the sun and chatting. Back at the house where for the next few days I have my own flat in the garden, I slept for a few hours. In the evening JT chooses a fish restaurant and I ate Balmain Bugs, a shellfish that looks like a large flea I am told, the sweetness of lobster and the lightness of scampi, rich but not over powerful. Then some John Dory, simply grilled with a little fresh tarragon, washed down with an Australian Chardonnay tasting quite strongly of oak. Fresh raspberries to end the meal, and when I said, 'I last had fresh raspberries in July,' John replied, 'Fortunate is the man who has fresh raspberries twice a year.'

Then a stroll down towards the harbour to a pub. At midnight the music stops, the doors are flung open, the walls become screens which swivel and the pub spills out on to the pavement. It is like a stage set for a play John has directed. All the car headlights are turned on, hooters blaring and as the hour strikes we all throw streamers and let off crackers. Amazing. If it was Britain I would recoil in embarrassment. Here, I love it, and we end the moment by all singing 'Waltzing Matilda'. Then back walking in a soft, warm drizzle.

What the diary did not say was that in the crowded pub (which was not a gay pub) at the stroke of midnight as streamers and crackers were going off around us, John had kissed me as we had kissed in 1958 and 1959. A kiss of intensity which only lovers give. I can recall at first thinking this is totally absurd, here I am in love with an English girl, being kissed by my old Australian lover in public, but as the kiss continued, the years vanished and something remarkable happened, something which seemed absolute, which would never fade or vanish, was there, *the fact of us*, a kind of indestructible, inviolate kernel. Looking back on it now, it was almost as if John was saying to me, 'Remember, this now is the last New Year's Eve we will kiss, after parting and quarrels, so remember, for this is the last full year I have.' Perhaps the diary does not mention it because I was embarrassed, or perhaps puzzled. I think the latter, as the former has never stopped me from writing the truth. I think I was profoundly bewildered and preferred not to think about it.

As we walked back in the rain, I remember noticing John had begun to show signs of a cold, and I heard myself say something about hoping I had not caught it. Must human beings always trivialize everything? We did not mention the incident on New Year's Eve, we did not discuss in that whole visit ourselves or what time had done to us. One evening I took him out to dinner and prefaced a story by saying it would amuse him: it was about my advertising in *Forum* and the answers I had had which involved one particular person. At the end of a saga which all other friends had found hysterically funny, John was still po-faced. 'You didn't find that amusing?' I asked. 'No,' he answered flatly, and there occurred one of *those* painful pauses. I saw his lips pursed with almost a kind of spinsterish disdain. I remember the same look in youth, when he was on his high horse. I regretted then his lack of fun in middle-age. I think now he was just sad to be shown these windows into my present life which he could not sympathize with, or perhaps he was alienated by my full and varied personal life. Perhaps at the core there was the same outrage as when my girl-friend rang up. However, such moments as these I pushed aside, not wanting to consider them. I curse myself now for not saying, why does it not amuse you?

There was one other sad incident which reflects how twisted up we still were in each other, as John was in my life and my past. On the first day I had arrived I had shown him with pride and pleasure photographs of my son, Jonathan, then aged twenty-six. But John looked at them without comment. A week later he gave a party which started in the early afternoon and ended in the evening. Full of far too much excellent Australian wine, we sat together after the guests had gone and quietly John confessed that he had a son too. I think he had quite forgotten that I knew he was infertile, but I know in that moment how important it was that I believed him. I asked whether I might meet the boy? John

246

was doubtful; he lived with his mother of course and was in his early twenties. I eased the conversation away from the fantasy, and I never referred to it afterwards. The fact that the sexual competitiveness was still so strong and urgent that a fantasy could ride upon it with the conviction with which it was related, troubled and moved me.

However, I think my immediate reflections on that visit were specious. I was too eager to wrap it all up. It was death that threw it all into a light by which I could at least attempt to scrutinize what had happened. Now there is no way of checking facts, of sifting evidence, there is only my subjectivity, interpreting emotions with an unreliable memory. I said above I had not reread John's letters until I came to write this memoir. I also said how one paragraph in a letter had always haunted me; even without rereading it had stayed with me, lodged in experience, refusing to grow vague in time. He wrote, 'Much of you is from me. Never think to escape that, when you are again in Florence, Venice or Vienna, sometimes when you swim at night, when you lie in a forest, when you fuss in a kitchen over something special or when snow lies on your window-sill.' For years I had performed daily tasks, travelled and read, swam at night and made something special in too many kitchens for too many lovers, and for all those years the whisper of John was at my back, in the air. A note of music, a shadow, a glimpse of a profile could trigger an explosion in my heart. He went on to write, 'Or reading a poem "somewhere my heart has never travelled", then suddenly you will know that I am there, you will smell that slight earthiness of my body or touch something which transforms itself into my body, or hear my laugh and see my eyes. We neither can escape. This is the love of my very life and I suspect deeper than all roses the core of yours. Then you will cry as I fear I do now, tears salt with longing and regret.'

A cry of such yearning and despair, of ardour and grief, it somehow got fixed upon the ether, indelible, a strident ghost. Still hungry, still unfed, it claws at the surface reality needing to tear all masks and disguises into shreds and has often left me breathless and vacant, staring at an empty wall, a book open and a glass unfilled. We used to quote from *Nightwood* the line about the graves of the separated lovers Nora and Robin, 'One dog will find them both.' We would believe, in the intensity of our own passion, that this was true of us. Yet while writing this book I have feared that I am missing some vital element which would explain why the ardour and the grief existed and go on existing. But little that I write, and no page of any letter I read, explain enough; they do not unravel the core of the mystery. A book such as this, I suppose, should somehow redefine love, or if that is too bold, at least paint it in more precise details, but the more I consider it, the more finally mysterious it becomes.

Why did John arrange that the letters be sent back to me after his death? Why was that the only message relayed to me once he was in the grave? Did he suspect that this would be my reaction and that finally something beyond those twenty-six months might exist? There are no clues to what was in his mind, nor in that time when he was dying did he wish to communicate with me to tell me ... anything or nothing? But I cannot get out of my mind a thought which nags and echoes that 'now I know in part; but later I shall know as I am known'. In his essay on Leon Bloy, *The Mirror of Enigmas*, Borges quotes from a letter of Bloy's: 'We are dreamers who shout in our sleep. We do not know whether the things afflicting us are the secret beginnings of our ulterior happiness or not.' Something that was ours, something that *is* ours, belongs to a restless dream, poignant and powerful one second, insubstantial the next. We are not what we are. We dream, we exist, we act out many forms and disguises (it was no accident that John was a director and I, a writer of fiction) and there is occasionally a fusion of all these identities, when the dream, the acting and the existing unite.

It matters not to me now whether one of us was male or not, was old or young, was a different nationality, colour, or culture, whether one lived or one died. I do know that whatever love is, that indelible kernel was part of it. That it is central amidst the restless dream, becoming part of all things whether awake or dreaming. That in the best of ourselves, the profound heart of things, we gave to each other something wholly remarkable and rare, which has pursued us ever since, not allowing us to deny its truth for long.

In that mutual gift as the poem 'Which of Us Two?' expressed, I am still uncertain which side of soil I'm on.

Appendix

•

from the Guardian *series* First Love, *2 June 1983*

The first romance must be when the string section of an orchestra steps out from behind mounting cumulus and surges into the Max Bruch violin concerto. That was the summer of 1953 and I was staring up at the sky quite often, as I was generally laid out flat on my back in a field, experiencing delicious new sensations. I was nineteen and besotted with Jan, a Pole. He was twenty-four and what we were doing on various Surrey wild grasses was illegal then, as it still is now for a lad of my age, in post-Wolfenden Britain.

I had just been discharged from the Army, after they had sent me bonkers in the first year of my National Service. While waiting to go to a teachers' training college I worked as a ward orderly in an old people's hospital in Croydon. Two years later my first short story was published in the *London Magazine*, based upon macabre events which occurred in that Dickensian place. Jan was not part of the story. He has never fitted into any story of mine, because that heightened phase appeared to be fiction at the time.

I had been working at the hospital for a few days when in a change of the day-shift Jan appeared. At this time I had a girl-friend in Cambridge and thought myself in love. That morning was to explain to me that one can have affairs of the intellect, which is one thing, but when you start to turn the mattress with a patient still in the bed, an unexpected and potent force has caused a traffic jam inside the brain.

Jan kindly tipped the patient back into the middle of the bed while glancing at me with alarm. He had that unnerving colour

249

combination of dark blue eyes and blond curly hair. We continued making beds until I found the tension so unbearable I spoke the truth. Never has a confession brought so much immediate reward.

One second as he made a hospital corner and I stared down at a mane of blond curls, I heard myself say, I love you. The next, we were in the nurses' locker room in a muscular clinch. After twenty minutes I reappeared in the ward with a love bite on each side of my neck and in a sensual haze began to redo the beds I had already made. I had stumbled on passion. I felt life would never be the same again. Nor was it.

The shattering experience was to discover that one's basic and urgent feelings were centred on a social taboo about which both the law and religion were paranoid. What I had been taught all my life, that men and women were natural lovers, struck me as a manipulative lie. Someone, somewhere was not telling all of the truth.

So with the newfound passion of a revolutionary convert I took Jan back home. My belief was that as my parents had accepted my sisters' husbands as part of the family, so the Pole should be accepted with the same affection and social graces.

I told my mother first. She said, 'Blimey,' or 'Crikey,' poured herself another sweet sherry and then asked me to ponder seriously on what the vicar would think. As the vicar was a Low Church Evangelical of 'strike the sinners dead' stance, we both had a pretty good idea that his mildest suggestion would be a cold bath and his most intemperate a bucket of hell fire.

Next I told my father who pretended not to hear. As he had a habit of declaiming, over a pint, randy monologues about his sexual adventures, my nature was a classically Freudian response, and in father's terms it could only dishonour his concept of virility, which is probably exactly what I wanted to do. I spoke earnestly and passionately of my experiences and all he did was to order a whisky chaser for us both. His need not to appreciate what I was doing brought on increasing deafness. I took Jan back to supper every evening, and in offering him at table tasty morsels in front of my parents I spread the endearments as thickly as the butter. My mother looked vague and father would rise and turn up the volume of the television.

Jan appeared to be highly delighted. He must have thought

that *petit bourgeois* scions were all in the habit of entertaining their foreign homosexual lovers in this open manner, for he was never embarrassed by my behaviour. If he had been, I would have lectured him severely on the subject of what would later be referred to as Gay Pride.

I did not realize how deeply naïve he was, partly because his experiences had been cruelly limited and distorted by the war. Jan was a young lad when Russia and Germany invaded his homeland. His home was a farm in Silesia and one of his most vivid memories was seeing the flat horizon grow dark and hearing at the same time the sound of distant rumbling while the earth shook beneath him. In the hour the dark shape was blacker and blacker, the noise louder and the farm animals were terrified. In another hour he could distinguish that the dark shape was composed of segments of a serpent which encircled the flat horizon. They were tanks and nothing would or could stop them.

By the end of the war Jan had been swept up into the Hitler Youth. At twelve he was trained to fire a rifle, throw a grenade and feed a machine gun with ammunition. His unit was prepared to start marching towards the Allied advance. In the confusion some of them deserted, some were rounded up and shot by the Nazis, and others escaped, including Jan, who made his way to Switzerland.

He was a gentle soul, infinitely kind and very sentimental. It always amazed me that this benign creature who was tender with spiders, children and raving geriatrics, was once part of Hitler's war machine and had suffered so much barbarity.

But I was to learn that the barbarians were not all led by Hitler. Jan suddenly disappeared from the hospital. On the second day I was told that he was off sick. Concerned, I pedalled up Shirley Hills where he had a room in a semi-detached house. His landlady opened the door and looked none too pleased at my request to see her lodger.

He was in bed with a heavy cold in a minute front bedroom. I sat on the bed, held his hand and muttered a lot of sweet nothings and cheery nonsense, oblivious to any creaking floorboards outside. After an hour I left and started to descend the stairs. The landlady was waiting for me at the bottom. As I started down the abuse flew up. She could have been the vicar's most ardent supporter. Her curses and language were then a revelation, but I suppose 'the shock was not so much the language as the violent enmity and loathing that she had for me. I wanted to vomit on the front door mat. I wish now that I had. The rain was falling like stalactites as I pedalled back home and I wept, for I had come across gross misinterpretation and felt the injustice of it acutely. I could not fathom how such a lyrical love could be considered this filthy insidious thing.

Jan had defended me, he told me later. He had arisen from his sick bed and told her he would leave the house if ever she spoke like that again. She had cried and begged for his forgiveness. The landlady was in love with him – Jan's 'little boy lost look' brought out the mother in nearly everyone – though we had not realized it.

He should have left the house there and then, for we had no bedroom between us and nowhere private to go. Hence those fields, behaving exactly as the vicar said – like beasts in the open. Jan had a motor bike and we used to zoom out of suburbia and into the Surrey Downs. There was something idyllic about the first romance having to be celebrated on the earth itself, something especially good about kisses and crushed wild flowers, something inherently right about the farming lad from Silesia finding his wild, demon lover in that most conformist of English counties. For part of homosexual love is the need to rebel. Same gender sex is an anarchic statement, aimed at the myths and fables necessary for society's status quo.

But our rural context was not the only conforming aspect. My Jan had been brought up as a Roman Catholic, but we had hardly discussed religion and I had thought it a subject of little interest. After we had been together for six months (I was then at college), Jan went to confession. He told me that we must never see each other again. He gave me no reason for the decision. The Bruch violin concerto stopped abruptly.

My nightmare was not knowing the reason, for it was difficult to believe that a powerful love just vanishes. Yet on the evidence I had, this seems to have been what happened. I went through a phase of cynicism until from a friend I discovered the part the priest had played. Jan had been convinced that he was in a dark state of mortal sin, that his love for me was, as the priest said, a malignant cancer that must be cut out from his soul. He did the surgery himself. It possibly hurt him more than it did me.

I felt betrayed by men, exactly my mother's pattern, and I turned to women, an option which had never occurred to mother. If it had I probably would have had a happier childhood.

Index

·

FOR THE BEST IN PAPERBACKS, LOOK FOR THE

In every corner of the world, on every subject under the sun, Penguin represents quality and variety – the very best in publishing today.

For complete information about books available from Penguin – including Puffins, Penguin Classics and Arkana – and how to order them, write to us at the appropriate address below. Please note that for copyright reasons the selection of books varies from country to country.

In the United Kingdom: Please write to *Dept E.P., Penguin Books Ltd, Harmondsworth, Middlesex, UB7 0DA.*

If you have any difficulty in obtaining a title, please send your order with the correct money, plus ten per cent for postage and packaging, to *PO Box No 11, West Drayton, Middlesex*

In the United States: Please write to *Dept BA, Penguin, 299 Murray Hill Parkway, East Rutherford, New Jersey 07073*

In Canada: Please write to *Penguin Books Canada Ltd, 2801 John Street, Markham, Ontario L3R 1B4*

In Australia: Please write to the *Marketing Department, Penguin Books Australia Ltd, P.O. Box 257, Ringwood, Victoria 3134*

In New Zealand: Please write to the *Marketing Department, Penguin Books (NZ) Ltd, Private Bag, Takapuna, Auckland 9*

In India: Please write to *Penguin Overseas Ltd, 706 Eros Apartments, 56 Nehru Place, New Delhi, 110019*

In the Netherlands: Please write to *Penguin Books Netherlands B.V., Postbus 195, NL-1380AD Weesp*

In West Germany: Please write to *Penguin Books Ltd, Friedrichstrasse 10–12, D–6000 Frankfurt/Main 1*

In Spain: Please write to *Alhambra Longman S.A., Fernandez de la Hoz 9, E–28010 Madrid*

In Italy: Please write to *Penguin Italia s.r.l., Via Como 4, I-20096 Pioltello (Milano)*

In France: Please write to *Penguin Books Ltd, 39 Rue de Montmorency, F-75003 Paris*

In Japan: Please write to *Longman Penguin Japan Co Ltd, Yamaguchi Building, 2–12–9 Kanda Jimbocho, Chiyoda-Ku, Tokyo 101*

A CHOICE OF PENGUINS

The Russian Album   Michael Ignatieff

Michael Ignatieff movingly comes to terms with the meaning of his own family's memories and histories, in a book that is both an extraordinary account of the search for roots and a dramatic and poignant chronicle of four generations of a Russian family.

Beyond the Blue Horizon   Alexander Frater

The romance and excitement of the legendary Imperial Airways East-bound Empire service – the world's longest and most adventurous scheduled air route – relived fifty years later in one of the most original travel books of the decade. 'The find of the year' – *Today*

Getting to Know the General   Graham Greene

'In August 1981 my bag was packed for my fifth visit to Panama when the news came to me over the telephone of the death of General Omar Torrijos Herrera, my friend and host...' 'Vigorous, deeply felt, at times funny, and for Greene surprisingly frank' – *Sunday Times*

The Search for the Virus   Steve Connor and Sharon Kingman

In this gripping book, two leading *New Scientist* journalists tell the remarkable story of how researchers discovered the AIDS virus and examine the links between AIDS and lifestyles. They also look at the progress being made in isolating the virus and finding a cure.

Arabian Sands   Wilfred Thesiger

'In the tradition of Burton, Doughty, Lawrence, Philby and Thomas, it is, very likely, the book about Arabia to end all books about Arabia' – *Daily Telegraph*

Adieux: A Farewell to Sartre   Simone de Beauvoir

A devastatingly frank account of the last years of Sartre's life, and his death, by the woman who for more than half a century shared that life. 'A true labour of love, there is about it a touching sadness, a mingling of the personal with the impersonal and timeless which Sartre himself would surely have liked and understood' – *Listener*

A CHOICE OF PENGUINS

Trail of Havoc   Patrick Marnham

In this brilliant piece of detective work, Patrick Marnham has traced the steps of Lord Lucan from the fateful night of 7 November 1974 when he murdered his children's nanny and attempted to kill his ex-wife. As well as being a fascinating investigation, the book is also a brilliant portrayal of a privileged section of society living under great stress.

Light Years   Gary Kinder

Eduard Meier, an uneducated Swiss farmer, claims since 1975 to have had over 100 UFO sightings and encounters with 'beamships' from the Pleiades. His evidence is such that even the most die-hard sceptics have been unable to explain away the phenomenon.

And the Band Played On   Politics, People and the AIDS Epidemic
Randy Shilts

Written after years of extensive research by the only American journalist to cover the epidemic full-time, *And the Band Played On* is a masterpiece of reportage and a tragic record of mismanaged institutions and scientific vendettas, of sexual politics and personal suffering.

The Return of a Native Reporter   Robert Chesshyre

Robert Chesshyre returned to Britain in 1985 from the United States, where he had spent four years as the *Observer*'s correspondent. This is his devastating account of the country he came home to: intolerant, brutal, grasping and politically and economically divided. It is a nation, he asserts, struggling to find a role.

Women and Love   Shere Hite

In this culmination of *The Hite Report* trilogy, 4,500 women provide an eloquent testimony to the disturbingly unsatisfying nature of their emotional relationships and point to what they see as the causes. *Women and Love* reveals a new cultural perspective in formation: as women change the emotional structure of their lives, they are defining a fundamental debate over the future of our society.

Stories   Satyajit Ray

'At once fantastic, realistically human, and occasionally frightening ... for sheer entertainment and pleasure Mr Ray's collection deserves the highest recommendation' – *The Times*

The Purple Decades   Tom Wolfe

From Surfers to Moonies, from *The Electric Kool-Aid Acid Test* to *The Right Stuff*, a technicolour retrospective from the foremost chronicler of the gaudiest period in American history. 'Like Evelyn Waugh, Wolfe is a maestro of savage hilarity and a moralist beneath the skin' – *Newsweek*

Sugar and Other Stories   A. S. Byatt

'Antonia Byatt's first collection of stories displays all her talents as a novelist, but spiced with an additional friskiness ... a bright sensual prose that seems to paint rather than describe' – Penelope Lively

The Moronic Inferno   Martin Amis

'Really good reading and sharp, crackling writing. Amis has a beguiling mixture of confidence and courtesy, and most of his literary judgments – often twinned with interviews – seem sturdy, even when caustic, without being bitchy for the hell of it' – *Guardian*

Elizabeth Alone   William Trevor

'With a fruitful marriage (and a quick, astonishing adulterous bounce) behind her, comfortable, amiable Mrs Aidallbery – Elizabeth – is in hospital for a hysterectomy ... A finely observed, gently sensitive comedy, delightful to read, like lived experience to remember' – *Daily Telegraph*

The Guide   R. K. Narayan

Raju, recently released from prison, used to be India's most corrupt tourist guide. Then a peasant mistakes him for a holy man – and gradually he begins to play the part. 'The best of R. K. Narayan's enchanting novels' – *New Yorker*

A SELECTION OF FICTION AND NON-FICTION

Cal   Bernard Mac Laverty

Springing out of the fear and violence of Ulster, *Cal* is a haunting love story from a land where tenderness and innocence can only flicker briefly in the dark. 'Mac Laverty describes the sad, straitened, passionate lives of his characters with tremendously moving skill' – *Spectator*

The Rebel Angels   Robertson Davies

A glittering extravaganza of wit, scatology, saturnalia, mysticism and erudite vaudeville. 'The kind of writer who makes you want to nag your friends until they read him so that they can share the pleasure' – *Observer*

Stars of the New Curfew   Ben Okri

'Anarchical energy with authoritative poise ... an electrifying collection' – Graham Swift. 'Okri's work is obsessive and compelling, spangled with a sense of exotic magic and haunted by shadows ... reality re-dreamt with great conviction' – *Time Out*

The Magic Lantern   Ingmar Bergman

'A kaleidoscope of memories intercut as in a film, sharply written and trimmed to the bone' – *Sunday Times*. 'The autobiography is exactly like the films: beautiful and repulsive; truthful and phoney; constantly startling' – *Sunday Telegraph*. 'Unique, reticent, revealing' – Lindsay Anderson

August in July   Carlo Gébler

On the eve of the Royal Wedding, as the nation prepares for celebration, August Slemic's world falls apart. 'There is no question but that he must now be considered a novelist of major importance' – *Daily Telegraph*

The News from Ireland   William Trevor

'An ability to enchant as much as chill has made Trevor unquestionably one of our greatest short-story writers' – *The Times*. 'A masterly collection' – *Daily Telegraph*